CHILD NURTURANCE

VOLUME 4
Child Nurturing in the
1980s

CHILD NURTURANCE

Series Editors
MARJORIE J. KOSTELNIK
Department of Family and Child Ecology
Michigan State University, East Lansing, Michigan
and
HIRAM E. FITZGERALD
Department of Psychology
Michigan State University, East Lansing, Michigan

A Continuation Order Plan is available for this series. A continuation order will bring delivery of
each new volume immediately upon publication. Volumes are billed only upon actual shipment.
For further information please contact the publisher.

CHILD NURTURANCE

VOLUME 4
Child Nurturing in the 1980s

Edited by

Robert P. Boger,
Gaston E. Blom, and
Larry E. Lezotte

*Michigan State University
East Lansing, Michigan*

SCHOOL OF
CALIFORNIA PROFESSIONAL
PSYCHOLOGY
LOS ANGELES

PLENUM PRESS • NEW YORK AND LONDON

Library of Congress Cataloging in Publication Data

Main entry under title:

Child nurturing in the 1980s.

(Child nurturance; v. 4)
Includes bibliographical references and index.
1. Child rearing—Addresses, essays, lectures. I. Boger, Robert P. II. Blom, Gaston
E. III. Lezotte, Larry E. IV. Series.
HQ769.C448   1984   649′.1   83-23073
ISBN 0-306-41505-4

©1984 Plenum Press, New York
A Division of Plenum Publishing Corporation
233 Spring Street, New York, N.Y. 10013

Printed in the United States of America

SERIES PREFACE

The United Nations' designation of 1979 as the International Year of the Child marked the first global effort undertaken to heighten awareness of the special needs of children. Activities initiated during this special year were designed to promote purposive and collaborative actions for the benefit of children throughout the world. Michigan State University's celebration of the International Year of the Child was held from September 1979 through June 1980. A variety of activities focused attention on the multiplicity of factors affecting the welfare of today's children as well as the children of the future. Many people involved with the university were concerned that benefits to children continue beyond the official time allocated to the celebration. The series *Child Nurturance* is one response to this concern. The first five volumes of *Child Nurturance* reflect directly the activities held on the Michigan State University campus and consist of original contributions from guest speakers and invited contributors. Subsequent biennial volumes will present original contributions from individuals representing such fields as anthropology, biology, education, human ecology, psychology, philosophy, sociology, and medicine. We hope the material presented in these volumes will promote greater understanding of children and encourage interdisciplinary inquiry into the individual, family, societal and cultural variables which influence their welfare and development.

We would like to express both our thanks and our admiration for Margaret Hall who not only typed the camera-ready copy for each of the volumes, but also served as general manager of the entire project. Although her contribution to the production of these volumes will not be noted in any chapter headings or indexes, each page reflects her devotion, care, and hard work. We also thank Mary Ann Reinhart for her careful and scholarly preparation of the subject index. Finally, we thank the editors and authors for their cooperation and for their concern for children and their families.

Marjorie J. Kostelnik
Hiram E. Fitzgerald
East Lansing, MI

PREFACE

Child Nurturing in the 1980s follows upon a series of lectures presented at Michigan State University in conjunction with the university's celebration of the International Year of the Child. The chapters, although far from an inclusive set, outline childrearing perspectives, issues and concerns relevant to the 80s and beyond. The authors have used different styles ranging from empirical review to essay.

The book is designed to provide those concerned with the nurturing of children in the United States with perceptions of what is and what could be. The initial chapter by Edward Zigler sets the stage for comments related to specific areas and modalities of child nurturing concerns for the decade. Some of the chapter authors are more futuristic than others in their perspective, but all have focused upon issues judged to be focal for those concerned with the nurturing of children in this culture during this period of our history.

The book is not addressed specifically to those who would set policy or those who would implement it. Rather, it is hoped that it can be read with benefit by a wide range of individuals including but not limited to parents, faculty members, child care workers and child agency personnel.

The editors wish to extend our appreciation to many individuals who made this effort possible. Funding of the IYC program was provided through the International Year of the Child Committee under the most able leadership of Andrew D. Hunt, M.D. The IYC lecture series, from which several chapters were drawn, was developed by the Child Nurturing and Development Committee which included Robert Boger, Pat Barnes-McConnell, Hiram Fitzgerald, Carol Fredrickson, Patricia Gage, Kay Ingram, Lawrence Lezotte, Lucetta Lyford, Pat Malony, John Mullins, Lilian Phenice, Richard Richter, Mark Roosa, and Marcia Rysztak.

The IYC child nurturing lectures would have been impossible without the dedicated efforts of Eileen (Beany) Tomber, whose efficient management made the series possible. We would also like to extend appreciation to Hiram Fitzgerald and Marjorie Kostelnik, the Child Nurturance Series editors, for their patience and support in assisting us with this volume, as well as Margaret Hall, Carolyn Boyd and the staff of the Institute for Family and Child Study at Michigan State University, for their assistance in the editing and typing of the manuscript.

From our perspective, little is more important than the nurturing of our children. The economic stress on families, as well as the scope and rate of social and technological change in our society, make the nurturance of America's children a true challenge for the 1980s. It is our sincere hope that this volume will be of assistance to parents and professionals involved with this most important of functions.

Robert P. Boger
Gaston E. Blom
Larry E. Lezotte
East Lansing, MI 1983

CONTENTS

CHILD NURTURING IN THE 1980s

STRENGTHENING SOCIAL POLICIES IN BEHALF OF

CHILDREN AND FAMILIES*(1)*

Edward Zigler and Kirby A. Heller

Department of Psychology
Yale University
New Haven, CT 06520

INTRODUCTION

The myth that we are a child-oriented society continues to exist in this country. Yet the condition of our nation's children is poor and getting worse. This condition is substantiated by a host of disturbing social indicators documented in several sources, such as the Carnegie council report, *All Our Children* (Keniston, 1977), and the 1976 report of the Advisory Committee on Child Development of the National Academy of Sciences (note 1). Problems faced by parents and children in four areas--health, child abuse, child care, and out-of-home child placements--will be described to highlight the invalidity of the myth.

SOCIAL INDICATORS

Infant Mortality

Although the United States is considered the world's most technologically advanced nation, *fifteen* countries have lower rates of infant mortality (Advisory Committee on Child Development, note 1). Even more shocking is the disparity in infant mortality rates between whites and minority groups, as well as between regions of the country. This country's ranking among nations drops to *31* when only non-whites, whose rate of infant mortality is twice as high as that of whites, are included. Similarly, there were 14.9 deaths per 1,000 births in the Pacific states in 1973, as compared to 21.6 deaths per 1,000 births in the southeastern section of the United States. This high mortality rate is due to a host of factors unrelated to our medical knowledge: poverty, poor sanitation, malnutrition of the mother, and lack of proper medical care. Statistics on

3

teenage pregnancies are enlightening. Complications during pregnancy and delivery as well as the risk of having infants in poor health are greatest for women below the age of twenty. Experts had believed that this was partially due to the physical immaturity of the young mothers. However, a recent study in Copenhagen found that teenage mothers given proper care had the least complications in childbirth (New Findings on Teen Pregnancy, 1979). This study illustrates that the high risk status of pregnant teenagers is due to societal rather than biological conditions.

Health

Statistics on the health care of children are also grim. Priorities in federal spending are clearly not directed to children. In 1970, only one out of seventeen federal dollars for health care was spent on children (Keniston, 1977). One-third of the nation's 60 million children received inadequate health care, with little access to primary care, immunizations, and early treatment of disease (Advisory Committee on Child Development, note 1). Despite the ability to eliminate infectious diseases through immunizations, epidemics continue to occur. For example, epidemics of measles in 1969, 1971, and 1974 were the result of nearly half of the children between the ages of one and four failing to get the proper inoculations (Knowles, 1977). Once again, poor children are the least likely to receive the necessary preventive care and have little access to health services until they enter school at the age of six.

Childhood accidents continue to be the greatest single cause of death for children between the ages of one and fourteen (Furrow, Gruendel, and Zigler, note 2). Among western countries, the United States has the *second* highest rate of childhood deaths due to accidents and is ranked first in deaths caused by firearms and poisonings. Motor vehicle accidents are the leading type of accidental death for children of all ages, yet there are few preventive efforts to protect children. Both children and parents need to be educated about traffic risks, and the use of infants' and children's automobile seats and restraints should be encouraged.

Foster Care

More than 500,000 children are not living with their families, but instead are in some type of out-of-home care (Edelman, 1979). The foster care system, presumably representing only temporary care until decisions about permanent placement can be made, subsidizes children indefinitely. Statistics on the number of children in foster care are difficult to collect--itself an indication of the poor state of monitoring of children in the system. It has been estimated that more than 250,000 children are in foster homes. In contrast, only 169,000 children were adopted in 1971 (Advisory Committee on Child Development, note 1). Children are moved from home to home and often attempts are not made to reunite the child with his family. In a survey conducted by the Children's Defense Fund (note 3), 52 percent of the children in foster care had been out of their homes for more than two years and 18 percent of the children removed from their homes had moved more than three times. The report by the Children's Defense Fund documents serious neglect by the state and federal governments of children for whom they are responsible as well as unnecessary separations of children from their parents, with little opportunity for reconstitution of the family. Despite the evidence that patterns of parental visiting best predict whether children will return home (Fanshel and Shinn, 1978), agencies have no specific policies concerning parental visits. For example, efforts are not made to place children with willing relatives, parents are sometimes not told where their child has been placed, children are placed far from their communities or even out of state, and parents are either not allowed to visit the child in their foster homes or are not given transportation subsidies. The child in the public welfare system is in a state of limbo; there is reluctance to either return the child back to his family or to terminate parents' rights so that the child may be adopted. Not surprisingly, minority and handicapped children are overrepresented in the population of children without permanent homes.

Institutional Care

Between 250,000 and 300,000 children are placed in public and private residential centers and institutions (Advisory Committee on Child Development, note 1). While many children need specialized services, public officials acknowledge that children are often inappropriately placed in institutions (Children's Defense Fund, note 3). The type of institutions, rather than the characteristics of the child, can determine the label the child receives (e.g., mentally retarded, emotionally disturbed). Occasionally an expose of an especially horrifying institution will catch the public's attention for a short time, but few long-term changes are made. For example, in 1965, Blatt and Kaplan visited five state institutions for the mentally retarded and described these field trips in their photo-essay, *Christmas in Purgatory* (1966). Ten years later, Blatt returned to find no substantial changes; still evident was the poor care, the lack of activities, education, and recreation. Even a new, small state institution costing $65,000 a year per resident contained no exceptional facilities nor services (Blatt, in press).

Child Abuse

Equally shocking are the statistics concerning child abuse and neglect. Although for a variety of reasons it is difficult to estimate the number of cases of child abuse per year (e.g., cases not reported, bias in the types of children who get reported, problems in the definitions of abuse and neglect), estimations range from a conservative 500,000 (Light, 1973) to four million adults who were aware of at least one incident of abuse (Gil, 1970). An estimate commonly quoted is that of the National Center on Child Abuse and Neglect--1,000,000 cases reported per year.

Perhaps even more frightening is the amount of physical violence found in the American home. Gelles (1979) reported that 63 percent of respondents in a survey described having at least one violent episode with a child between the ages of three and seventeen in one year. Extrapolating from the data based on his survey, he found that between three and four million children have at some time been kicked, bitten, or punched by parents, between 1.4 and 2.3 million children have been beaten up, and between 900,000 and 1.8 million children have had a parent use a gun or knife on them. In one year (1975), between 1.4 and 1.9 million children were vulnerable to physical injury from parental violence. Clearly, the less than $20 million provided by the Child Abuse and Treatment Act can barely begin to address the problem.

Instances of legalized child abuse occur in America's public institutions--e.g., schools, correctional settings, and homes for the mentally retarded or otherwise handicapped. Documentation of institutional abuse is found in Blatt and his colleagues' research, described above (Blatt, in press; Blatt and Kaplan, 1966) and Wooden's *Weeping in the Playtime of Others* (1976). The Supreme Court's decision on corporal punishment is an indication of the nation's attitude towards children. Ruling on a case in which two junior high school students received severe beatings, the Court upheld the use of corporal punishment in the schools (Ingraham vs. Wright). The message clearly conveyed to parents is that corporal punishment is not an inappropriate method of discipline. Violence toward children is sanctioned when it is labeled corporal punishment; abhorred when it is labeled child abuse. This contradiction and its ramifications are highlighted by Newberger and Bourne's (1979) discussion of the court case of Landeros vs. Flood in which a physician could be sued for malpractice by not reporting bruises that were *legally* inflicted by a teacher.

Child Care

The last area to be described concerns the need for child care. This issue does not elicit the emotional reaction associated with child or institutional abuse. There is no widespread public outcry for day care. Child advocacy, labor, and women's rights groups have failed to form a single effective lobby capable of overcoming the public fears and myths about day care. Yet the need for alternative child care arrangements exists. In 1977, 6.4 million children under six and 22.4 million children between the ages of 6 and 17 had working mothers. Data from HEW in 1976 indicate that only 1.6 million licensed child care openings exist in centers and family day care homes. While some of the needs for child care are being met by informal arrangements (e.g., care in one's home by a relative), unmet needs also lead to lengthy waiting lists, unaffordable private care, and less than optimal arrangements. In addition, more than two million children between the ages of seven and thirteen come home at the end of the school day to an empty house (Congressional Record, 1979). In a study of 11- and 12-year-olds in Oakland, Rubin and Medrich (1979) found that 47 percent of the children had to babysit for younger siblings after school. Children who are themselves in need of supervision are instead solely responsible for providing it.

Not much is known about the modal kind of care children are receiving, since research tends to focus on high quality day care centers, the least common type of substitute care. An exception to this pattern of research was the study by the National Council of Jewish Women (Keyserling, 1972), in which 11 percent of all licensed non-profit centers were rated as poor in quality, 51 percent were rated as fair, 28 percent were rated as good, and only 9 percent were rated as superior. Proprietary centers fared worse: 50 percent were considered poor, 35 percent were fair, 14 percent were good, and 1 percent was superior. Finally, the percentages for family day care were: 14 percent were rated as poor, 48 percent were fair, 31 percent were good, and 7 percent were superior. These figures probably overestimate the quality of child care, since most care is provided in unlicensed homes that are not accountable to public authority. Yet unlicensed settings are not the only culprits in this situation. Even among licensed centers, standards and monitoring are often lax. Staff/child ratios that are part of the Federal Interagency Day Care Requirements (FIDCR) for children from six weeks to six years have been suspended since 1975. After four years of study and consideration, the new standards presented to the public in June, 1979 do not promote the optimal development of children in child day care. In fact, the suggested standards are less stringent than many state licensing requirements. One suggested option for a staff/child ratio is one adult for *five* infants. These recommendations do not differentiate three-month-old infants from 2½-year-old toddlers, but include all children younger than 2½ years. These proposed standards are truly regressive. The debate concerning day care can no longer focus on whether it is or is not good for children. Rather, ways to improve and expand the current system need to be explored.

SOCIAL TRENDS

The needs of children, outlined above, should be considered against the backdrop of two recent social trends. The first is the increased labor participation of women. Dramatic changes in the number of working mothers have occurred in the last two decades, especially mothers of children under six. For example, in 1950, 22 percent of all mothers were working. Of mothers having children under six, 14 percent were employed. In 1960, the comparable employment figures were: 30 percent of all mothers and 20 percent of mothers having children under six. In 1978, 54 percent of all mothers, 44 percent of mothers having children under six, and 60 percent having children between the ages of six and seventeen were employed (Rivlin, 1978). The percentages are higher for mothers in single parent households: in 1978, 56 percent of mothers with children under six and 71 percent of mothers with children over six were employed (Rivlin, 1978). Clearly, the mythical American family with two parents, one working and one taking care of the children, does not describe the majority of American families today. Programs providing services to children and families will have to take into account these changes in the status of families.

The second important social trend is the increasing cutbacks in spending. In recent years, both inflation and unemployment have been high, producing hardships for many families. A survey by Yankelovich, Skelly, and White in 1974-75 found that Americans had less faith in the economy than they previously had, and no longer were optimistic about future prosperity. In addition, tax revolts such as the one leading to Proposition 13 have led to cutbacks in spending on social services by state and federal governments. Thus, it is unlikely that new programs designed to fulfill the needs of children and families will be funded.

The lack of funding is not the only problem in the delivery of necessary social services. Many public services that are currently provided have an anti-family bias and are not cost-effective. One such system is out-of-home care. The average monthly payment for foster care is $254; the average monthly payment for institutions is $575. Preventive services to families at risk as well as adoption subsidies to insure a permanent home for children could be considerably cheaper than both of these (Edelman, 1979). The Children's Defense Fund report on out-of-home care (note 3) described the removal of three preschool children from their home and their placement in foster care because their mother could not afford to pay $250 to fix the broken furnace. Blatt (in press) presented statistics from two studies in New York comparing types of care for mentally retarded individuals. Costs per year for residents in small group homes were $6,700. The best residential care provided for the mentally retarded that Blatt observed was a community-based service by foster parents costing $8,500 per year. In institutions, costs were $35,000 per individual per year. High quality care for people with special needs is not necessarily provided by the most expensive alternative.

What are the solutions to this array of problems? More specifically, how can the knowledge that we have gained about the nature of the developmental process be applied to implement solutions to these problems and begin to meet the needs of children? In some cases, an adequate knowledge base does not exist. For example, the dynamics producing child abuse are not well enough understood to *predict* which abused children will grow up to themselves abuse their own children and which of them will not. In most cases, however, social science research that can be useful in the formation and implementation of policy concerning children and families does exist. Is this information utilized by this nation's policy makers? The answer to this question is complex. Too often, solutions to children's problems seem to be based on social fads and questionable assumptions about development. An effective utilization of social science knowledge and a meaningful collaboration between social scientists and governmental decision-makers do not seem to be the norm.

In recent years, interest in studying the utilization of social science knowledge in policy making has grown. The questions that we have raised related to the apparent lack of use of research in child development apply to most areas of social science and public policy. While an extensive review of this work is beyond the scope of this paper, a brief digression exploring some of the issues in the utilization of social science research is useful. In the next section, problems, myths, and unrealistic expectations in the application of research to policy making will be described. More realistic approaches to the utilization of knowledge about human development to constructive social policy will be offered.

PROBLEMS IN THE UTILIZATION OF SOCIAL SCIENCE KNOWLEDGE

One problem that is commonly cited as causing a failure in the utilization of social science knowledge is the conflict in values between social scientists and policy makers (Mayntz, 1977; Weiss, 1977, note 4; Weiss and Bucavalas, 1977). Social science is presumably value-free while policy decisions are made in a value-laden context. This dichotomy is misleading, however. Research in the social sciences is not value-free, and even the most basic research takes on the values of the investigators. These are evident in the questions that are asked, the methodologies used, the presentation of results, and the interpretation of the data. Research in child abuse demonstrates the influence of the values of the investigators on the way that problems are studied. Three approaches to understanding child abuse will be briefly compared (See Parke and Collmer, 1975, for a detailed analysis of each approach). In the psychiatric analysis of child abuse, investigators assume the causes of abuse are within the parent, who is ill or abnormal. The research, therefore, focuses on identifying those traits or characteristics that are common to abusive parents. The solution to abuse advocated by those working within this model is typically individual or group psychotherapy. The second approach, the sociological model, views child abuse as a response to stress and frustration in one's everyday life, as well as the social values of one's culture. Conditions such as the cultural attitude toward violence, housing conditions, job-related stress, unemployment, poverty, family size, and social isolation, rather than inherent factors in the individual, contribute to child abuse. Control of abuse in this framework results from changes in societal values and conditions (e.g., the elimination of poverty). Researchers working within the social-situational model of child abuse study the patterns of interaction between abusing parents and their children and the conditions under which abuse occurs. Factors such as use of discipline, the child's role in abuse, and interferences in mother-child attachment are viewed as important contributors to child abuse. Because the cause is not the individual but the context in which abuse occurs, intervention efforts emphasize the modification of maladaptive behaviors by both partners in the interaction. From this brief description of three approaches to child abuse, the close relation between the values of the scientist, the hypotheses proposed, and the outcomes of research can be seen.

Another example of the value-laden nature of psychological research is the tendency to blame the individual for his problems, rather than look for causal factors within the situation (Caplan and Nelson, 1973). Although two of the models of child abuse discussed above did identify the cause of the problem in the environment, these analyses were not typical of psychological approaches. The nature of the discipline leads to the study of intrapsychic causes of phenomena. Solutions, therefore, would not be externally based but should result from change within the target group. Thus, researchers studying the underachievement of minority children label the children and their families as "problem groups," rather than identifying the school and the educational system as the roots of the problem.

A second conflict between social science research and policy making frequently cited is that research is often viewed as basic, not applied, and irrelevant to social problems. This position clearly is not accurate. Within the last decade, there has been a dramatic increase in the amount of funding for applied research. In 1977, the federal government spent nearly $2 billion on the production and application of social knowledge, a majority of which went to research (Study Project on Social Research and Development, note 5). In addition, evaluation requirements are written into many new social programs. Clearly, the federal government is looking toward social scientists for answers to their questions.

Perhaps the major problem in the utilization of social science research is that social scientists are perceived as not providing clear answers to appropriate policy questions, while policy makers are not asking questions in ways that would lead to valid and reliable research. Each group, therefore, does not supply the information necessary for effective collaboration.

Expectations concerning the types of questions that social science research can answer need to be revised. Those who expect single studies to have an impact on policy are likely to be disappointed, for the effects of such studies are usually small or nonexistent (Cohen and Garet, 1975; Cohen and Weiss, 1977; Weiss, 1977; Weiss, note 4; Rich and Caplan, note 6). Furthermore, answers that single-study research can provide are more likely to come from an in-house research staff of a federal agency (Caplan and Rich, note 7).

If single studies do not have an impact on policy, what is the effect of accumulated research in any one area? Typically, the result of the proliferation of research on a topic is not to more adequately or definitively answer a policy question but to introduce additional complications (Cohen and Garet, 1975; Cohen and Weiss, 1977). This seemingly negative consequence does, however, have advantageous effects. Although research may not provide a consensus from which to draw undisputed solutions, it can lead to a clarification of differences and perspectives as well as improved research methodologies. Evaluations of

Head Start exemplify how research can be both contradictory and complex while leading to a more sophisticated and useful understanding of the effects of early intervention. After the early and primarily negative findings of the Westinghouse evaluation of Head Start in 1969, questions about proper assumptions, subject selection biases, analyses, and program goals arose. Improved statistical techniques (e.g., the Campbell-Evans debate concerning regression artifacts), a range of methodologies (e.g., Shipman, et al. case study approach), an interest in outcome variables other than school achievement (e.g., changes in community institutions, utilization of special education classrooms), and a focus on process within individual programs all contributed to a complex and murky picture of how early intervention programs affect children. Yet this is not a regrettable situation. When the question asked is complicated, it deserves more than a simple "yes/no" answer (see Datta, 1976, 1979; for an analysis of the effects of evaluations on Head Start).

Based on the above discussion, it is obvious that in order to understand how social research is used in social policy, one must clarify the meaning of the term "use". Weiss (note 4) has discussed at length many possible uses of research in policy making and a summary of some of these interpretations will be described below.

USES OF RESEARCH IN SOCIAL POLICY

Ideally, research can be used for problem solving. This is the most common understanding of the relation between research and policy, yet the link least likely to occur. This approach assumes that a concrete and well-defined problem needs to be solved and that empirical evidence can be used to help generate a solution or choose among several alternatives. The more subtle assumption is that there is consensus among decision makers on the goals for the policy in question, a condition rarely met. Caplan (1975; Caplan and Rich, note 7; and Rich and Caplan, note 6) interviewed 204 policy makers in the executive branch of the federal government who were asked: "On the basis of your experience in the federal government, can you think of instances where a new program, a major program alternative, a new social or administrative policy, legislative proposal, or a technical innovation could be traced to the social sciences?" Although 82 percent of the respondents replied yes to this question, their examples were not empirical studies, nor did the information they cite guide specific policies. Rather, their use of social knowledge was a subtle process, relying on ideas and principles derived from the social sciences.

Research can create its own use. Weiss (1977; note 4) refers to this model of social science utilization as the "knowledge driven model." Borrowed from the physical sciences, it assumes that due to the compelling nature of basic research, applications are bound to follow. This is unlikely to occur in the social sciences.

Research can be used as political ammunition. Even after policy makers have reached decisions and are unlikely to be influenced by research, they may use social science knowledge to bolster their argument. This is neither an unethical nor unimportant use of research, as long as the information is not distorted and is accessible to all sides.

Related to the above use is research that advances self-interest. For example, policy makers can delay taking an action, arguing that the needed evidence is not available. This was the case in the four-year moratorium on staffing regulations in the federal day care standards, pending the results from the ABT National Day Care Study and the "Appropriateness Report" from HEW to Congress. Social scientists also serve their own interests by having an influence on policy, gaining governmental funds, and advocating their own, usually liberal, views.

The last use of social science research to be discussed is the most amorphous, but perhaps the most important: "research as conceptualization" (Weiss, 1977). This definition of use encompasses sensitizing policy makers to new issues, turning research problems into policy issues, clarifying alternatives, and supplying a common language. Although this is a "softer" use of research than is commonly desired, it can have far-reaching implications. Generalizations from the accumulation of research in an area can, over time, change the climate of ideas and become a part of the social consciousness. The negative aspect of this type of use of research in policy is that myths and social fads become part of the knowledge that is accessible and utilized by the public. Unfortunately, these myths often remain unquestioned and become the basis for new policy and further research.

This use of social science research can be clearly seen in the formation of Project Head Start. Social and political forces in combination with the prevailing social science theories converged in the mid-1960s to form this important social program (see Zigler and Anderson, 1979, for a more detailed description). The revival of scientific interest in the role of the environment in human development and the design of educational intervention efforts for children of the disadvantaged in combination with the Civil Rights era and the War on Poverty combined to influence the development of Head Start. A novel alliance between child development experts and social policy makers was created.

Thus, the use of broad principles based on social science knowledge can and does affect social policy. In the remainder of this paper, several principles of development, based on decades of work in child development, will be outlined. Examples of policies that are contrary to these principles, as well as examples and suggestions for ones that are consistent with our knowledge, will be offered.

PRINCIPLES OF DEVELOPMENT

The first principle is that a child's development is continuous, and that the child benefits if he has a sense of continuity, both between the stages of his life and between the spheres of his life. For the past twenty years, workers in the field of child development have sought some magic time in a child's life in which to optimize development. Some have claimed that this magic period is the nine months in utero, others have emphasized the first three years of life, while others have said that the true critical period is the first three years of elementary school.

According to the principle of continuous development, each of these periods is a magic period. Intervention programs for children should be designed in such a way that the child's needs at that specific stage are met. Of course, it is advantageous to begin meeting the child's needs as early in life as possible. However, it is never too late to intervene effectively to optimize the development of the child.

The principle of continuity also implies that the child will benefit from consistency in his environment. On a most obvious level, the lives of children removed from their homes need to be stabilized. Earlier in this paper, the number of children in out-of-home placements and the number of times children in foster care changed homes were described. Revisions of child welfare laws are needed. The current child welfare bill in Congress targeting funds for adoption subsidies as well as preventive and support services is a first step. Children who must be removed from their families should be placed in the least restrictive setting, preferably with relatives, and close to their families. Reviews of children in the welfare system should be made periodically and if the child is not to be returned to his family, termination of parental rights should be hastened. Above all else, a permanent, secure, and supportive home for the child should be found.

Consistency in one's environment does not apply only to children in foster care or institutions, but to those who spend some time away from home each day. Children who attend day care programs, from the most informal to the most structured, need consistency. The status of child care providers needs to be upgraded to avoid rapid staff turnover. Family day care workers are responsible for about half of the children in care who are under six. They suffer from isolation, underpay, and inadequate training. An expansion of the Child Development Associate program could begin to address the problem of staff training. Caregivers are certified through competency examinations, so that child care workers with experience, but without academic degrees, can qualify for a CDA degree. Innovative programs such as family day care networks, toy lending libraries, and affiliations between family care providers and more stable centers can also aid in solving some of the problems in the family day care system.

Parents should be encouraged to participate in the child's out-of-home setting. Although many working families may not be able to find the time to actively work in the child's day care setting or classroom, they should remain in close contact with the child's other providers. In order to provide a child with a sense of continuity, genuine partnerships must be established between professionals and the families that they serve. A model for such a partnership exists in the Head Start Program, in which parent involvement is critical. Programs such as the Brookline BEEP project are demonstrating the value of parental involvement in elementary schools as well.

Related to the first principle of continuity is the second principle of child development: The most important influence on the development of the child is the family. Children need a one-to-one relationship with a caring adult. The growing recognition of this principle has led to the development of programs designed to improve parenting skills. Thus, in Home Start, professionals work not with children but with parents. Such programs help parents develop realistic expectations for their children's behavior and to gain confidence in their childrearing abilities.

Recently, child development education has been expanded to reach people before they become parents. George Hecht, the founder of *Parents Magazine*, has observed that young people are almost completely unprepared to assume the responsibilities of childrearing. The Education for Parenthood program was developed to introduce students to the topic of child development. More importantly, students are given the opportunity to gain firsthand experience with children in supervised settings.

The need for primary prevention has been emphasized throughout this paper. With some outside aid, parents can often handle the stresses and frustrations that all too frequently result in the break-up of the family. Home visitors or parent aides can help the abusive or potentially abusive parent deal with some of the problems he or she faces by being a role model, a teacher, and a good listener (Adnopoz, note 8). Crisis day care centers and parents' groups have also been developed to help control child abuse. Ideally, not only families at known risk, but all American families would have access to needed services.

The most important support that could be offered to families would be for one parent to have the option of raising a child at home, without having to sacrifice necessary income. This may involve income-maintenance policies, family allowances, maternity or paternity benefits, or flexible working hours (Kamerman and Kahn, 1979). Many European countries have successfully implemented these policies.

The third principle is that children as a group are heterogeneous and show great variability on every characteristic that can be measured. This variation relates only minimally to social class and ethnic factors. Children with diverse abilities have diverse needs, and rather than expect children to match the characteristics of any single program, programs should be developed that can be tailored to fit the needs of each child and his family. The ideal intervention effort would not consist of one uniform national program, but centers in every community with a variety of programs to meet the range of needs represented by children and families. The model for this policy of the future already exists in the Child and Family Resource Program. This community-wide delivery system links a variety of programs and services to children and families in areas such as early childhood education, parent involvement, health, and nutrition.

Parents need options in child care that match their lifestyles and philosophies. The present system tracks children so that poor children attend one type of center while more affluent children go elsewhere. Government funds for day care should subsidize whatever options the parents choose: babysitting in the home by relatives or non-relatives, family day care, or center care. The criteria that parents use to choose child care are complex. While several surveys have shown that cost, location, and convenience of hours are critical to the decision-making process (Unco, Inc., 1976), an intensive research project based on a case study approach indicates that this is too simplistic. Lein (1979) found that parents sought a caregiver who was reliable, warm, and protected their children from physical danger. She also found that parents varied in how important they considered certain features of day care such as an emphasis on cognitive development, supervision, exposure to different values, and discipline and control provided. Options in child care that mesh with parents' needs and desires can augment, rather than undermine, family life.

Certain groups of children and families have special needs and deserve priority in receiving support. Three groups of children should be considered first in expanding and designing new programs: children from families with low income and/or with a single, working parent, handicapped children, and bilingual children.

Attempts to meet the variable needs of children do not imply that programs should try to change children to fit into one uniform mold. Pluralism and diversity are healthy, and cultural variation must be respected. Our emphasis on options reflects this belief. Caution by professionals is always required to avoid the tendency to believe that as "experts," no one, including parents, can make better decisions for children.

The fourth principle is that full human development involves more than the formal cognitive system. Development of character, personality, and values is equally as important as the acquisition of intellectual skills. This "whole child" principle leads to the rejection of the view that higher IQ scores and school grades are the ultimate goals of educational intervention efforts.

For this reason, the "back to basics" movement represents a threat to educators committed to the whole child view. Skills in reading and mathematics are important, but social competence should be the ultimate goal of education and intervention. At least three factors must be considered in a definition of social competence: physical and mental health, formal cognitive development, and optimal emotional and motivational development. Unfortunately, measures of social, emotional, and motivational development are difficult to construct and validate. Yet many adequate measures of such variables (e.g., effectance motivation, expectancy of success, self-image, learned helplessness, and creativity) do exist (Zigler and Trickett, 1978) and child development researchers can contribute by refining these measures as well as by developing new indicators of social competence.

The fifth principle concerns the relation between the child and his social and nonsocial environment. In the past, the direction of causality was perceived to be unidirectional; from environment to child, and from parent to child. A more accurate description would include the reciprocal effects of both the child on the environment and the environment on the child. Of course, if the environment falls below a minimum level of quality, the damage to the child can be drastic. But recent views of child development have emphasized the nonpassive nature of the child (Bell, 1968; Piaget, 1952). Based on this principle, programs designed to alter only one partner in an interaction are not adequate. The focus of change should be on the interaction and all participants' perceptions of this interaction. Revising a course curriculum is not enough if the child expects to fail and the teacher expects the child to fail. Therapy for abusing parents is not enough if the child's contribution to the abuse and the eliciting conditions are not taken into consideration.

Social policy that is based on the notion that hereditary factors are all-important or environmental factors are all-important is doomed to failure. Expectations based on the complete malleability of the child (e.g., expecting compensatory education to erase differences in achievement levels across all children) or lack of hope in the possibilities for change (e.g., expecting that schooling will not have an effect on future success) ignore the complexities of the individual in his changing environments.

The final principle to be discussed is the broadest, for it concerns all the institutions that influence the development of the child. The child's development is not determined only by the parents' childrearing techniques. The child encounters many environments and social institutions in his development and is affected by all of them. The family is, of course, critical, but so are the schools, the community, and the media. America's children are affected by social forces such as the state of the economy, the length of the industrial work day, the geographical mobility of industrial employees, the availability of day care, the ever-changing regulations concerning the availability of food stamps, and a thousand other decisions made at the federal, state, and local levels of government.

Advances in research are not enough to improve the lives of children. While we believe that the principles that have been outlined should be the base upon which effective social policy is formed, we also believe that helping our nation's children should not wait for all the necessary or relevant knowledge to be produced. As we have discussed, social science research is often underutilized, misinterpreted, and above all, takes an exceedingly long time to influence the social consciousness of the public. We must, therefore, take a broad view of our responsibilities to children and their families. When the media manipulates and exploits the child consumer, we must speak out. When government policy, by commission or omission, threatens our children's well-being, we must speak out. If we are concerned about the lives of America's children, we must become nothing less than social activists in their behalf.

REFERENCE NOTES

1. Advisory Committee on Child Development. *Toward a national policy for children and families.* Washington, D.C.: National Academy of Sciences, 1976.

2. Furrow, D., Gruendel, J., and Zigler, E. *Protecting America's children from accidental injury and death. An overview of the problem and an agenda for action.* Unpublished manuscript, Yale University, 1979.

3. Children's Defense Fund. *Children without homes.* Washington, D.C.: Author, 1978.

4. Weiss, C. H. Improving the linkage between social research and public policy. In Study Project on Social Research and Development (Eds.). *Knowledge and policy: The uncertain connection.* Washington, D.C.: National Academy of Sciences, 1978.

5. Study Project on Social Research and Development. *The federal investment in knowledge of social problems* (Vol. 1). Washington, D.C.: National Academy of Sciences, 1978.

6. Rich, R. F., and Caplan, N. *Instrumental and conceptual uses of social science knowledge in policy-making at the national level: Means/ends matching versus understanding.* Unpublished manuscript, University of Michigan, 1976.

7. Caplan, N., and Rich, R. F. *Open and closed knowledge inquiry systems: The process and consequences of bureaucratization of information policy at the national level.* Unpublished manuscript, 1977.

8. Adnopoz, J. *Parent aides: Effective supports for families.* Unpublished manuscript, Yale University, 1979.

REFERENCES

Bell, R. Q. A reinterpretation of the direction of effects in studies of socialization. *Psychological Review*, 1968, *75*, 81-95.

Blatt, B. The pariah industry. A diary from purgatory and other places. In G. Gerbner, C. J. Ross, and E. Zigler (Eds.), *Child abuse reconsidered.* New York: Oxford University Press, in press.

Blatt, B., and Kaplan, F. *Christmas in purgatory.* Boston: Allyn and Bacon, 1966.

Caplan, N. S. The use of social science information by federal executives. In G. Lyons (Ed.), *Social research and public policies.* Hanover, NH: Dartmouth College, 1975.

Caplan, N., and Nelson, S. On being useful: The nature and consequences of psychological research on social problems. *American Psychologist*, 1973, *28*, 199-211.

Cohen, D. K., and Garet, M. S. Reforming education policy with applied social research. *Harvard Education Review*, 1975, *45*, 17-43.

Cohen, D. K., and Weiss, J. A. Social science and social policy. Schools and race. In C. H. Weiss (Ed.), *Using social research in public policy making.* Lexington, MA: Lexington Books, 1977.

Congressional Record, January 15, 1979, pp. S76-S77.

Datta, L. The impact of the Westinghouse/Ohio evaluation of the development of Project Head Start: An examination of the immediate and longer term effects and how they came about. In C. C. Abt (Ed.), *The evaluation of social programs.* Beverly Hills, CA: Sage, 1976.

Datta, L. What has the impact of Head Start been: Some findings from national evaluations of Head Start. In E. Zigler and J. Valentine (Eds.), *Project Head Start: A legacy of the war on poverty.* New York: MacMillan: Free Press, 1979.

Edelman, M. W. Children instead of ships. *New York Times*, May 14, 1979, p. A19.

Fanshel, D., and Shinn, E. B. *Children in foster care: A longitudinal investigation.* New York: Columbia University Press, 1978.

Gelles, R. J. Violence toward children in the United States. In R. Bourne and E. H. Newberger (Eds.), *Critical perspectives on child abuse.* Lexington, MA: Lexington Books, 1979.

Gil, D. *Violence against children: Physical child abuse in the United States.* Cambridge, MA: Harvard University Press, 1970.

Kamerman, S. B., and Kahn, A. The day-care debate: A wider view. *Public Interest*, 1979, *54*, 76-93.

Keniston, K. *All our children.* New York: Harcourt, Brace, Jovanovich, 1977.

Keyserling, M. D. *Windows on day care.* New York: National Council of Jewish Women, 1972.

Knowles, J. H. (Ed.), *Doing better and feeling worse. Health in the United States.* New York: W. W. Norton, 1977.

Lein, L. Parental evaluation of child care alternatives. *Urban and Social Change Review*, 1979, *12*, 11-16.

Light, R.   Abused and neglected children in America: A study of
    alternative policies. *Harvard Educational Review*, 1974, *43*, 556-598.
Mayntz, R.   Sociology, value freedom, and the problems of political
    counseling.   In C. H. Weiss (Ed.), *Using social research in public
    policy making.* Lexington, MA: Lexington Books, 1977.
Newberger, E. H., and Bourne, R. The medicalization and legalization of
    child abuse.   In R. Bourne and E. H. Newberger (Eds.), *Critical
    perspectives on child abuse.* Lexington, MA: Lexington Books, 1979.
New York Times. New findings on teen pregnancy, April 29, 1979, p. E7.
Parke, R., and Collmer, C. Child abuse: Interdisciplinary review. In E.
    M. Hetherington (Ed.), *Review of child development research*, (Vol.
    5). Chicago: University of Chicago Press, 1975.
Piaget, A.   *Childcare and preschool: Options for federal support.*
    Washington, D.C.: U.S. Government Printing Office, 1978.
Rubin, V., and Medrich, E. A. Child care, recreation and the fiscal crisis.
    Urban and Social Change Review, 1979, *12*, 22-28.
Unco, Inc. *National child care consumer study: 1975.* Washington, D.C.:
    U.S. Government Printing Office, 1975.
Weiss, C. H. Introduction. In C. H. Weiss (Ed.), *Using social research in
    public policy making.* Lexington, MA: Lexington Books, 1977.
Weiss, C. H., and Bucuvalas, M. J. The challenge of social research to
    decision making. In C. H. Weiss (Ed.), *Using social research in public
    policy making.* Lexington, MA: Lexington Books, 1977.
Wooden, K. *Weeping in the playtime of others.* New York: McGraw Hill,
    1976.
Yankelovich, Skelly, White, Inc.   *The General Mills American family
    report 1974-75.* Minneapolis: General Mills, 1975.
Zigler, E., and Anderson, K.   An idea whose time had come: The
    intellectual and political climate for Head Start. In E. Zigler and J.
    Valentine (Ed.), *Project Head Start: A legacy of the war on poverty.*
    New York: MacMillan: Free Press, 1979.
Zigler, E., and Trickett, P. K. IQ, social competence and evaluation of
    early childhood intervention programs. *American Psychologist*, 1978,
    33, 789-798.

FOOTNOTE

(1) This chapter is drawn from Dr. Edward Zigler's keynote address
"Child Nurturance: A System's Perspective for the 1980s" presented on
January 29, 1980 as part of the Michigan State University's International
Year of the Child "To Rear a Child" lecture series.

PERINATAL NURTURANCE:

THE BEGINNINGS OF A HUMAN RELATIONSHIP

Ann L. Wilson

Departments of Pediatrics and Psychiatry
School of Medicine
University of South Dakota
Sioux Falls, SD 57105

INTRODUCTION

The period of time from the twentieth week of pregnancy to the twenty-eighth day of an infant's life comprises what has been identified as the perinatal epoch. Perinatal medicine reflects a unique merging of subspecialists in obstetrics and pediatrics, as well as a concept of collaborative care for the mother, developing fetus, and newborn. However, this period encompasses much more than the cooperation of medical specialists who care for the pregnant woman and her baby. It includes all of the factors surrounding the baby's entry and early days in the world.

Intrauterine life represents a complex system of physiological, psychological and social interactions occurring in a cultural milieu. Nutrition (Worthington, Vermeersch, and Williams, 1979), genetic inheritance (Apgar and Beck, 1972) and the presence or absence of disease or pathological conditions (Sokol, Stojkov, and Chik, 1979), are some aspects which affect a woman's pregnancy and the growth and development of the fetus. How she will adjust to the pregnancy, labor and delivery and to caring for the newborn is determined by her present mental health, response to stress, and past and current life experiences and attitudes (McDonald, 1968). Fetal behavior, as well, has been shown to be affected by such psychological variables (Ottinger and Simmons, 1964).

The social circumstances presiding during this period further affect how the woman will respond to the major physiological adjustments demanded by each perinatal event (Nuckols, Cassel, and Kaplan, 1972).

21

Socioeconomic status and access to perinatal health care and services certainly also play crucial roles (Osofsky and Kendall, 1973). Additionally, the cultural context of birthing determines by whom, how and where care is provided for a mother during labor and delivery (Mead and Newton, 1967). The interactions of these biological, psychological, social, and cultural circumstances encompassing the expectant woman and her family impact on the outcome of the pregnancy.

Though application of the perinatal concept to the practice of speciality medicine is relatively new, less technologically advanced peoples through their cultural practices have understood for generations the need to respect the interaction between a pregnant woman's social, emotional and physical environments. Though mortality for mothers and babies in nonindustrialized nations remains high, established customs, beliefs, and practices provide nurturance for the pregnant and parturient woman and her newborn.

This book on child nurturing in the 1980s reflects a contemporary need to focus on the life sustaining care which children must receive so that they may achieve their human potentials. A particular focus on perinatal nurturance reflects more specifically the necessity of responding to this awareness by attending to the needs of families during the period of time from pregnancy through the first month of their new baby's life. In today's work where much technology has been applied to routine prenatal and intrapartum care, attention to nurturance for the family is timely. How do prospective parents who now frequently live substantial distances from their own parents receive nurturance while they are experiencing the changes of pregnancy and adjusting to impending parenthood? With ultrasonic examinations of fetal development, fetoscopy, amniocentesis and prenatal diagnosis, much can be done to nurture the growth of the fetus, but what is being done to respond to parents' own needs for nurturance during pregnancy, labor and delivery and during the early days following delivery? How are parents being helped to nurture their newborn who must receive such care to thrive physically, emotionally and socially?

This chapter includes two sections. First, current knowledge about issues related to nurturance during the perinatal period will be presented. This will include a review of the declining mortality rates, bonding, the sensitive period, neonatal behavioral capabilities and contemporary views on care of the newborn. This section will be followed by descriptions of programs and approaches geared toward caring for families as they begin to interact and form a lifelong relationship with their new baby. How new babies receive nurturance has long-term consequences for their own future ability to receive and, in turn, provide nurturing care.

CURRENT KNOWLEDGE OF HOW HUMAN RELATIONSHIPS
BEGIN DURING THE PERINATAL EPOCH

Today we can afford the luxury of examining with a broad perspective human development issues as they relate to childbearing. Health
care professionals have been the target of angry attacks in recent years
by those who feel the rights of the obstetric patient have been denied
(Arms, 1975; Elkins, 1977). Today many routine hospital rules and
restrictions seem to have outlived their original purposes. In the not too
distant past, however, the rationale for such rigidity in care reflected the
very real threat to the lives of mothers and newborns posed by infection.
Sobering evidence for this is apparent in the past 30 years of statistics on
neonatal morality. The death rate for the neonate (first 28 days of life)
has dropped from 20.5 per thousand live births in 1950 to 9.4 in 1978
(Wegman, 1979). This decline in morality can be attributed, in part, to
the use of antibiotics in the management of infections. Further, in more
recent years, the institution of regionalized intensive care units with
transport systems for high risk mothers and infants has also contributed to
the decline in neonatal mortality and morbidity (Harris, Isaman, and Giles,
1978). With such advances in care now available, issues such as how
perinatal care impacts on family dynamics and how family dynamics
affect responses to perinatal events can be examined.

Graven (1978) has outlined how perinatal health care providers have
come to this point of professional interest and development. He identifies
five eras in the past 50 years representing different areas of concern for
the medical practitioner caring for the pregnant woman and her infant.
During the first era, from 1930 through the 1940s, the primary concerns
of physicians and nurses was the assurance of the safety of the mother
through her pregnancy. At a time when maternal mortality was of great
concern, efforts were focused upon reducing the risks pregnancy and
childbearing represented to the health of a woman. During the late 1950s
and 1960s, the second era, efforts began to focus upon reducing neonatal
mortality. As already described by statistics, this goal continues to be
achieved. In the third era, during the late 1960s and 1970s, interest in
fetal monitoring focused attention on the well-being of the fetus, and
during the fourth era, occurring in the middle 1970s, concerns turned
toward reducing neonatal morbidity through improvements in the management of labor and delivery. In the late 1970s, the fifth era, interest has
grown around the issues of how the provisions of care affects the
beginnings of family relationships.

The fifth era has come at a time when much has been done to assure
the survival of mothers and babies. Now, Graven notes, issues related to
ethical concerns and the management of families are sources of discussion
and controversy. Care providers are examining the role they play in
creating a proper environment for the families of expectant women.
Studies have been initiated to explore the characteristics of the earliest
interactions between newborns and their parents. The discovery of the

phenomena of bonding, identification of the sensitive period, recognition of the newborn's sensory capabilities and alternative approaches to infant care are topics relevant to the concerns of the present era and therefore will be discussed over the following pages.

Discovery of the Bonding Phenomenon

Current interest in examining how perinatal care affects the behavior of pregnant women and their families has led to great professional and public interest in what is now commonly described as "bonding". In this paper, bonding will be defined as the parental behavior of claiming a baby following birth as parents' feelings of closeness develop toward their newborn.

The psychological, psychiatric and pediatric literature have well described the negative consequences for babies when they do not receive care for more than their physical needs (Gardner, 1973). Spitz (1946) coined the term, "hospitalism" to describe the aberrant behavior and development of institutionalized infants. Bowlby (1969) has described the necessity of a primary caregiver for an infant to develop the capacity to form an attachment. Fraiberg (1967) has discussed the significance of an infant's attachment for his or her future emotional development and well-being. These clinicians and researchers highlighted the important role primary caregivers play in an infant's development of an attachment and the significance of this early attachment to the infant's future development. Interest in bonding, a precursor to attachment, emerged from medical professionals' concern for how parents begin to express nurturance for their newborn infants.

By the nature of their work and concern for the welfare of children, pediatricians have traditionally been aware of how parents begin to relate to their babies (Cone, 1979; Kennell and Rolnick, 1960). The advent of intensive care nurseries and advances in medical care which led to the survival of very small preterm infants required that this traditional interest accommodate new concerns and issues. Clinicians, through observations of parents with their preterm infants, noticed hesitance and discomfort as mothers and fathers first interacted with their babies who had been cared for in an intensive care nursery (Klaus, Kennell, Plub, and Zuehlke, 1970). During the early years of neonatal intensive care, parents were not permitted to enter the nursery or to interact with their babies until hospital discharge. Investigators began and continue to identify some disconcerting findings when examining neonatal outcome data. Noted by several investigations is a disproportionate number of cases of failure to thrive, child abuse and indications of parenting failures among infants who had been separated from their parents to receive intensive care following birth (Elmer and Gregg, 1967; Klein and Stern, 1971; Shaheen, Alexander, Truskowsky, and Barbero, 1968). The question raised by these findings is, are babies lives being saved by new medical technology at the expense of risking the care they will receive later from their parents?   Though more than simply being separated from their parents distinguishes ill from healthy newborns, the role of separation has been considered important and, therefore, has been investigated.

In the 1960s the feasibility of allowing parents entry to an intensive care nursery was examined in a study conducted at Stanford University to determine if more bacteria would be introduced to the nursery if parental visiting were not restricted (Barnett, Leiderman, Grobstein, and Klaus, 1979). Findings from this study showed that parents' entrance into the nursery did not increase the babies' risk for infections. Studies further examined the effects of parental visitation on the behavior of mothers with their infants at the time of hospital discharge (Leifer, Leiderman, Barnett, and Williams, 1972; Seashore, Leifer, Barnett, and Leiderman, 1973).   In studies conducted at Stanford and Case Western Reserve Universities, data revealed behavioral differences between parents permitted visitation and those restricted from entering the nursery. At Stanford the observation was made that the experimental group of primiparous mothers, those allowed to enter the nursery seemed more confident with their infants at the time of discharge than the control mothers who were allowed to have only visual contact with their infants during the first three weeks of life (Seashore et al., 1973). The Case Western study showed that mothers who were allowed contact were more responsive to their babies during a feeding at the time of discharge and the babies subsequently performed better on standardized tests of development than did infants whose parents were denied the opportunity to have early contact with them (Klaus and Kennell, 1976).

The findings of these early studies brought attention to the timing of parent-infant contact and its importance for bonding as measured by positive maternal care. The very stressful experience of having a less than healthy preterm infant combined with the imposing barriers presented by an intensive care nursery certainly can impede parents' efforts to get to know their baby. Though statistics reveal a greater likelihood of severe parent-baby interaction problems for families of preterm infants, most parents adapt to the stress such an experience imposes and accept their babies. Research reveals, however, that prolonged separation of mothers and babies is associated with observed discomfort during initial interactions (Harper, Concepcion, Sokal and Sokal, 1976). Additionally, mothers interact differently with preterm than with full-term infants (Bakeman and Brown, 1980a). Controversy exists concerning the long-term impact of these initial interactions of the baby's future behavior and development (Bakeman and Brown, 1980b; Cohen and Beckwith, 1979).

Though methodological limitations make study findings difficult to interpret, there is much clinical evidence that separation of mother and infant affects the developing relationship. Parents of infants in an intensive care nursery comment that their baby doesn't feel like "theirs"; that they "have had a baby--but not really". Bonding or feeling close is difficult under such circumstances. Yet, such circumstances first brought the importance of early parent-baby contact to the forefront of public and professional attention.

That the importance of bonding has been accepted is evidenced by the 1977 statement by the American Medical Association (American Medical Association, 1977). Approximately 10 years after the first published descriptions of the often deleterious consequences of separation, the AMA's House of Delegates, the organization's policy making body, urged hospital medical staffs to develop new guidelines to humanize the birth experience to promote parent-infant bonding for all families. The studies which prompted such a statement investigated the importance of early parent-newborn contact for full-term as well as for ill infants. These studies will now be reviewed.

Testing the Sensitive Period Hypothesis

Once the significance of early parent-infant interaction in the intensive care nursery was recognized, discussion and attention turned to the nature of contact parents were permitted to have with their full-term infant while in hospital. If allowing parents to have contact with their preterm infant affects bonding and the nature of developing relationships, what are the effects of routine short-term separation of parents from their newborn?

The often cited studies which explored this question and which have stimulated much controversy and thinking about this issue were conducted at Case Western Reserve University (Klaus, Jerauld, Kreger, McAlpine, Steffa and Kennell, 1972; Ringler, Kennell, Jarvella, Navojosky, and Klaus, 1975; Ringler, Trause, Klaus, and Kennell, 1978). An experimental study was conducted with 28 primiparous women. One half the sample received 16 additional hours of contact time with their newborns during the first three days of life. The control group received the usual amount of time with their babies including scheduled time during feedings.

Follow-up studies have shown significant differences between these two groups over time. One month following birth the mothers who received extra contact with their infants were more responsive toward their babies (Klaus et al., 1972) and at one year *they* were observed *still* to be significantly more responsive with their infants than were the control mothers (Kennell et al., 1975). At two years, the linguistic behavior of the two groups of mothers with their children was compared (Ringler et al., 1975). Differences were identified as the mothers who had extended contact were observed to speak to their children with fewer commands, more questions and more elaborate sentences. Five years following birth the children who experienced extra contact with their mothers had significantly higher IQ scores than did those children who had received routine nursing care (Ringler et al., 1978). A variety of methodological problems inherent in these studies requires that their findings be cautiously interpreted. Attrition in sample size over time, low

socioeconomic status and limited knowledge about the personal backgrounds of the mothers raise questions about the implications of the
findings for different populations of families.

In Sweden, de Château and Wiberg (1977) conducted similar research
which revealed comparable findings. They examined the effects of 30
minutes of skin to skin contact between mother and baby. An experimental group was permitted such contact immediately following birth
while the control group was not. At 36 hours the mothers in the
experimental group held their infants more (de Château and Wiberg,
1977a), also at three months (1977b) and one year following birth the
experimental group displayed more nurturant caregiving with their infants
than did the mothers in the control group (de Château, Cajander,
Engstrom, 1978). A variety of other studies report short-term effects of
early mother-baby contact on mothers' nurturant behavior with their
babies (Schaller, Carlsson, and Larsson, 1979; Taylor, Campbell, Taylor,
Maloni, Dickey, and Rubenstein, 1979).

In a publication entitled "Defining the Limits of the Maternal
Sensitive Period", Hales, Lozoff, Sosa, and Kennell (1977) compared the
effects of providing 60 Guatemalan mothers one of three different
postpartum experiences with their newborns. Twenty mothers had contact with their newborns during episiotomy repair immediately after
delivery. Following this, they were allowed to have skin to skin contact
for 45 minutes in a private room. Twenty mothers in a second group were
given their newborns 12 hours following delivery for 45 minutes of skin to
skin contact whereas a control group of 20 mothers briefly saw their
newborns in the delivery room and again 12 hours later when they were
brought from the nursery to be fed. At 36 hours following birth, mothers
in the early contact group showed significantly more affectionate behavior with their newborns than was observed for the other two groups.
Similar differences were not observed in regard to the mothers' proximity
maintaining or caretaking behavior. In their discussion of the findings
from this study, the authors comment upon the important role the
newborn may play when a mother is allowed to be with her baby
immediately following birth. During this time the baby is very alert and
responsive and consequently reinforcing to the mother as they first spend
time together.

Studies examining the effects of early and extended contact for
mother and baby have also been conducted to examine such effects on
breastfeeding. Frequently the insufficient milk syndrome, or nursing
failure is observed as breastfeeding becomes an abortive effort for many
mothers (Gussler and Briesemeister, 1980). In developing countries, infant
mortality and morbidity is associated with early cessation of breastfeeding. Studies from both industrialized (Johnson, 1976; de Chateau,
1976) and developing nations (Kennell, Trause, and Klaus, 1975; Sosa,
Klaus, Kennell, and Urutia, 1976) show that early mother-baby contact
and the opportunity for suckling to occur increase the likelihood of more

prolonged breastfeeding. These findings have much significance for societies where breastfeeding plays such an important role in contributing to the potential for survival.

Though the studies which have explored the role of early contact have focused primarily upon maternal behavior, several investigations (Greenberg and Morris, 1974; Parke and O'Leary, 1975; Peterson, Mehl, and Leiderman, 1979) have explored the father's response to his newborn. Greenburg and Morris (1974) have used the term "engrossment" to describe a father's reaction to his newborn following birth. Engrossment occurs as a father experiences heightened feelings of excitement following the birth. Parke and O'Leary (1975) have done a series of studies using observational techniques to describe the father's style of interaction with his new baby during its first three days of life. Data from these studies provide striking evidence that the father is as active a participant in interaction with the baby as is the mother. Peterson et al. (1979), in a study of fathers' involvement throughout the perinatal period, found that participation in the birth and attitude toward it are most significant in predicting later attachment to the infant.

The research reviewed provides evidence of what, in 1972, was coined as the "Sensitive Period" for the development of human attachment (Klaus et al., 1972). The series of studies reported here has led to the assertion that the period of time immediately following birth affords a unique opportunity for bonding. When parents have the opportunity to be with their newborn following birth they may experience a special closeness that can affect the long-term parent-baby relationship and the baby's development. These concepts have been challenged by Campbell and Taylor (1979). Some attempts to replicate findings have failed to show similar long-term significant effects (Senechal, 1979). What cannot be refuted, however, are maternal and neonatal psychophysiological responses to birth. These complement the early contact studies by contributing to an understanding of how reciprocal parent-newborn behavior begins during the early hours post-partum. Much of this understanding has come from research describing the nature of a newborn's sensory capabilities and how these promote the beginning of an interactional sequence between parents and their infant.

Recognizing the Newborn's Sensory Capabilities and Unique Behavior

In the last 20 years scientific publications have confirmed what many mothers have always known: newborns can see, hear, and further are able to smell, taste, and initiate and respond to social interaction as they express their unique behavior. The recognition of these capabilities has added to the growing awareness of the importance of the early hours and days following birth for the beginning of the parent-baby relationship. During the immediate hours following birth an infant is in an alert, attentive state and is quite responsive to caregivers (Emde, Swedberg, and Suzuki, 1975).

Interaction between a mother and her baby, however, begins long before birth as fetal movement is felt and the unborn baby responds to the mother as she changes positions. Recently, research has begun to identify the prenatal development of sensory responsiveness (Liley, 1972) and new technology has made it possible to monitor the states of consciousness of a fetus (Rosen, Dierken, Hertz, Sorokin, and Timor-Trisch, 1979).

Following birth, the interaction which has already begun between a baby and mother continues as the baby adjusts to extra-uterine life. Studies have shown that infants who are cared for by one as opposed to many different caregivers more easily develop patterns in their rhythms of hunger, sleep and waking behavior (Burns, Sanders, Stechler, and Julia, 1972). With one caregiver the babies also showed less distress and were better able to regulate their individual behavior patterns to those who care for them.

Mothers of several children will describe behavioral differences they have noted with their babies and longitudinal research has shown that behavioral characteristics of infants are significant to personality development over time (Thomas and Chess, 1977). Each newborn has a unique style of behavior which can be observed with the Brazelton Neonatal Assessment Scale. This scale describes a newborn's interactive capabilities, response to stress, state liability and motor capabilities. Information from the observations gathered through administration of the scale can be shared with parents to help them better understand their baby's unique behavior.

A newborn uses his senses to communicate with those caring for him and parents can be shown how their individual baby is able to respond to them. Eye to eye gaze is inherent to human communication and from the time of birth, babies look into the eyes of those who speak to them. Not only can they see, but they can fixate upon and follow a moving target (Fantz, Fagan, and Miranda, 1975). Amazingly, newborns focus best upon objects eight to twelve inches away from them, which is just the distance between the caregiver's and baby's faces during a feeding. Newborns are also responsive to sounds and are selectively responsive to sounds resembling human speech (Eisenberg, 1976). Parents are particularly impressed when it is demonstrated how their baby is able to turn and visually fixate upon their eyes as they talk off to the side of their newborn. Between adults, a rhythmic interaction can be observed as two individuals speak to one another. Condon and Sander (1974) have shown that this can also be observed between a newborn and caregiver and reflects how new babies are already able to nonverbally respond and contribute as partners in the interactions they have with those who care for them.

Research has shown that newborns are innately responsive to odors and will avoid an adversive odor by turning away from it (Reiser, Yonas, and Wikner, 1976). MacFarlane has demonstrated that from the time of birth newborns are able to discriminate the odor of their mother's breast pad from that of an unused breast pad. Crook (1978) has shown that newborns are also differentially responsive to varying tastes.

Newborns also respond to movement and will quiet when lifted to a shoulder (Korner and Thoman, 1970). Many baby care activities include movement and proprioceptive-vestibular stimulation which calms and alerts a baby and makes positive interaction with a caregiver possible.

Interaction between a mother and infant thus begins during pregnancy as the baby develops unique traits which are expressed in the baby's individual behavior. Using amazingly developed sensory capabilities, the baby is able to respond to those caring for him from the time of birth.

Re-examination of Approaches to Caring for Mothers and Babies

The amassment of knowledge about the sensory and behavioral characteristics of newborns has increased respect for their unique and amazing capabilities. In a psychology textbook written in 1890 James wrote that the new infant perceives the world as one great blooming, buzzing confusion (James, 1890). Such a description denies the infant personhood and displays little respect for a baby's ability to perceive and selectively respond to the environment and caregivers with his or her very own style of behavior. In spite of the many professional and popular publications which discuss the sensory capabilities of newborns, one can frequently hear lay people and professionals make comments such as "babies only see shadows."

While today such ignorance is inexcusable among those who work with parents of new infants, in the past the perception of the newborn as an unresponsive, unfeeling organism may well have served a function by protecting caregivers from emotional investment in a baby whose chances of survival were always very guarded. Mead and Newton (1967) have commented that in some societies where neonatal and infant mortality is high, the infant is not considered a person at all and remains unnamed and unmourned if it dies. In our modern society where the chances of neonatal death are minimal and still decreasing, we can comfortably accept newborns as persons possessing behavioral capabilities which allow them to perceive their world and respond discriminatingly to those around them.

We have much, however, to learn from cultures which do not have the luxuries of modern technology and medical care. In his 1979 Armstrong Address to the Ambulatory Pediatric Association entitled, "Are We in the Midst of a Revolution?", Kennell (1980) drew on anthropological studies of maternal care to highlight how technological societies may be less sophisticated in providing responsive care to babies than those peoples who have not experienced the many conveniences of modern life. He described as an example the doula or traditional birth attendant in

Guatemala. The doula, by her caring and support, helps a mother during labor and delivery and can ease her anxieties so that lactation is initiated and maintained. Interestingly, the presence of a doula is also associated with a lower incidence of difficulties during labor and delivery (Sosa, Kennell, Klaus, and Urrutia, 1979).

Feeding practices vary across cultural contexts. Though breast-feeding has experienced an increase in popularity in the United States and recently has been endorsed by the American Academy of Pediatrics (Nutrition Committee of the Canadian Pediatric Society and the Committee on Nutrition of the American Academy of Pediatrics, 1978), the use of formulas and feeding schedules has been the predominant feeding style in our modern world (Berg, 1973).

In their paper, "Infant Care: Cache or Carry," Lozoff and Brittenham (1979) contrast infant feeding styles in industrialized and nonindustrialized societies. The authors note that in the nonindustrialized societies and among hunting-gathering peoples, infants are carried by their mothers 80 to 90 percent of the time during their early months. Infants in such societies typically sleep with their mothers at night, and breastfeeding is continuous.

Lozoff and Brittenham report that in the United States infants spend much less time in body contact with their mothers, up to approximately one-third of the time until three months of age and only 16 percent by nine months of age. Though sleeping together is advocated by some (Thevenin, 1976), typically separate sleeping arrangements for mothers and their babies are recommended in our country. Lozoff and Brittenham conclude that in modern societies infant care resembles that observed in mammals who cache their young and produce breast milk high in fat and protein, allowing the very young animal to be left alone for periods of time while the mother hunts. The pattern of frequent feedings observed in nonindustrial societies is in keeping with the composition of breast milk. Being a dilute, low fat fluid having relatively low protein content, breast milk is quickly digested and efficiently absorbed. However, as digestion is quick, a baby must nurse frequently to remain satiated.

Many contemporary parents who have identified the discrepancy between what is typically called modern baby care and what can be considered sensitive care appropriate to the basic needs of a baby have developed new trends in caring for infants. The LaLeche League provides support and information to the mother about lactation and nursing (LaLeche League, 1963). Parent-baby distancing, represented and experienced with buggies, strollers and the more traditional means of transporting an infant, is not as popular as it once was. Today, baby carriers, slings, and backpacks are frequently used to provide a baby with the calming comfort of body warmth and movement.

ENABLING THE PARENT-BABY RELATIONSHIP TO BEGIN POSITIVELY

In recent years there has been a recognition of the changing patterns of social supports available to families. Many new mothers and fathers face the responsibilities of parenthood with little or no experience caring for babies. There is, as well, an increased awareness that many adults encounter parenthood with a personal background ill-suited to providing responsive care to their new baby (Boger and Light, 1976; Helfer, 1978; Steele and Pollock, 1974). Health care personnel, parent educators and others who provide services to families have begun integrating the growing knowledge about early parental and neonatal behavior with new approaches to care, services and education in response to the perceived need to support new families. The perinatal epoch is the ideal time to provide such programs; not only to prevent severe problems, but to also foster the nurturance every new baby needs.

Kempe and his associates at the University of Colorado brought national attention to the issue of child abuse and neglect through initial publications, presentations at professional meetings and clinical work which identified the Battered Child Syndrome (Kempe, Silverman, Steele, Droegemueller, and Silver, 1962; Helfer and Kempe, 1968). As the problems of child abuse became well defined and its etiology understood, attention focused on its prevention, as the treatment of such a complex family problem has proved to be most difficult and frequently unsuccessful. One vanguard study which examined how child abuse and neglect could be prevented and how families could be supported during the perinatal epoch was conducted by Gray, Cutler, Dean and Kempe (1979). This study used observations made during prenatal visits to an obstetric clinic and during labor, delivery and postpartum hospitalization. From these observations mothers were identified as either high or low risk for parenting problems. Half the mothers in the high risk group received "additional services" which included assignment to one pediatrician responsible for their baby's care, weekly visits by a public health nurse, and frequent phone contact between the family, physician and nurse. The remaining high risk mothers received the usual services of the pediatric well-baby clinic.

Follow-up data comparing the outcome of these children when they were between 17 and 35 months old (mean 26.8 months) revealed striking differences between the study groups. More children in the high risk group experienced abuse, failure to thrive, abnormal scores on the Denver Development Screening Test and accidents than in the low risk group. Significantly more children required hospitalization for an injury secondary to what was defined as "abnormal parenting practices" in the high risk-no intervention group than in the high risk group that received additional services. The data from this study clearly support the significance of hospital observations of mother-baby interaction, as 77 percent of the high risk sample could be predicted from the labor and delivery observations without the prenatal or postpartum measures of the mother's behavior.

Though such findings have powerful implications for the identification of those at risk for parenting failure, caution must be exercised
in the use of behavioral rating scales to identify categories of risk without
more complete descriptions of an individual's social history and situation.
Further, the perinatal epoch is not only a time to identify and hopefully
provide additional services to families believed to require assistance for
child rearing, but is also a time to reinforce and support those parents
who are positively responding to the major life event the birth of a baby
represents. Much can be done to help parents learn to respond and adjust
positively to their new baby while the mother and baby are still in the
hospital together. Prenatal education, supportive environments for birth,
rooming-in, educational programs focused upon modeling and supporting
parents as they learn to communicate with the newborn, and the use of
home visitors will be reviewed. Each of these services will be discussed
as a response to the need for individualized care to strengthen family
relationships at a time of beginning.

Prenatal Support and Education

A mother's feeling of closeness to her child begins during pregnancy
(Kennell, Slyter, and Klaus, 1970). A woman's previous experiences
including her own mother's response to pregnancy (Uddenberg, 1974),
parental loss during childhood (Frommer and O'Shea, 1973a) and her
present marital adjustment (Porter and Demeuth, 1979) have been shown
to affect her adjustment to pregnancy. Study findings further indicate
that adaptation to caring for a baby is strongly related to her adaptation
to pregnancy (Shereshesky, Liebenberg, and Lockman, 1973). Maladaptive
responses to pregnancy may signal problems in caring for the newborn
(Cohen, 1979). Interestingly, a woman's failure to experience nurturance
from previous and present family relationships is highly associated with
adaptive problems during the perinatal epoch. Identification of these
problems before or during pregnancy and the provision of special aid to
such parents may help them better adapt to a baby's needs for nurturant
care (Frommer and O'Shea, 1973b; Helfer, 1978).

Though previous experiences can adversely affect a woman's response to pregnancy, almost all women emotionally experience pregnancy
with some degree of uncertainty, fear and ambivalence. Prenatal
education can play an important role in helping prospective parents
anticipate a variety of responses to pregnancy. Courses for parents
covering various aspects of pregnancy, nutrition, and preparation for labor
and delivery have become increasingly popular. Based on the philosophy
that knowledge reduces anxiety, educational courses for parents prior to
birth aim to educate prospective parents so that they may be more knowledgeable about the physical changes they are experiencing and be better
prepared for labor and delivery. Little data are available about the effect
of such learning on the actual parent-baby relationship. However, studies
do provide some information on the effects of prenatal education on labor
and delivery (Charles, Norr, Block, Meyering, and Meyers, 1978; Highley,

McElin, and Young, 1978).   In one study, parents who participated in
Lamaze training showed no obstetric differences from controls, but had
lower levels of pain and higher levels of enjoyment (Charles et al., 1978).
In a similar study, different findings emerged (Highley et al., 1978).   Using
500 Lamaze participants with 500 matched controls, Highley found that
those with Lamaze training had one fourth the number of Caesarean
sections, one fifth the amount of fetal distress, one-third the amount of
postpartum infection, less serious perineal lacerations, one-third the incidence of toxemia, and one-half the number of preterm newborns.   The
hypothesis can be advanced that the less traumatic the labor and delivery
and the more comfortable the experience for the parents, the easier the
adaptation to parenting can be for them.   Certainly, bonding following an
uncomplicated labor and delivery can transpire more easily and naturally.

Creating a Physical and Social Environment for Birth

In the 1970s many routine practices of hospital care began to be
questioned, especially in regard to the birth process.   Whereas birth has
historically been a time for family togetherness and celebration, in the
hospital it is often accompanied by alienation and isolation.   As a reaction
to this, many families began to opt for delivering their babies at home
with either lay or professional assistance (Sousa, 1976; Stewart and
Stewart, 1976; Lang, 1972).   Parents expressed their preference for such
an experience as it offered them optimal contact with their newborn in a
relaxed environment, free from restrictions, where friends and family can
share the joyous moments surrounding the birth of the baby.   In response
to such a reaction against traditional obstetrical care, increasing consumer pressure, and a declining birth rate, hospitals and perinatal health
care providers began to examine many routine practices surrounding labor
and delivery which had become institutionalized.   Several major changes
and alternatives in care have subsequently developed.

Maternity centers, independent but in close proximity to hospitals,
are now available in some communities (Faison, Pisani, Douglas, Cranch,
and Lubic, 1979).   These centers are usually administered by certified
nurse midwives who also serve as primary caregivers.   The centers provide
a relaxed home-like environment where a woman at low risk for obstetrical difficulties can labor and deliver in the same room in the
company of her family and friends.   Though controversial, siblings
sometimes have also been included in such birthing settings (Leonard,
Irvin, Ballard, Ferris, and Clyman, 1979).

Similar services may be offered on in-patient hospital wards.
Alternative birth centers, pending or birthing rooms, also provide a home-
like atmosphere but in a hospital (Ballard, Ferris, Read, Clyman, Leonard,
and Irvin, 1978).   In such a setting a woman is allowed to be with family or
friends and remains in the same room throughout labor and delivery.   With
this care a woman can then stay with her newborn following delivery, and
discharge home may take place less than 24 hours following birth.

Follow-up care is provided by public health nurses and out-patient pediatric visits.

Changes in routine care have also occurred for the family who receives more traditional hospital obstetric services for labor and delivery. Sensitivity to the needs of fathers is increasing nationally as rules are now relaxed and fathers are permitted and sometimes encouraged to attend the delivery. In many places fathers are present for Caesarean births as well as for normal vaginal deliveries. As already discussed, the role of a supportive person during labor has been shown not only to affect the mother's later behavior with her newborn, but also to decrease complications during labor and delivery (Sosa et al., 1979). Many routine nursery check-in procedures such as injection of vitamin K, eye drops, measuring and washing are now delayed until parents have an opportunity to see, hold and nurse their baby if this is desired. Administration of prophylactic silver nitrate is now commonly delayed until parents have been able to interact with their baby following birth when the period of alert behavior enhances opportunities for positive eye to eye gazing (Butterfield, Emde, and Platt, 1978).

During the immediate minutes following birth parents can express their exhilaration as they reach out and hold their new baby. Studies have demonstrated that placing a naked, dry newborn on a mother's bare chest and covering the baby with a warm blanket are as effective as placing the baby under a heat panel for the maintenance of appropriate body temperature (Gardner, 1979). Hospitals and personnel can do much to allow for such positive experiences. At the same time they must provide care for babies as they physiologically adapt to extrauterine life, and for mothers as they recover from childbirth. However, this care can be adapted so as to accommodate the parents' needs for contact with their newborn.

Rooming-In

In an article published in *Parents Magazine,* Jackson (1947) described a new hospital care arrangement for mothers and babies called rooming-in. Borrowing this term first used by Gesell and Ilg (1943), Jackson, Olmstead, Foord, Thomas and Hyden (1948) wrote about their experience in New Haven, Connecticut of providing care to mothers and babies together in the same room for the sake of mother-baby closeness and understanding. They discussed the very favorable responses of mothers and fathers to such an arrangement but also pointed out the adjustments demanded of the nursing staff by this situation. At about this same time, rooming-in was instituted as a compulsory care arrangement at Duke Hospital in order to prevent an infection epidemic (McBryde, 1951). In his report of the advantages of such care, McBryde (1951) stated that there was a reduction in infections, an increase in the amount of breastfeeding and less infant crying when mothers cared for their own newborns. McBryde stated that with rooming-in the mother is better able to observe her infant's hunger rhythm and the baby "gets as good care as a puppy and a kitten, who thrive nutritionally and psychologically better than many human offspring" (p. 626). McBryde also reported that following the use of rooming-in there was a 90 percent decrease in the number of telephone calls back to the hospital by mothers with questions about the care of their baby. This system of care was also reported to be less costly.

.These studies conducted over 30 years ago highlighted the practicality of such care for pragmatic concerns including infection control, cost, and the psychological benefit to mothers and babies. Recent studies on the effects of rooming-in on the developing parent-baby relationship continue to provide evidence of advantages. Greenberg, Rosenberg and Lind (1973) note that mothers who were randomly assigned to room-in with their newborns judged themselves to be more confident and competent in baby care, thought they would need less help in caring for their infants at home and could attribute more to their babies' cries than the mothers who were not assigned to the rooming-in treatment.

A second recent study was conducted as part of a large investigation of factors predictive of child abuse (O'Connor, Vietz, Sherrod, Sandler, and Altemeier, 1980). With a sample of women receiving care from a large hospital/medical school clinic, mothers were assigned to either room-in with their new babies or to receive the standard nursing care which allowed mothers and babies to be together for the first time seven hours following delivery. The results of this study showed that between 12 and 21 months later (mean 17 months) only one child, among the 143 who room-in, experienced what was identified as substantial inadequate parenting. Nine children from the control group of 158 received parenting judged to be substantially inadequate by evidence of inappropriate growth, more than one hospitalization for remedy of parental inadequacy, investigation by Protective Services, abnormal development, parental relinquishment of caretaking responsibility, or physical abuse. The different outcome observed in the two groups is both significant and dramatic.

Evidence from these years of experience with rooming-in documents the helpful role it can play in fostering positive interaction between parents and their new baby. Certainly, as a relatively easy to manage was of providing care, hospitals can facilitate and encourage mothers and fathers to play a major caregiving role with their baby prior to discharge home.

Helping Parents Communicate with their Newborn

The sensitive period hypothesis emphasizes that the immediate hours and days following birth offer a special time for parents to experience closeness with their newborn. Providing time for parent-baby contact immediately after delivery by delaying transfer of the newborn to the transitional nursery, and during the subsequent postpartum days through rooming-in, enables parents to, if nothing more, become accustomed to their newborn's behavior and feel more comfortable giving care. However, more than simply allowing parents and their newborn time together is necessary. One frequently hears parents say, "Well, the baby will become more fun once he can respond to me more. Now he just eats and sleeps." Maternal-child nursing care has traditionally been involved in teaching parents how to care for a baby's basic physical needs. This mission must continue but in a broadened form, and recently attention has been focused upon helping parents get to know their newborn.

Communicating with a newborn demands that an adult use a mode of behavior not primarily involved in every day adult-to-adult conversations. Adults communicate with language, writing and nonverbal expressions. An infant uses his sensory capabilities to initiate interaction and to respond to the behaviors of those interacting with him. An adult learns to interpret this behavior and to respond to it using his or her own facial expressions, vocalizations, touch, and through cuddling and movement. This does not happen automatically; parents need help through modeling practice and supportive feedback for their efforts as they begin to get to know and communicate with their baby.

Although most practicing pediatricians are more actively adhering to a biosocial approach to well child care, these efforts typically do not begin until the commencement of routine office visits (Casey and Whitt, 1980; Wolfson and Bass, 1979). Literature has documented the many concerns and problems that mothers telephone to their pediatrician's office prior to their first visit (Sumner and Fritsch, 1977). One may speculate about the role in-hospital care, focused upon assisting parents as they learn to communicate with their baby, could play in minimizing these concerns by helping parents to develop greater comfort in caring for their new baby.

Emotional and Social Postpartum Support with Home Visitor

The definition of the perinatal epoch includes the first 28 days of life. Assistance to families should continue after the baby's discharge from the hospital nursery.

Kempe (1976) has proposed that a lay health visitor program be offered to all mothers during their postpartum hospitalization. This could provide an outreach to families and be instrumental in preventing the incidence of child abuse and neglect. European countries offer several models of such programs. These have been used as demonstration projects for home health visitors in the United States and Canada. To evaluate the efficacy of implementing Kempe's (1976) proposal, two lay home health visitor programs have been initiated in the Denver area (Gray, Kaplan, and Kempe, 1980; Butterfield, van Doorninck, Dawson, and Alexander, 1979).

During an 18-month period, the program conducted by Gray et al. (1980) offered to all mothers who delivered a baby at Colorado General Hospital and lived within a specified area the services of a home visitor as part of their routine pediatric care. The visitor, either a mother or a woman well experienced in working with children, was selected for her ability to provide warmth, flexibility, empathy and high self-esteem. She functioned as a socially supportive person to a new family and provided information about child development, behavior and home safety. These women received a salary of minimum wage for their time. From the 550 families who received such services, only two children received minor injuries thought to be secondary to nonaccidental injury. Though formal evaluation of this program is in process, its strength has been perceived to lie in the supportive care provided by the visitor in helping to link the family and the community. Further, it has served as a lifeline in times of crisis.

In order to evaluate the effect of home visitors and parent groups on maternal adjustment Butterfield et al. (1979), randomly assigned women from public health maternity clinics to control or treatment groups. Complete follow-up data from this study is not yet available. However, parental acceptance of the program has been noted to be quite favorable (Dawson, 1980).

A Canadian study also has examined the efficacy of home visitors and compared the relative effectiveness of beginning the onset of services during the mother's pregnancy, beginning six weeks following delivery or providing no services (Larson. 1980). This program provided care to families through the baby's first 18 months of life. Findings show that independent evaluations of the home environment, mother-infant interaction and child health outcomes reveal significant differences between families in the three groups. The group which began to receive services prenatally had fewer accidents, more positive maternal behavior, fewer feeding problems, fewer mother-infant interaction problems and less non-participant fathers. There were few differences between the group that began to receive services following the birth of the baby and the control group that received no services. It was concluded that mother-infant pairs derived significant benefit from the home visitor, and early involvement of the visitor has a positive effect upon outcome measures. The authors speculate that a bonding between visitor and family occurred during the early perinatal period which strengthened the effectiveness of the former's role in supporting parents as they adjusted to parenthood.

A comprehensive program of perinatal support for first time parents has been developed by Boger and his colleagues at Michigan State University (Boger and Richter, 1980). This program, entitled Perinatal Positive Parenting, involves the delivery of information and positive support beginning in the hospital room of the new mother, with follow-up home visitation and parent group programming during the first six weeks postpartum. Volunteers, who are experienced mothers, are provided training in communication skills and infant development.   Videotapes, which include anticipatory guidance on newborn behaviors and suggestions for enhancing family life with a new baby, are shown in the mother's hospital room. The primary goal of this program is to provide support to new families facilitated through relationships between the new mothers and the experienced volunteers.   Such support helps parents feel good about themselves so that they can better meet the needs of their new baby.

SUMMARY

In the 1980s a woman can conceive knowing her chances of surviving pregnancy and childbirth are excellent. Referral centers are available for the care of the woman with a high-risk pregnancy, so that if problems arise she can receive specialized care for herself and her unborn baby. For newborn babies, too, the chances of surviving have never been better. Through efforts being made to reduce the risk of delivery for a preterm or ill newborn, smaller and smaller infants are surviving without experiencing handicapping conditions.

Lozoff, Brittenham, Trause, Kennell and Klaus (1977) have noted that advances in perinatal medicine have decreased maternal and neonatal morbidity, but also have altered the initiation of the mother-child relationship.   These authors state, "some mother-infant pairs may be strained beyond limits of their adaptability" (p. 1). Though inadvertent, the effects of hospital care most definitely can interfere with the developing synchrony of the infant-parent relationship (de Château, 1979).

Studies which have experimentally explored the effects of altering care for mothers and babies have used measures of maternal and paternal behavior as dependent variables.   Bonding, a term used to describe the feelings of closeness between parents and their newborn, has also been studied by observations of parental behavior.   The issue of bonding has become controversial.   Its critics and its proponents often have cast it as an all or nothing phenomenon.   It has too often been confused with attachment which refers to the mutual affectual tie that develops between infant and caregiving adult(s) over a longer period of time. Investigations of bonding have relied on actual observations of nurturant behavior, behavior long assumed and accepted as essential for proper positive development.   The results continue to support the new importance now being shown this early postpartum experience between parents and infant.

Nurturance is the behavior of caring for and loving a baby. For a baby to grow and thrive, food, warmth and supportive handling are needed. A woman's body can give all of this to a newborn when close contact between mother and newborn occurs over time. A father's supportive care and handling can also greatly enhance the newborn's ability to thrive. By providing nurturance, parents are also able to experience and express their feelings toward baby which have been developing long before birth. These feelings are reinforced as the baby responds to them. What results is a progression of expanding transactions. This appears to have been nature's plan for babies and their families. Science has assisted in the development of programs for infants and their mothers, and has documented how essential nurturance is for survival. It is very important that those involved with human services foster parents' ability to nurture their newborn children. This nurturant care is the beginning of a positive parent-baby relationship which will have major impact on the nature of the baby's early life and later development.

REFERENCES

American Medical Association. News release, Dec. 21, 1977.

Apgar, V., and Beck, J. *Is my baby alright?* New York: Simon and Schuster, 1972.

Arms, S. *Immaculate deception.* Boston: Houghton Mifflin, 1975.

Bakeman, R., and Brown, J. V. Analyzing behavioral sequences: Differences between preterm and full term infant-mother dyads during the first months of life. In D. B. Sarvin, R. C. Hawkins, II., L. O. Walker, and J. H. Penticuff (Eds.), *Exceptional infant: Psychosocial risks in infant-environment transactions* (Vol. 4). New York: Brunner/Mazel, 1980. (a).

Bakeman, R., and Brown, J. V. Early interaction: Consequences for social and mental development at three years. *Child Development,* 1980, *51,* 437-447. (b)

Ballard, R. B., Ferris, C., Read, F., Clyman, R., Leonard, C., and Irvin, N. Safety of a hospital based alternative birth center (ABC). *Clinical Research,* 1978, *26,* 179. (Abstract)

Barnett, C. R., Leiderman, P. H., Grobstein, R., and Klaus, M. Neonatal separation: The maternal side of interactional deprivation. *Pediatrics,* 1970, *45,* 197-205.

Berg, A. *The nutritional factor: Its role in national development.* Washington, D.C.: Brookings Institute, 1973.

Boger, R. P., and Richter, R. A. *The perinatal positive parenting program: An overview,* (occasional paper). Institute for Family and Child Study, Michigan State University, 1980.

Boger, R. P., and Light, H. Education for parenting: A preventive approach to child neglect and abuse. *Midwest Parent Review,* Fall, 1976.

Bowlby, J. *Attachment and loss series, Attachment* (Vol. 1). New York: Basic Books, 1969.

Brazelton, T. B. *Behavioral Neonatal Assessment Scale.* Philadelphia: J. B. Lippincott, 1973.

Burns, P., Sanders L. W., Stechler, G., and Julia, H. Distress and feeding: Short term effects of caregiver environment on the first ten days of life. *Journal of American Academy of Child Psychiatry,* 1972, *11,* 427-439.

Butterfield, P. M., van Doornick, W. J., Dawson, P., and Alexander, H. *Early identification of dysparenting*. Paper presented at the biennial convention of the Society for Research in Child Development, San Francisco, March, 1979.

Butterfield, P. N., Emde, R. N., and Platt, B. B. Effects of silver nitrate on initial visual behavior. *American Journal of Diseases of Children*, 1978, *132*, 426.

Campbell, S. G., and Taylor, P. Bonding and attachment: Theoretical issues. *Seminars in Perinatology*, 1979, *3*, 3-13.

Charles, A. G., Norr, K. L., Block, C. R., Meyering, S., and Meyers, E. Obstetric and psychological effects of psychoprophylactic preparation for childbirth. *American Journal of Obstetrics and Gynecology*, 1978, *131*, 44-52.

Casey, P. H., and Whitt, J. K. Effect of the pediatrician on the mother-infant relationship. *Pediatrics*, 1980, *68*, 815-820.

Cohen, R. L. Maladaptation to pregnancy. *Seminars in Perinatology*, 1979, *3*, 15-24.

Cohen, S. E., and Beckwith, L. Preterm infant interaction with the caregiver in the first year of life and competence at age two. *Child Development*, 1979, *50*, 767-776.

Collias, N. E. The analysis of socialization in sheep and goats. *Ecology*, 1956, *37*, 228-239.

Condon, W. S., and Sander, L. W. Neonate movement is synchronized with adult speech: Interactional participation and language acquisition. *Science*, 1974, *183*, 99-101.

Cone, T. E. *History of American Pediatrics*. Boston: Little, Brown and Company, 1979.

Crook, C. K. Taste perception in the newborn infant. *Infant Behavior and Development*, 1978, *1*, 52-69.

Dawson, P. Personal communication, May, 1980.

de Château, P. Neonatal care routines, influences on maternal and infant behavior on breast feeding. *Umea University Medical Dissertations* (new series), No. 20, 1976.

de Château, P. Effects of hospital practices on synchrony in the development of the infant parent relationship. *Seminars in Perinatology,* 1979, *3*, 45-60.

de Château, P., Wiberg, B. Long term effect on mother-infant behavior of extra contact during the first hour postpartum. I. First observation at 36 hours. *Acta Peadiatrica Scandinavica*, 1977, *66*, 137-144. (a)

de Château, P., and Wiberg, B. Long term effect on mother-infant behavior of extra contact during the first hour postpartum. II. Follow up at three months. *Acta Peadiatrica Scandinavica*, 1977, *66*, 145-151. (b)

de Château, P., Cajander, K., and Engstrom, A. C. Long term effect of early postpartum contact: One year follow-up. In *Proceedings of Fifth International Congress on Psychosomatic Obstetrics and Gynecology*. New York: Academic Press, 1978.

Eisenberg, R. B. *Auditory competence in early life: The roots of communicative behavior*. Baltimore: University Park Press, 1976.

Elkins, V. H. *The rights of the pregnant parent*. New York: Two Continents Publishing Group, 1977.

Emde, R. N., Swedberg, J., and Suzuki, B. Human wakefulness and biological rhythms after birth. *Archives of General Psychology*, 1975, *32*, 780-783.

Faison, J., Pisani, B. J., Douglas, R., Cranch, G., and Lubic, R. The childbearing center: An alternative birth setting. *Obstetrics and Gynecology*, 1979, *54*, 527-532.

Fantz, R. L., Fagan, J. F., and Miranda, S. B. Early visual selectivity as a function of pattern variables, previous exposure, age from birth and conception and expected cognitive deficit. In L. B. Cohen and P. Salapatek (Eds.), *Infant perception: From sensation to cognition*. New York: Academic Press, 1975.

Fraiberg, S. The origins of human bonds. *Commentary*, 1967, *44*, 47-57.

Frommer, E. A., and O'Shea, G. The importance of childhood experience in relation to problems of marriage and family building. *British Journal of Psychiatry*, 1973, *123*, 157-160. (a)

Frommer, E., and O'Shea, G. Antenatal identification of women liable to have problems in managing their infants. *British Journal of Psychiatry*, 1973, *123*, 149-156. (b)

Gardner, L. Deprivation dwarfism. In Scientific American, *The nature and nurture of behavior, developmental psycho-biology*. San Francisco: Scientific American, 1973.

Gardner, S. The mother as incubator after delivery. *Journal of Nurses Association of American College of Obstetrics and Gynecology*, 1979, *8*, 174-176.

Gesell, A., and Ilg, F. *Infant and child in the culture of today*. New York: Harper and Brothers, 1943.

Graven, S. N. Perinatal health promotion: An overview. *Family and Community Health*, 1978, *1*, 1-11.

Gray, J. D., Cutler, C. A., Dean, J. G., and Kempe, C. H. Prediction and prevention of child abuse. *Seminars in Perinatology*, 1979, *3*, 85-90.

Gray, J., Kaplan, B., and Kempe, C. H. Eighteen months experience with a lay health visitor program. In R. E. Helfer and C. H. Kempe (Eds.), *The battered child* (3rd Ed.). Chicago: University of Chicago Press, 1980.

Greenberg, M., and Morris, N. Engrossment: The newborn's impact upon the father. *American Journal of Orthopsychiatry*, 1974, *44*, 520-531.

Greenberg, M., Rosenberg, I., and Lind, J. First mothers rooming-in with their newborns: Its impact upon the mother. *American Journal of Orthopsychiatry*, 1973, *43*, 783-788.

Gussler, J. D., and Briesemeister, L. H. The insufficient milk syndrome: A biocultural explanation. *Medical Anthropology*, 1980, *4*, 1-24.

Hales, D. J., Lozoff, B., Sosa, R., and Kennell, J. H. Defining the limits of the maternal sensitive period. *Developmental Medicine and Child Neurology*, 1977, *19*, 454-461.

Harper, R., Concepcion, S., Sokal, S., and Sokal, M. Observations on unrestricted parental contact with infants in the neonatal intensive care unit. *Journal of Pediatrics*, 1976, *89*, 441-445.

Harris, T. R., Isaman, J., and Giles, H. R. Improved neonatal survival through maternal transport. *Obstetrics and Gynecology*, 1978, *52*, 294-300.

Helfer, R. E. *Childhood comes first* (Evaluation edition). Box 1781, East Lansing, Michigan, 1978.

Helfer, R. E., and Kempe, C. H. *The battered child.* Chicago: University of Chicago Press, 1968.

Hersher, L., Richmond, J., and Moore, A. Maternal behavior in sheep and goats. In H. R. Reingold (Ed.), *Maternal behavior in mammals*. New York: John Wiley and Sons, 1963.

Highley, M. J., McElin, T. W., and Young, T. Maternal and fetal outcome of Lamaze-prepared patients. *Obstetrics and Gynecology*, 1978, *51*, 643-647.

Jackson, E. Mothers and babies together. *Parents' Magazine*, 1947, *22*, 18-19.

Jackson, E., Olmstead, R. W., Foord, A., Thomas, H., and Hyden, K. Hospital rooming-in unit for four newborn infants and their mothers: Descriptive account of background, development and procedures with a few preliminary observations. *Pediatrics*, 1948, *1*, 28-43.

James, W. *Principles of psychology.* New York: Holt Rinehart and Winston, 1890.

Johnson, N. W. Breast feeding at one hour of age. *American Journal of Maternal Child Nursing*, 1976, *1*, 12-16.

Kempe, C. H. Approaches to preventing child abuse: The health visitor concept. *American Journal of Diseases of Children*, 1976, *130*, 941-947.

Kempe, C. H., Silverman, F. N., Steele, B. F., Droegemueller, W., and Silver, H. K. The battered child syndrome. *Journal of the American Medical Association*, 1962, *181*, 17-24.

Kennell, J. H. Are we in the midst of a revolution? *American Journal of Diseases of Children*, 1980, *134*, 303-310.

Kennell, J. H., and Rolnick, A. Discussing problems in newborn babies with their parents. *Pediatrics*, 1960, *26*, 832-838.

Kennell, J. H., Slyter, H., and Klaus, M. The mourning response of parents to the death of a newborn infant. *New England Journal of Medicine*, 1970, *283*, 344-349.

Kennell, J. H., Trause, M. A., and Klaus, M. Evidence for a sensitive period in the human mother. In Ciba Foundation Symposium 33 (new series), *Parent infant interaction*. Amsterdam: Elsevier Publishing, 1975.

Klaus, M., Jerauld, R., Kreger, N. C., McAlpine, W., Steffa, M., and Kennell, J. H. Maternal attachment: Importance of the first postpartum days. *New England Journal of Medicine*, 1972, *284*, 460-463.

Klaus, M. H., and Kennell, J. H. *Maternal infant bonding.* St. Louis: C. V. Mosby, 1976.

Klaus, M., Kennell, J. H., Plumb, N., and Zuehlke, S. Human maternal behavior at first contact with her young. *Pediatrics*, 1970, *46*, 186-192.

Klein, M., and Stern, L. Low birth weight and the battered child syndrome. *American Journal of Diseases of Children*, 1971, *122*, 15-18.

Korner, A. F., and Thoman, E. B. Visual alertness in neonates as evoked by maternal care. *Journal of Experimental Child Psychology*, 1970, *10*, 67-78.

La Leche League. *The womanly art of breastfeeding*. Franklin Park, IL: Author, 1963.

Lang, R. *Birth Book*. Ben Lomond, CA: Genesis Press, 1972.

Larson, C. P. Efficacy of prenatal and postpartum home visits on child health and development. *Pediatrics*, 1980, *66*, 191-197.

Leifer, A. D., Leiderman, P. H., Barnett, C. R., and Williams, J. Effects of mother infant separation on maternal attachment behavior. *Child Development*, 1972, *43*, 1203-1218.

Leonard, C. H., Irvin, N., Ballard, R. A., Ferris, C., and Clyman, R. Preliminary observations of the behavior of children present at the birth of a sibling. *Pediatrics*, 1979, *64*, 949-951.

Liley, A. The foetus as a personality. *Australian and New Zealand Journal of Psychiatry*, 1972, *6*, 99-105.

Lozoff, B., and Brittenham, G. Infant care: Cache or carry. *Pediatrics*, 1979, *95*, 478-483.

Lozoff, B., Brittenham, G. M., Trause, M. A., Kennell, J. H., and Klaus, M. The mother-newborn relationship: Limits of adaptability. *Journal of Pediatrics*, 1977, *91*, 1-12.

MacFarlane, J. A. Olfaction in the development of social preferences in the human neonate. In Ciba Foundation Symposium, 33 (new series), *Parent infant interaction*. Amsterdam: Elsevier Publishing, 1975.

McBryde, A. Compulsory rooming-in in the ward and private newborn service at Duke Hospital. *Journal of the American Medical Association*, 1951, *145*, 625-628.

McDonald, R. L. The role of emotional factors in obstetric complications: A review. *Psychosomatic Medicine*, 1968, *30*, 222-237.

Mead, M., and Newton, N. Cultura patterning of perinatal behavior. In S. A. Richardson and A. F. Buttmacher (Eds.), *Childbearing--its social and psychological aspects*. Baltimore: Williams and Williams, 1967.

Nuckolls, K., Cassel, J., and Kaplan, B. Psychosocial assets, life crises and the prognosis of pregnancy. *American Journal of Epidemiology*, 1972, *95*, 431-441.

Nutrition Committee of the Canadian Pediatric Society and the Committee on Nutrition of the American Academy of Pediatrics. Breast Feeding. *Pediatrics*, 1978, *62*, 591-601.

O'Connor, S., Vietz, P. M., Sherrod, K. B., Sandler, H. M., and Altemeier, W. A. Reduced incidence of parenting inadequacy following rooming-in. *Pediatrics*, 1980, *66*, 176-182.

Osofsky, H. J., and Kendall, N. Poverty as a criterion of risk. *Clinical Obstetrics and Gynecology*, 1973, *16*, 103-109.

Ottinger, D., and Simmons, J. Behavior of human neonates and perinatal maternal anxiety. *Psychology Reports*, 1964, *14*, 391-394.

Parke, R. D., and O'Leary, S. Father-mother-infant interaction in the newborn period: Some findings, some observations, and some unresolved issues. In K. F. Riegel and J. Meacham (Eds.), *The developing individual in a changing world, Vol. 2, Social and environmental issues.* The Hague: Mouton and Company, 1975.

Peterson, G. H., Mehl, L. E., and Leiderman, P. H. The role of some birth related variables in father attachment. *American Journal of Orthopsychiatry*, 1979, *49*, 330-338.

Porter, L. S., and Demeuth, B. R. The impact of marital adjustment on pregnancy acceptance. *Maternal Child Nursing Journal*, 1979, *8*, 103-113.

Rieser, J., Yonas, A., and Wikner, K. Radial localization of odors by human newborns. *Child Development*, 1976, *47*, 856-859.

Ringler, N. M., Kennell, J. H., Jarvella, R., Navojosky, B. J., and Klaus, M. Mother to infant speech at two years--effects of early postnatal contact. *Journal of Pediatrics*, 1975, *86*, 141-144.

Ringler, N. M., Trause, M. A., Klaus, M., and Kennell, J. H. The effects of extra postpartum contact and maternal speech patterns on children's IQs, speech, and language comprehension at age five. *Child Development*, 1978, *49*, 862-865.

Robson, K. S. The role of eye to eye contact in maternal-infant attachment. *Journal of Child Psychology and Psychiatry*, 1967, *8*, 13-25.

Rosen, M. G., Dierker, L. J., Hertz, R. H., Sorokin, Y., and Timor-Tritsch, I. Fetal behavioral states and fetal evaluation. *Clinical Obstetrics and Gynecology*, 1979, *22*, 605-616.

Sanders, L. W., and Julia, H. L. Continuous interactional monitoring in the neonate. *Psychosomatic Medicine*, 1966, *28*, 822-835.

Schaller, J., Carlsson, S. G., and Larsson, K. Effects of extended postpartum mother-child contact on the mother's behavior during nursing. *Infant Behavior and Development*, 1979, *2*, 319-324.

Seashore, M. H., Leifer, A. D., Barnett, C. R., and Leiderman, P. H. The effects of denial on early mother infant interaction on maternal self confidence. *Journal of Personality and Social Psychology*, 1973, *26*, 369-378.

Senechal, P. K. Long term effects of early mother-infant contact. *Journal of Family Practice*, 1979, *8*, 511-516.

Shaheen, E., Alexander, D., Truskowsky, M., and Barbero, G. Failure to thrive--a retrospective profile. *Clinical Pediatrics*, 1968, *7*, 255-261.

Shereshesky, P., Liebenberg, B., and Lockman, R. *Psychological aspects of a first pregnancy and early postnatal adaptation.* New York: Raven Press, 1973.

Sokol, R. J., Stojkov, J., and Chik, L. Maternal-fetal risk assessment: A clinical guide to monitoring. *Clinical Obstetrics and Gynecology*, 1979, *22*, 547-560.

Sosa, R., Klaus, M., Kennell, J. H., and Urrutia, J. J. The effect of early mother-infant contact on breast feeding, infection and growth. In Ciba Foundation Symposium 45 (new series), *Breast feeding and the mother.* Amsterdam: Elsevier Publishing, 1976.

Sosa, R., Kennell, J. H., Klaus, M., and Urrutia, J. The effect of a supportive woman on mothering behavior and the duration and complications of labor. *Pediatric Research*, 1979, *13*, 338. (Abstract)

Sousa, M. *Childbirth at home*. Englewood Cliffs, NJ: Bantam Books, 1976.

Spitz, R. Hospitalism: A followup report. *Psychoanalytic Study of the Child*, 1946, *2*, 113-117.

Steele, B. F., and Pollock, C. B. A psychiatric study of parents who abuse infants and small children. In R. E. Helfer and C. H. Kempe (Eds.), *The battered child*. Chicago: University of Chicago Press, 1974.

Stewart, D., and Stewart, L. *Safe alternatives in childbirth*. Chapel Hill: National Association for Parents for Safe Alternatives for Childbirth, Inc., 1976.

Sullivan, D. L., and Leake, R. D. Significant effect of Brazelton Neonatal Behavioral Assessment Scale in maternal training. *Pediatric Research*, 1980, *14*, 439. (Abstract)

Sumner, G., and Fritsch, J. Postnatal parental concerns the first six weeks of life. *Journal of the Nurses Association of the American College of Obstetrics and Gynecology*, 1977, *6*, 27-32.

Taylor, P. M., Campbell, S., Taylor, F. H., Maloni, J., Dickey, D., and Rubenstein, G. Short term effects of mother-first born contact. *Pediatric Research*, 1979, *13*, 338. (Abstract)

Thevenin, T. *The family bed*. Box 16004, Minneapolis, Minnesota, 1976.

Thomas, A., and Chess, S. *Temperament and development*. New York: Brunner/Mazel, 1977.

Uddenberg, N. Reproductive adaptation in mother and daughter: A study of personality development and adaptation to motherhood. *Acta Psychiatrica Scandinavica* (supplement 254), 1974.

Wegman, M. E. Annual Summary of Vital Statistics--1978. *Pediatrics*, 1979, *64*, 835-842.

Wolfson, J. H., and Bass, L. W. How the pediatrician can foster optimal parent-infant relationships. *Seminars in Perinatology*, 1979, *3*, 101-105.

Worthington, B. S., Vermeersch, J., and Williams, S. R. *Nutrition in pregnancy and lactation*. St. Louis: C. V. Mosby, 1977.

CHILD NURTURING AND TELEVISION IN THE 1980s

Bradley S. Greenberg

Department of Communication
Michigan State University
East Lansing, MI 48824

INTRODUCTION

Television in the early 1980s is a focal point of parental concern. Surveys of adults reflect several principal concerns. For one, there is guilt which emanates from the belief that one's children spend too much time watching television. There is anxiety that some kinds of content, notably violent and sex-oriented content, are likely to induce unacceptable behaviors or dispositions. There is uneasiness in dealing with children's demands for advertised products without an accompanying expectation of fiscal responsibility from the child. Overarching these issues is the growing realization that the television phenomenon may be spiraling out of parental control. Direct access, without parental intervention, is easier to obtain, e.g., the home has more sets, there are more channels available, single parent households or two parents working make monitoring more difficult. All these concerns generate some very common questions from parents:

> How much should my child watch? What's good to watch? What's bad to watch? Am I depriving my child by not permitting him/her to watch? How come they like to watch such dumb things?

Before dealing specifically with television throughout this decade, let us identify what it consists of at the start of the decade.

The typical home in the 1980s has at least two working television sets, one fairly centrally located for family viewing with the other in a bedroom. That bedroom is often a child's. If not, it is the room the child is dispatched to if a parent chooses one show and the child another. The central set is in operation between six and seven hours a day, with the second set adding half again that number of hours to a daily total. The preschool child watches television four hours a day, whereas the elementary and middle school child average somewhat more than that. Individual differences are substantial; a sizeable proportion watch merely one or two hours a day, whereas a like proportion will be watching six or more hours a day. The non-viewing child is as difficult to locate as the non-television household. By the age of ten, 90 percent of the programs being watched were designed for an adult audience, not for children. That programming originates with the commercial networks; public television comprises a tiny portion of the viewing diet and even tinier when the youngster graduates from "Electric Company" to "Three's Company." Network programming remains the main staple of television watching; cable systems now feed alternative channels into about 32 percent of American homes. Without cable, the typical home can receive five or six channels, with one or two of those redundant in programming during prime time; with today's cable, there are 12 to 35 channels available. The preponderant viewing remains loyal to the commercial networks, but there is rapid erosion of that loyalty. In one recent study we found less than half of all cable viewing focused on network offerings.

However, this chapter is to focus on the 1980s. My main assertion is that television in 1989 will be so significantly different than at the start of the decade that to focus on what is and what has been would be very misleading. An appropriate thesis for this chapter is, "You ain't seen nothing yet." Grammarians might object, but communication technologists and researchers will not. To focus heavily on child nurturing in the context of today's television could be rapidly outdated by what will be introduced into a large mass of homes in this country in this decade. Let us provide some details regarding the changes. This is not a futuristic, pie-in-the-sky introduction to items which will be experimental, overly expensive, or minimally developed. No industry is today outstripping the information industry in terms of growth rate. In order to pose appropriate child nurturing issues in the context of the family and television, it is first imperative to attempt to describe what television or, more appropriately, telecommunication will consist of for large proportions of American families.

THE NEW TELEVISION

Cable Television

What was anticipated for the 1970s will occur in the 1980s: A majority of all homes will have cable television. Cable is now in nearly 25 million U.S. homes and increasingly available to many millions more. In major urban areas, cable is now feasible because of viewer willingness to pay for channels in addition to those available off the air. About 40 percent of the cabled homes now buy an additional channel. Home Box Office, for example, is a strong financial success, and the soon-to-be-realized income from these extra channels will be a significant factor in television production as well. The cable systems now being proposed for major cities have at least 50 available channels rather than the traditional dozen in the older cable systems. Segmenting the audience into smaller groups on the basis of viewing interests will be a key target with the presumption that viewers will seek more of what they already want to glut on and will pay for it. Audience segmentation is likely to occur from most of the technological changes we will describe. The challenge of filling those channels remains, but a best guess is that we will have an analog to the format of highly specialized magazines. There is current evidence of this in the form of all-news channels, all-sports channels, all-movie channels, and soft-porn channels. When television is not so scarce a resource, non-entertainment uses also are likely to multiply, e.g., government, instructional, and minority programming channels.

The growth expectation identified here is minimal. If even 30 percent of all homes had cable, the monthly income would enable the cable industry to compete provocatively with the commercial networks. Indeed, if just five million homes bought the added service of HBO, far less than its current availability, the annual income would be half a billion dollars. At the 30 percent level, we can anticipate more than a curious interest from advertisers; they would virtually insist on access to that size market, and that insistence would be received positively by the cable industry.

The cable of the 1980s will be increasingly interactive, or two-way, in which the home user will be able to make a variety of immediate responses to the originating system, sending a signal back through the channel selector box to a computer. Families will make product purchases or answer marketing surveys, children will participate in quiz games and in achievement tests. Such cable systems will receive immediate feedback from viewers for program rating information, as well as more qualitative program evaluation responses. The interaction capability will again require a fiscal basis for its installation, but the direct use of cable for home security systems, such as fire and burglar alarms, and stock market and shopping transactions will continue to transform the television system into a home utility beyond its entertainment focus. These video systems will permit complex interactions with computers, instructors, entertainers, etc.

Cable itself as a piece of equipment may be short-lived. The rapid development of optical fiber need only be understood here so far as to stipulate that currently manufactured glass fibers can carry more than 100 television signals in about the thickness of a human hair. What to do with all those signal potentials remains the ultimate software problem. The emerging conception is that this single wire into the home will carry the phone, television, computer-based informational data, and high-fidelity audio, and that it will provide the linkage among television, computers and allied pieces of communication technology.

Satellites

Satellites in the home in the 1980s?   It's not a question but a statement.   The 1979 feature item in the Neiman-Marcus Christmas catalog was a backyard satellite receiver for $35,000.   Current expectations are that by the mid-1980s the necessary converter and satellite receiving dish will be marketed for about $300.   The antenna that comes off the roof when a cable wire goes into the home will be replaced by a small receiving dish.   Such a price would make the item desirable and reasonable for home consumption.   Direct broadcast to home via satellite will be manifestly available and it may be originating in Canada or Mexico or England, as well as New York and Los Angeles.   Satellites will be most important in less populated areas where cable is not economically possible and where the variety of mass media opportunities is narrower.

Equally important, programming could originate from anywhere in this country.   Uplinks from stations to the satellites would constitute the basis for additional programming to be fed across the country, threatening the concept of purely local programming as individual stations expand their audience expectations.   Channel capacity for individual satellites is also increasing.   Further, satellites can be used to interconnect stations, networks, cable systems and other elements of the telecommunication industry to feed a nearly infinite variety of messages into family viewing quarters.

Videotape and Videodisc

Video recorders are now in about three million homes.   Used largely to record off-air broadcasts for later playback, the potential for in-home adoption will be enlarged during the 1980s.   First, prices for individual units have decreased rapidly; new models now go for $300 to $400.   The home videotape library and the "tape-of-the-month club" can be anticipated to develop much like the record industry.   When there are enough recordings available, then the unit itself becomes secondary.   Canned programming for home videotape units provides another set of options for family decision-making: new video stores spring up in shopping centers weekly.   Additionally, the rapidly decreasing price of cameras for home television production purposes is a largely untapped expectation for family activity.   Both uses make television more of an initiating activity, the passive observer may be more of an anomaly.   There is now scarcely a home without an audiorecorder; the same may be true for video recorders before this decade is concluded.

Videodisc development may be more problematic.   The disc looks like a phonograph record.   It is much cheaper than a tape by a factor of perhaps ten to one, and the cost of playback equipment is only half that of cassette units.   The major drawback is that the home videodisc player has no recording capability.   Without a resolution of that problem, the marked growth of videotapes remains the best prediction.   However, the inexpensive nature of the disc system may itself be a significant enough advantage; it could be coupled with external exchange systems for home borrowing and lending of discs. For example, city libraries will provide such services as they now provide audio cassettes and records.

Although it fits as well with any of the other telecommunication innovations described, add here the opportunity to view such material on a larger-than-life screen, perhaps in new homes with a wall-to-wall-to-floor-to-ceiling screen. Consider the learning potential, as well as the dramatic potential, of a biology lesson, the birth of a calf, gore, a candy bar, and an argument in those size dimensions, by contrast with our current typical 21-inch limit.

Electronic Text

The presentation of alpha-numeric textual information on home television sets can be accomplished through the vertical interval between frames of a television picture. This can be disseminated over the air, by phone lines, or by cable. One version, Teletext, is now in operation in Britain. In this relatively primitive version, pages of information are stored on computers and fed to a television station's transmitter. The information stored can include textbooks, bus schedules, menus, achievement tests, sports scores, etc. This one-way format functions *ad seriatim*, i.e., it proceeds page-by-page through the stored information and the viewer has to wait for what is desired. The next stage will be interactive access to electronic texts, so that the viewer can tap into whatever page, line or section of stored information is desired. Then the inclusion of such items as yellow page sections from the phone directories and catalog information as Sears is now creating will become reasonable for searching purposes. Of course, what is stored in one computer can be linked, via satellite or even phone lines, to most other computers, further extending the range of potential information. In the 1980s, a number of U.S. daily newspapers have been experimenting in cable markets with interactive data retrieval systems, making their news content accessible through home television receivers.

For those wanting a printed output of such material, the technology for facsimile reproduction is now well into a developmental cycle.

Minicomputers

The final component we will add to the home telecommunication center of the 1980s is that of the small home-based computer, now being marketed at prices as low as $100 with a capacity for most things conceivable in the home. This information system will continue to drop in cost as more sophisticated generations are developed. This prognosis stems from the experiences of the 1970s in which all forms of electronic equipment costs ran counter to the national cost trend. Hand-held calculators and watches are the most visible examples. There is little reason for minicomputers and the other pieces of technology described in this chapter not to follow the same trend. Linking this computer to the home television set as a display terminal will perhaps complete the 'gaming' uses of television during the 1980s. Programming the family budget, income tax and banking information, as well as tomorrow's math assignment, will be practical uses of home computers. But the anticipation of what else there will be to 'play' or 'play with' on the unit will likely be a major factor in product purchase decisions. The most ready extension is to realize that this home computer can be interfaced with other computers outside the home and their stored elements. For a user fee, of course, one will be able to access the computer libraries of the world.

PARENTING AND CHILD NURTURING IN THE 1980s

Before speculating as to specific implications of the new media environment in the home, let me provide an empirical base from recent research on parents, television and children. The origin of much of the research synthesized here stems from two longitudinal projects at Michigan State University. One, Project CASTLE, was funded from 1975-1978 by the Agency for Children, Youth and the Family. It focused on social role and social behavior learning from television, with a particular emphasis on the role of parental mediation. Mother-child pairs (n = 293) were interviewed separately. Portions of the project also focused heavily on comparisons between Black and White children in the fourth, sixth and eighth grades in Wisconsin, Michigan and California. The second, Project CASA, began in 1980 and continues, funded by the Gannett Company, Inc. In that project, the television behaviors of Hispanic and Anglo children yield input for this discussion, including the youngsters' perceptions of their parents' television mediating behaviors. These children came from the fifth and tenth grades in cities in California, Arizona and New Mexico.

Beginning with the former project, these findings characterize best what parents do with their children:

...Two-thirds of the mothers, but only half the children, say that the parent "almost always" knows what programs the child is watching.
...Twenty percent of the mothers say their child can watch past 10 p.m., compared to 40 percent of the children.
...When the child is found watching a program considered inappropriate, 80 percent of the mothers say they "never let the child watch anyway," compared to 33 percent of the children.
...Two-thirds of the mothers say they do not allow the child to watch violent movies; 40 percent of their offspring agree.
...When asked whether they prohibit the viewing of 13 specific network television series, a per show average of 24 percent of the mothers said those shows were banned, compared to 13 percent of the youngsters; more shows were banned more often for fourth graders than

for sixth graders, and more for sixth graders than for eighth graders; more shows were banned in the Eastern time zone (Michigan) where prime time is 8 to 11 p.m., than in Central time zone (Wisconsin), where prime time is 7 to 10 p.m.

The conclusion emerges that mothers and their children show substantial disagreement in their reports of parental activities. From one-third to one-helf the children, on most of the individual items, do not perceive the control or intervention behavior reported by the parent as a normative parental response. And this is with mothers, primarily non-working mothers, who would be expected to be better aware than fathers of what is happening with the child and television. No firm evidence exists for fathers; anecdotal wisdom proposes that they know even less in this area of child behavior.

These same studies demonstrate a substantial relationship between the mother's general level of concern over television and her engagement in a variety of monitoring, interpretative, prohibitive and controlling behaviors. Table 1 correlates a set of individual parental intervention styles with each other. Perhaps the bottom line is the most revealing. Co-viewing with the child primarily increases the mother's perception that she is very aware of what the child is watching; in a lesser fashion, co-viewing is related to the specific intervention behaviors interpreting show content. The table also shows that setting time limits on how much television may be watched is the best correlate of a variety of other measures, particularly show prohibitions. Thus, there are two major clusters of intervention styles. One consists of most of the *prohibition* elements; the second connects the *interpretation* ones. Large numbers of mothers are oriented to each of these quite different patterns.

Data were collected from separate samples of Black and White youngsters in San José and Berkeley, California, and Detroit, Michigan. Data were not collected from their parents. The findings tend to falsify the proposition that minority youngsters receive less guidance or control. Normally that proposition includes the caveats that Black homes are poorer, more disorganized, contain less parental supervision in general, are more likely to have single parents, and are less likely to have parents at home at any given time. Even without controlling for these factors there is no support for the lack of guidance thesis. Table 2 contains the results of principal interest here.

First, Black youngsters experience closer control over television exposure than Whites. One-third said that their parents "make more rules about TV" compared to most kids their age, while one-fifth of the Whites reported this. Half of each group said that their parents "almost always" knew what programs they were watching, and a higher proportion of Blacks said their parents "care very much" about the shows they watch. In addition, the Black youth are no more likely to be allowed to stay up late to watch television on school days and they have just as many pro-hibitions against watching shows their parents don't approve.

TABLE 1

Intercorrelations Among Parental Intervention Styles

Monitors Program Viewing	Monitors Viewing	Limits	Controls	Prohibits Dramas	Prohibits Movies	Prohibits Comedies	Interdicts	Encourages Pro-Social	Interprets Dramas	Interprets Comedies	Interprets Pro-Social	Comments
Limits Late Viewing	.29											
Controls Strictly	.24	.51										
Prohibits Violent Dramas	.20	.51	.41									
Prohibits TV Movies	.22	.51	.40	.44								
Prohibits Insult Comedies	.15	.39	.34	.64	.32							
Interdicts During Viewing	.22	.28	.37	.32	.40	.29						
Encourages Pro-Social Shows	.20	.16	.14	.22	.24	.24	.16					
Interprets Violent Dramas	.22	.18	.18	.21	.29	.31	.12	.34				
Interprets Insult Comedies	.14	.20	.28	.22	.35	.29	.22	.30	.43			
Interprets Pro-Social Shows	.15	.23	.24	.22	.33	.25	.24	.49	.48	.57		
Comments About Programs	.17	.17	.14	.10	.11	.23	.12	.11	.30	.21	.24	
Co-Views With Child	.28	.06	-.01	-.02	.05	.08	-.05	.13	.21	.13	.17	.10

TABLE 2

Black and White Youth Reports of Parental TV Intervention Strategies

		Black	White
How late do your parents let you stay up to watch TV on school days?	8:00	24%	17%
	8:30	20%	17%
	9:00	9%	22%
	9:30/10	10%	18%
	10:30/11	21%	19%
	Later	16%	7%
Compared to other kids your age, do your parents make more rules about TV or less rules about TV, or is it about the same as your friends?	MORE	31%	20%
	SAME	28%	36%
	LESS	41%	44%
How often do your parents know what programs you are watching on TV?	ALMOST ALWAYS	51%	51%
	USUALLY	23%	26%
	SOMETIMES	23%	16%
	ALMOST NEVER	3%	7%
How much do your parent care what you are watching on TV?	CARE VERY MUCH	35%	28%
	CARE PRETTY MUCH	30%	31%
	CARE A LITTLE	24%	30%
	DON'T CARE AT ALL	11%	11%
When your parents see you watching a program that they don't think you should watch, what do they do about it? (percent saying "usually")	TURN OFF THE TV SET OR CHANGE CHANNELS	27%	24%
	EXPLAIN WHY YOU SHOULD STOP WATCHING	29%	24%
	SUGGEST THAT YOU DO SOME OTHER ACTIVITY	25%	28%
	SEND YOU OUT OF THE ROOM	28%	21%
	LET YOU WATCH ANYWAY	29%	25%
Does your parent suggest or tell you to watch any of these programs? (percent saying "yes")	AVERAGE OF 12 NON-BLACK SHOWS	29%	27%
	GOOD TIMES	41%	21%
	SANFORD AND SON	53%	33%
	FAT ALBERT	28%	14%
	THE JEFFERSONS	41%	21%
Do your parents ever tell you that the families on TV are like real families?	YES	12%	8%
	NO	88%	92%
Do your parents ever tell you that the families on TV are not like real families?	YES	24%	22%
	NO	76%	78%
Do your parents ever say good things to you about families they see on TV?	YES	32%	33%
	NO	68%	67%
Do your parents ever say bad things to you about the families they see on TV?	YES	21%	17%
	NO	79%	83%
Now please look at each show in this list. Circle each show if you "usually" watch it with your mother or your father.	FAT ALBERT	39%	15%
	GOOD TIMES	84%	32%
	THE JEFFERSONS	86%	34%
	SANFORD AND SON	84%	39%
	THAT'S MY MAMA	67%	20%
	GRADY	56%	11%

Second, parents of Black youngsters are reported to be more likely to provide quidance toward approved programs on television. For a set of four programs featuring Black performers, an average of 40 percent of the Black parents compared with 22 percent of the White parents suggested that their child should watch. For programs with substantial pro-social content, such as "The Waltons" and "Little House on the Prairie," about one-fifth of each were advised to watch the shows. Parental suggestions to watch non-Black shows occurred equally in the two groups.

Third, Black parents were reported to be somewhat more likely to actually sit down and watch television programs with their children. This was especially the case for Black shows during prime time when more than 80 percent of the Black parents watched with their child. For 37 of 46 different network series, a higher proportion of Black than White youth reported their parents watched with them.

Fourth, Black and White parents provided equivalent amounts of interpretation of television depictions. About two-fifths of the Black and White youths said that their parents tell them about the real and unreal elements in televised protrayals of occupations, family roles, racial roles, and sex roles.

The table suggests what is normative, parental behavior with regard to television, as perceived by the child:

...The individual youngster believes he/she has fewer home rules about television than their friends.
...Three fourths believe their parents know pretty well what shows they are watching.
...More than a third of the youngsters don't perceive their parents as caring about what they watch on television.
...A fourth of the children get to watch the shows their parents don't think they should watch.

Now, let us look at a small portion of the study which deals with Hispanic and Anglo youngsters in the Southwest. Table 3 presents the major results, separately for the ethnic groups and also for the fifth and tenth graders. As with the Black youth, the Hispanic youngsters are no less likely than Anglos to be monitored, controlled and guided by their parents. In fact, where there are differences, they are in the opposite direction.

First, the banning of shows is less likely to occur in Anglo homes than in Hispanic homes, and somewhat later night viewing is tolerated more in the former than in the latter. On all other guidance variables in Table 3--extent of television viewing rules, co-viewing with parents, talking while co-viewing, and show guidance--there are no ethnic differences.

TABLE 3

Hispanic and Anglo Youth Reports of Parental TV Intervention Strategies

	Anglo	Hispanic	5th	10th
Are there any TV shows your parents won't let you watch?				
NONE	59%	47%	29%	68%
1 OR 2	11%	17%	19%	11%
A FEW	17%	21%	28%	13%
SEVERAL	9%	10%	16%	6%
A LOT	5%	5%	9%	2%
How late can you stay up on a school day to watch TV? 8:30	5%	9%	11%	4%
9:30	26%	22%	45%	10%
10:30	26%	33%	24%	33%
11:00	43%	36%	19%	53%
How do your TV rules compare to other kids' your age?				
LESS RULES	40%	39%	35%	43%
ABOUT THE SAME	46%	51%	50%	49%
MORE RULES	14%	10%	16%	8%
How often does a parent watch TV with you?				
NOT AT ALL	9%	7%	7%	7%
NOT MUCH	28%	31%	31%	29%
OFTEN	45%	42%	38%	47%
VERY OFTEN	19%	20%	24%	16%
How often do you talk with a parent about a show while watching together?				
NOT AT ALL	10%	11%	12%	10%
NOT MUCH	39%	41%	38%	41%
OFTEN	43%	34%	34%	41%
VERY OFTEN	8%	14%	16%	8%
How often does a parent tell you to watch certain shows?				
NOT AT ALL	33%	29%	21%	36%
NOT MUCH	48%	36%	37%	45%
OFTEN	13%	23%	27%	14%
VERY OFTEN	6%	11%	15%	5%
Has a parent ever told you you're watching too much TV?				
NO	54%	52%	49%	55%
YES	46%	48%	51%	45%

Second, the consistent age-group differences demonstrate from two to three times as much parental activity for fifth graders as for tenth graders, e.g.:

...Twenty-nine percent of the fifth graders have zero shows banned compared to 68 percent of the tenth graders.
...One-fourth of the fifth graders can watch at 11 p.m. or later compared with 53 percent of the tenth graders.
...Surprisingly, nearly two-thirds at each age level report that a parent co-views with them "often" or "very often."

Third, the normative tendencies across the entire sample of youngsters suggests these patterns:

...Nearly half the youngsters have no shows banned.
...Two-thirds can stay up until 10 p.m. to watch television.
...Two-fifths have fewer rules than their friends, they believe.
...Half report a parent watches with them frequently.
...Talking with parents about a show while watching the show is nearly as frequent as co-viewing.
...Half the youths say that their parents have told them they watch too much; half have not had that mandate.

These studies intersect to permit some tentative generalizations:

1. The parent's perceptions of the television watching situation is discrepant from the child's perception;
2. There is considerable viewing of late-night prime time television among children from fourth through tenth grades;
3. The banning of shows by parents is minimal, according to the children, and often not enforced;
4. The youngsters think their peers have more rules than they do;
5. Minority group children are no less prone to parental mediation efforts than majority group children;
6. Co-viewing of television by parents and children is more prevalent than anticipated.

Bower (1973), Mohr (1976), and Corder-Bolz and Marshall (1980) have reported quite similar results in separate studies on these different issues.

So what? If these are descriptions of what parents now do, what evidence is there that what parents do makes any difference? Here, the research evidence is more slim.

One study central to this issue is that reported by Atkin and Greenberg (1977). Essentially, they examined the extent to which parental mediation (in the forms of discussing television program content with children and parental co-viewing of television) would impact on the relationship between television exposure and specific social behaviors. Included were two anti-social behaviors--physical and verbal aggression--and two pro-social behaviors--altruism and affection. Exposure to shows depicting varying levels of each of these social behaviors was specifically assessed. Taking the straightforward correlation between television exposure to content rich in each of those behaviors and the behavioral disposition of the child to perform those behaviors as the baseline, they found that *under conditions of high parental mediation* in the form of interpretative comments about content, (a) the correlation between exposure to verbal aggression and the verbal aggression of the child was lower than with low parental mediation; (b) the correlation between exposure to both types of pro-social behavior and the pro-social behavioral tendencies of the child was higher than with low parental mediation; and (c) the correlation between exposure to physical aggression and the physical aggressiveness of the child was higher with high parental mediation, contrary to expectations, an anomaly also reported by Chaffee and Tims (1976). However, for the youngest age group, mediation did function to weaken the association between exposure and physical aggression. Hicks (1965) executed an experiment in which an adult's positive or negative comments about a violent program impinged on the aggression of the children in a post-viewing situation, such that positive comments yielded more aggression and negative comments less aggression.

When co-viewing was entered as a second form of mediation, the expected results were obtained consistently, i.e., high co-viewing weakened the correlation between exposure and both physical and verbal aggressive behaviors. Generally, then, one or both forms of parental mediation facilitated the impact of pro-social television content exposure and mitigated against the impact of anit-social television content.

To summarize the roles that parents can assume with regard to their children's use of television, the main emphases of researchers have centered on these areas:

1. The amount of television exposure and the time frame in which that amount is located;
2. The extensiveness and selectivity of content monitoring, e.g, good shows to watch but, particularly, bad shows to avoid watching;
3. The extent of co-viewing with the child;
4. The amount and direction of interpretative comments regarding television content;
5. The models the parents actually provide in terms of their own television behaviors and their attitudes toward television;
6. The alternatives to television provided within the household.

From this context, then, let us proceed into the remainder of the decade, taking with us our new sensitivity to television as it is likely to be, rather than what it is today or last year. What central issues accompany the wish to be nurturing of the child in a vastly different television environment?

In the space remaining, I wish to discuss four central concerns related to the family and television and to the positive growth and development of children in that context. Because we speculate about the future, it is sufficient to pose and describe the problems without also attempting to resolve them here. We will give a specific emphasis to the communication process components of child nurturing, but we pose significant research questions in doing so and significant coping problems for the current generation of new parents.

First, consider the increased complexity of *decision-making* within the family with regard to the telecommunication options that will exist. Today, in uncabled homes, there is presumably some process, some decision-making scheme by which a selection is made from among four or five television programming options; in cable homes today, someone picks from 12 to 18 options. In truth, no research now available identifies how that is accomplished, let alone what will be done when the choices included (a) 40 to 50 television channels on a cable system, (b) adjustment of the home dish antenna to choose from among several dozen national and international satellite offerings, (c) retrieving a pre-recorded tape from the home videotape library whether produced by the family or borrowed through the local videotape exchange club, (d) tapping the electronic text options for income tax forms, classified ads, and birthday purchases for grandparents, or (e) working with the video display terminal for purposes of creating computer graphics as a substitute for the coloring books.

By what means will the family arrive at the decision which would allocate leisure time to such activities? I suggest there is a strong need to probe into current family decision-making strategies and processes in order to even conceptualize what might be done in the future. For example, what information sources are now used? What credibility do they have? What information is contained in these sources that is evaluated highly enough to be accepted? What roles are offered different family members to participate in the final set of decisions which allocate family economic resources which in turn direct the allocation of family time resources? Where do the criteria come from by which the decision-making occurs? To what extent do contemporary models of family decision-making with regard to television issues--laissez faire, consensual, authorization, etc.--continue unchanged in such an advanced communication environment?

Let me exemplify that point by identifying a current issue which might provide significant leads for subsequent investigations. In the fall of each year, the commercial networks provide us with the "new season." Later, of course, we are recipients of the second and third seasons because of the abysmal failure of most of the contributions to that new season. Nevertheless, in the fall there appear about 30 weekly series on television and, on the average, two-thirds of them have not aired before. American children sift, sort, sample and select from among these offerings. They decide what they want to watch and what not. We do not know how this takes place, what role parents and peers play, and perhaps most critically, we do not know why shows A....E are accepted as regular members of the family's viewing habits for the year and shows F....P are rejected. We do know that the choices made in the fall persist through the full year with remarkable stability. And if this task seems overly awesome, we could content ourselves with the Saturday morning viewing decisions alone. That would focus most directly on the child. There is virtually no parental input to Saturday viewing decisions; the child alone makes those choices in the vast majority of American homes. How that comes about seems like a useful question in attempting to project how it will occur in an expanded telecommunication system later in this decade.

Second, the television of the 1980s provides a distinct shift from *reactive to proactive uses* of television. Today, we are entirely subject to television content and schedules which have been initiated and originated elsewhere. One-way cable increases the options we choose from, but the specification of the options begins elsewhere. We have virtually no say in what is available to us other than market demand forces which will remove what we reject by non-viewing. I suggest that the initiation of activity will be far more at the option of family members with the larger set of telecommunication services described. In particular, the computer options, the two-way interactive systems and electronic text material will be more subject to proactive activities in the family. The current passivity in viewing television will be considerably diminished. The individual may still opt to do very little in an initiating sense; he or she could continue to focus most heavily on the mass-oriented entertainment vehicles.

How will the child be prepared, perhaps even trained, to become proactive in television choices? The parent's own training as a television viewer was primarily through trial and error. Recent work sponsored by the National Institute of Education on creating curricula of critical viewing skills may be valuable in this context. O'Bryant and Corder-Bolz (1978) have outlined half a dozen methods parents might use in facilitating a child's acquisition and use of critical television viewing skills: (1) limiting television viewing in the context of prioritizing it among other shared and independent family activities; (2) controlling content by encouragement or discouragement of specific program watching; (3) creating purposeful viewing, such that television watching is not merely habitual but is derived from some reasoning process; (4) mediating television watching through interpretative comments, discussion and explanation; (5) indirect mediation through the parent's own behavior with television, in terms of viewing selections and inter-parent discussion and evaluation of programs and of the act of viewing itself; and (6) transference of television program content to contemporary family and social issues, such as, taking the occurrence of violence on television and using it as the basis for discussing playground violence or societal violence, or taking sex on television as the basis for parentally-sponsored sex education lessons.

These same skills could be examined within our third issue area, that of *self-control*. We use that term in two quite different ways. For one, there is the notion that the available options in television will become more controllable by the individual user. You have more choices among devices; within devices, you have a spiraling number of choices as to what to do with the device. The availability of extensive programming directed at special-interest audience segments will permit and necessitate the development of discriminating television preferences for each individual viewer. The entire concept of audience segmentation and diversification is dedicated to making many options available and is not dependent on the most massive audiences for commercial success. One-hundred-thousand children dedicated to math may warrant the availability of that option in some telecommunication form. Means for exercising that personal control, the basis on which it is done, encouraged, maintained and evaluated seem relevant issues. The alternative examination of self-control is more threatening to the growth and development of the child. Having fixed on an interest that is served by television, what is an acceptable level of immersion? If a cartoon channel provides cartoons 8 to 16 hours a day each day, what is to inhibit the child from choosing that option alone, repeatedly and incessantly? Here the issue of self-control may be the absence of self-control. Perhaps the freedom which comes with variety and access may be abdicated by individual choice. The potential exists for developing varied interests and accessing information on a large set of those interests. The structure and process that encourages the child to take advantage of multiple cultural, social and academic opportunities, and the role of parents and schools in instigating them, is increasingly complex as the child's direct access to media choice points increases.

Finally, it seems appropriate to raise some questions about *family communication processes*, in addition to those decision-making areas discussed earlier. Let us posit the extreme typologies derivable from the impact of these technologies on family communication processes. Perhaps the least desirable type would yield a new generation of "tech freaks." This is an offspring of the "computer freak" common to most college settings. The individual creates an anthropomorphic relationship with the computer, lives with it, talks to it, hears it talk back, plays games with it, and essentially becomes wedded to the computer center or takes on an office partner in the form of a remote terminal. Each member of the family, in this conception, could be wedded to one or another of the family of television units we have described, with prodigious time allocations to sorting through available electronic texts, vicarious interactions with impersonal others on two-way cable systems, or incessant searching for satellite offerings much in the manner of ham radio operators.   A nearly opposite alternative is to conceive of the *interdependence* that will be required in families to utilize the new media. Rather than the individual as the unit of analysis, it is equally possible to posit that the family as a unit will have greater inter-communication needs in arriving at optimal uses of what we have described.   Such interdependence will require additional role definitions, the allocation of time and economic resources, scheduling, monitoring, and specifically the opportunity and need to communicate with each other about this potentially enlightening set of telecommunication experiences.   Family communication styles, the content of family discussions, and the linkages among family members are prime areas for examination in such a conception.

Television in the 1980s will not be the television we have had available since 1950.   Correlative child nurturing practices by parents about television must undergo an intensive examination and likely alterations.   Rather than that being a dismal prospect, this chapter has attempted to capture some sense of the excitement and of the expansive nature of the opportunities which will quickly overtake us.

REFERENCES

Atkin, C., and Greenberg, B.   Parental mediation of children's social behavior learning from television. *CASTLE report #4.* Department of Communication, Michigan State University, August, 1977.

Corder-Bolz, C. R., and Marshall, A. M.   *Family interaction and TV viewing.*   Paper presented at the 1980 Annual Meeting of the American Educational Research Association, Boston, April 8, 1980. (a)

Genovese, M. Electronics boom: A gamble or sure bet. *Presstime,* Dec., 1980, 4-9.

Gunn, H.   Window on the future: Planning for public television in the telecommunications era. *PTR,* July/August, 1978, 5-54.

Hicks, D. J. Imitation and retention of film-mediated aggressive peer and adult models. *Journal of Personality and Social Psychology,* 1965, 2, 97-100.

Mayer, M. For commercial TV, either a new beginning or the end. *Next,* Feb., 1981, 34-39.

Mohr, P. J.   *Television, children and parents.*   Unpublished report, Department of Speech Communication, Witchita State University, 1978.

O'Bryant, S. L., and Corder-Bolz, C. R.   Can people affect television: Teacher vs. program. *Journal of Communication,* 1978, 28, 97-103.

CHILDREN WHO COPE:

SOME IMPLICATIONS FOR INTERVENTION AND PREVENTION

Gaston E. Blom

Department of Psychiatry
University Center for International Rehabilitation
Michigan State University
East Lansing, MI 48824

INTRODUCTION

Behavioral scientists have become preoccupied with the language and concepts of disorder, deficit, illness, disability, handicap and disease as applied to the range of human behavior. They invariably see the minority of children and adults who are not coping and leading satisfactory lives. Concepts about child behavior, development and personality functioning have been strongly influenced by this biased perspective. In studying pathology at the neglect of normality, adversity has been given the highest percentage of attention. What is overlooked is that the majority of children and adults is able to lead satisfying, gratifying lives even under conditions of adversity, chronic stress and handicap.

CONSEQUENCES OF THE PATHOLOGY ORIENTATION

Imbalances and consequences have resulted from this exclusive interest in things that go wrong. One consequence is advocating an ever increasing number of human service professionals to meet the needs of more people who are identified as psychologically disturbed. One answer to the psychosocial problems of society seems to be to train more professionals to deal with the populations affected as if they were mentally ill. For example, a projection of the need for 50,000 psychiatrists in the year 1990 has been made by a graduate medical education advisory committee (Psychiatric News, 1980). There can be legitimate needs for more human service professionals but one is concerned about how this is determined. From this author's perspective, a more important emphasis should be placed on their distribution, accessibility, efficacy and coordination rather than on their number.

A second consequence of the pathology orientation is the influence of well-publicized statistics on the extent of human problems in our child and youth populations. It is a discouraging experience to confront such data. Examples from various sources (Keniston, 1977; Snapper and Ohms, 1977; Children's Defense Fund, 1979) cite the following:

- Some 10.9 million, or roughly one-sixth, of children, in the United States live in single-parent families.

- One million children are victims of abuse and neglect.

- An estimated 500,000 to 750,000 children grow up outside their homes in foster, group and institutional care.

- One million children run away from home each year.

- Each year more than 550,000 teenagers become mothers.

- Almost three times as many youngsters committed suicide during 1977 as did in 1950, an increase from 4.5 to 11.8 per 100,000.

- An estimated 3.3 million problem drinkers exist in the fourteen- to seventeen-year age bracket, representing 19 percent of this population.

- Of all seventeen-year-olds in school today, 13 percent are functionally illiterate.

However, the incidence and prevalence of these and other problems may have been overestimated. Studies reveal different results probably based on methodological errors. Statistics are many times "guesstimates" and "guesstimates" may be wrong.

A presentation at a national professional conference illustrates both a pathology bias and the use of "guesstimates," presented as statistics (*Psychiatric News*, 1980). The authors cite that 15 million is probably a conservative estimate of the number of American school children with alcoholic parents. This number represents 23 percent of the total population of children below 18 years of age! Furthermore, the authors refer to these children as having "impairments" ranging from minimal to severe; they display terror, loneliness, restlessness, anger and frustration. Their homes are depicted as conflictful, inconsistent, disorganized, uncaring and chaotic. The authors acknowledge that not all children of alcoholics are psychologically disturbed, yet they make recommendations for their identification, intervention and treatment as if this was so.

In contrast, it is refreshing to encounter a comparison study of childbearing and childrearing experiences of carefully sampled teenage and older age mothers (Roosa, Fitzgerald, and Carlson, 1981). Both groups of mothers had first pregnancies. In general, the findings on the infants and mothers in the teenage group showed a more positive picture than usually reported. The negative consequences which did occur seemed to be the result of the teenage mothers not continuing education and having limited job opportunities and reduced earning power. The authors of this study were able to divest themselves of pathology seeking and finding and of prejudicial attitudes towards teenage mothers that exist in society, as well as in the professional literature (Barzerman, Sheehan, Ellison, and Schlesinger, 1971; Stewart, 1976). The tendency to view adolescent pregnancy as having reached "epidemic" proportions suggests a disease pathology orientation. A careful analysis of demographic data indicates that the rate of teenage pregnancies and births actually decreased between 1957 and 1975, particularly for older age teens (Eddinger and Forbush, 1977). However, the number of women in the age group, 15 to 19 years of age, increased so that the actual number of teenage pregnancies was larger.

A third consequence of the pathology emphasis is the concept of normality as the absence of pathology or close to pathology but not quite. Mental health is viewed as not being mentally ill or too ill, rather than having a positive health definition. Normality is equally as complex as pathology. It is complex in that human beings find many ways to deal successfully with life situations. These ways of adapting are fascinating and worth studying in their own right.

It is rather striking when one thinks about the training of mental health specialists such as social workers, psychologists and psychiatrists. They rarely study and observe normal people as a required part of professional training. Mental health professionals do not talk in depth with normal people within their natural life settings. Yet, those who have been trained to know a great deal about the problems of people are turned to for advice and guidance about normal living. These same professionals have very little experience and training in knowing how people cope and how they live effective and satisfying lives. Books written by professionals on how to rear children often consist of what not to do and of pathology warnings rather than positive suggestions and possibilities for parents to follow which are associated with favorable outcomes.

A fourth consequence of the focus on pathology has been an interest in child vulnerability and at-risk life situations. A public health model of primary, secondary and tertiary forms of prevention of mental illness has evolved. Primary prevention for various types of psychological disorders has been proposed. An expectation has developed that, through changing environments and providing individual inputs early in life to children and families, one can reduce the incidence of schizophrenia, delinquency, learning disabilities, mental retardation and other disorders. It is a very immodest and unrealistic idea on the part of professionals who believe that such psychosocial engineering is possible. Coupled with it is the notion that intervention as early as possible in life is more effective. Not only is this not so but also Brazelton and Als (1979) warn about the possible danger of negative expectations from early infant intervention. They state "we have been stuck for too long in a nonreciprocal therapeutic model of judgements, criticisms, looking for pathology and ignoring strengths in mother-father-infant triads." Negative expectations can have undesirable effects at any age.

Yet studies of at-risk and vulnerable children have resulted in findings about children who cope. It has been found that children at risk often do not have the future pathologies predicted for them. This has led professionals to the realization that it is just as interesting to understand the greater majority of children who seemed to do adequately as compared to the minority who display predicted negative outcomes.

HISTORICAL PERSPECTIVES

Lois Murphy in "The Widening World of Childhood" (1962) presents an historical perspective on the twentieth century preoccupation with behavioral pathology. Studies of childhood have developed a vast problem literature. Clinical thinking and fascination with the psychological problems of adults biased professionals to study the origins of maladjustment. Interest in positive adjustment and the successful management of life problems has lagged behind. In support of Murphy's perspective, the author surveyed eight quarterly issues of the Child Development Abstracts and Bibliography for the years 1978-1980. Of over 3,500 articles cited, only twelve (3%) were indexed under coping and competence. In contrast, 75% of the articles dealt with psychopathology.

One of the issues that came up during the great society programs of the 1960s was a professional conflict about their guiding philosophy. These programs were developed to facilitate greater potentialities for children and adults to participate in the opportunities of American society. What emerged was the clinical versus competence controversy. The controversy represented, on one hand, professionals who were interested and invested in the generating of strengths, skills and adaptiveness. Against them were those who advocated that interventions should be based upon clinical approaches of removing obstacles to development such as disturbed feelings and problems in human relationships. This controversy was never resolved. A harmony between clinicians and those who advocated the development of strengths was not attained and conflict between these views still remains.

Another historical perspective comes from the recent development of social policies regarding disabled persons and the assurance of their civil rights. They are represented in federal legislation, Section 504 of Public Law 93-112 of 1973 and Public Law 94-142 of 1975. The implementation of this legislation has emphasized deinstitutionalization, least restrictive environments, normalization, independent living and mainstreaming. These trends challenge labeling, negative expectations, and deficit and pathology programming which have influenced traditional forms of services to disabled people.

REVIEW OF THE EVIDENCE ON COPING

Everyday Life Examples

One can regularly find newspaper, magazine and television reports and accounts of adaptive, if not heroic, responses on the part of children and adults to personal danger, collective threats and catastrophic events. There are also many examples of persons who overcome handicaps, either congenital or acquired. Too frequently these reports are dismissed as extraordinary rather than being within the grasp of a majority of people.

Newspaper stories provide ongoing examples of children who overcome adversity and danger. Their headlines call attention to children who cope:

. SHORT, SPUNKY IS HER STYLE
. A PROGRESSIVE HANDICAPPER, ACHIEVES GOALS
. HE DISLIKES WORD 'HANDICAP'
. CUB SCOUT, 10, PROOF HEROES DON'T HESITATE
. BORN WITHOUT LEGS, JOHN FRY LEARNS TO BE A SKYDIVER
. KIDS, WAITING TO DIE, LEARN HOW TO LIVE
. TEEN SKATER REFUSES TO GIVE UP
. A CHAIR-CAR-ELEVATOR SETS HIM FREE
. BOY SOLE SURVIVOR OF PLANE CRASH
. SPECIAL KIND OF GYMNAST OVERCOMES
. YOUTH PUTS OUT TRAIN FIRES, AVERTS DISASTER
. HE WALKS WITH HELP--AND COURAGE
. SCOTT, 5, IS A HERO BY INSTINCT
. PATTY, A FREE SPIRIT WITH SPUNK
. TEEN GIRL HONORED AS MOST COURAGEOUS ATHLETE
. CHILDREN OF WAR, OUT OF THE HORROR, AMAZING
  STRENGTH
. SIX-YEAR-OLD SAVES DAD'S LIFE
. BOY, 14, WINNING BIG FIGHT
. RULING FREES ROLLING TEEN FOR A LIFE ON THE ROAD
. ACCIDENT VICTIM PREPARES TO GRADUATE

One of these newspaper accounts is cited.

HE WALKS WITH HELP--AND COURAGE

Rochester, N.Y.--Freddie Dove's metal legs squeak and bend as he rotates his hips to lift one leg in front of the other.

The artificial limbs are four inches too short for
him, so Freddie, 9, looks awkward and dwarfish to his
friends.

One afternoon in May 1977, he and some friends
hopped aboard the last of a slow-moving Conrail train.
When the train began to go faster, Freddie tried to jump
off. He slipped and fell beneath the wheels. His legs
were severed above the kneecaps. Freddie spent two
months in a hospital before returning home.

"From the first, he was determined to adjust to his
handicap," said his first grade teacher at the school.
"Most victims of this kind of accident go through a long
period of depression. Freddie didn't stay down very long.
He had a great spirit and self-confidence."

"He's very well liked by everyone in the room -----.
He's accepted as a regular child and that's the best thing
in the world for him."

----- But little things--like the slick waxed floors
at the school, which send Freddie sprawling when he walks
too fast--remind him of his handicap. "I hate Mop-N-
Glow," he smiled.

"He's rough," his mother says. "He's worn out three
pairs of shoes right through the toe this year. You can't
stop him."

Freddie gets around the house faster without the
artificial legs, but Mrs. Dove encourages him to wear
them. "They (the legs) are his best friends," she said. "He
might as well wear them here (at home), because he'll
have to wear them in the real world" (*The State Journal*,
February 15, 1980, Lansing, Michigan).

From the concepts of pathology, this and other examples might be
viewed as illustrations of the defenses of denial, counterphobia, identification with the aggressor, repression and reaction formation. Such
simplistic formulations are neither correct nor do they do justice to
complex behavioral mechanisms and environmental events.

LONGITUDINAL DEVELOPMENTAL STUDIES

A new look is emerging from the longitudinal developmental studies
that began in the 1930s. Information about adult outcomes are now
available as new methods of complex data analysis have been developed
(Block, 1971). One aspect that comes from these long-range studies of

development has been that professionals have been surprised. What has been a surprise is that many children were viewed to be at-risk for later disturbances but they did not turn out that way. Children in ongoing unfavorable life situations were able to obtain restitutive experiences later on in life or have favorable outcomes for reasons not clearly understood.

There also have been studies that have taken another look at the outcomes of prematurity at birth which represents an at-risk situation (Sameroff and Chandler, 1975). This evidence indicates that environmental experiences, if not quality of life environments, as well as improved neonatal treatment and care results in much more favorable outcomes than was earlier predicted and found.

Recent long-term follow up of headstart intervention has also provided a new look (Lazar, Hubbell, Murray, Rosche and Royce, 1977; Lazar and Darlington, 1978). Comprehensive studies of low-income children who attended head start programs in the 1960s have shown conclusively that these children were far less likely to require special education, be retained in grade, or drop out of school than similar children without preschool training. These differences could not be attributed to variations in family background or intelligence.

Preschool paid off in other ways. Children who had attended head start were more likely to express pride in specific achievements and rated themselves as better students than did similar children who did not attend preschool programs. Mothers whose children attended preschool were more likely to have higher aspirations for their children than similar low-income mothers whose children had not attended preschool.

Further evidence on coping comes from the rediscovery of earlier studies and publications. White developed the concepts of competence and competency to account for behavioral phenomena that could not be explained on the basis of drive, affect and conflict motivation (White, 1959; White, 1979). He viewed exploratory and motor practicing activities directed at the body self and at the outside inanimate and social worlds from earliest infancy as part of the development of reality relations. These activities created effects and consequences on the body, inanimate objects and people from which their properties could be extracted. Furthermore, the ability to create effects and the feelings associated with them were called respectively the effectance motive and the sense of efficacy. Collective experiences from multiple transactions over developmental time gave rise to competence and a sense of competency in the normative situation of child and environment.

Also in 1959, Harris published findings of in-depth case studies of 54 normal boys and girls, ages eight and nine, and their mothers (Harris, 1959). The children were nominated by teachers as normal based on their social and academic adjustment to school. The lives of these children and their families were not stress free in the past or present. What was more universally present were the capacities of the children and their mothers to deal with stress and adversity. A wide range of types of successful adjustments of the children were found as well as differences in mother-hood themes with successful mothering.

RISK RESEARCH STUDIES

Another area of evidence on coping has emerged from "risk re-search" studies of children who are at-risk for present or future develop-mental and psychological disturbances. The at-risk situation can be individual child vulnerability or family/environmental stressful situations.

Robert Coles' original book, *Children of Crisis* (1964), is a good example of case studies of heroic children who were faced with the environmental stress of racism and dealing with schools that did not welcome them and communities that opposed their being part of the mainstream of society. The case studies are remarkable stories of children who coped and who in adult life are doing well in various endeavors.

In studies of first relapses, recovery and chronicity in adult schizo-phrenia, Garmezy (1973) found that recovery seemed to be associated with early signposts of competence as obtained from retrospective historical data. Garmezy then became interested in the children who were at high risk of developing schizophrenia because either one or both parents had diagnostically established schizophrenic disorders. The like-lihood of children from families where one or both parents have schizo-phrenia also developing schizophrenia increases considerably. In following a sample of these children, while a small percentage of them showed the beginning of disturbed behavior in adolescent or young adult life, what struck him was that the great majority of these children did remarkably well (Garmezy, 1974). "Remarkably" is the term used because profes-sionals are surprised and because their thinking has led them to not expect positive outcomes.

Bleuler (1974) has also studied the offspring of schizophrenic adults. Of 164 children followed for 20 years, he found that somewhat close to 75 percent seemed to have learned well and to have graduated from school. They have jobs, are married, and seem to lead quite adequate lives.

Mednick (1977) found in his longitudinal study of children from schizophrenic parents in Denmark that 88 percent do not become schizo-phrenic in adult life. Twelve percent of the children did show schizo-phrenic-like disorders in growing up to adulthood, which is greater than its incidence in general population studies. But again, the great majority of the children did "remarkably well."

Studies of inner city children from Chicago and New York who are not only disadvantaged by poverty but also by skin color have revealed that not all of them are delinquent. Not all of them are destined to become school dropouts and unemployable (Neuchterlein, 1970).

There have also been epidemiological studies of children raised in disadvantaged environments of inner London (Rutter, 1976). Rutter found that of the children who are at-risk for delinquency at least 25 to 30 percent do not turn out to have any delinquent trends in adolescence or young adult life. They do not develop an antisocial career (Rutter, 1979). Rutter has been interested in the issues of risk or vulnerability from the standpoint of additive stressors. He has also pointed out facilitating factors in the child's life experiences that may balance out the at-risk situations. One of the important facilitators is school achievement.

Rutter and his collaborators have recently published the results of a three-year study of 2,700 pupils from twelve secondary schools in a large urban area of inner London (Rutter, 1979). The results showed that there were clear differences between those schools that promote success and those associated with failure. A careful examination of school life features pointed to differences that could be related to contrasting academic and social behavior outcomes when intake measures of pupil adjustment were taken into account. High school attendance, pro-social behaviors, high level of outgo examination success and low delinquency rates were strongly correlated. These positive behaviors were associated with certain school characteristics such as positive teacher expectations, more child work displayed on classroom walls, more actual teaching discipline interventions and high teacher attendance and punctuality. Rutter's work points to the importance of school environments in modifying at-risk situations even as late as the secondary school level.

In a recent book, Segal reviews some of the findings from at-risk research in a chapter entitled, "Children Who Will Not Break" (Segal, 1978). However, the concept of an unbreakable child sounds neither human nor accurate. Other terms which have been used such as "Super Kids" and "invulnerables" are equally unsatisfactory. Stress resistant children is a more reasoned concept. Segal summarizes studies of children from families where the parents were physically ill or had severe psychological disturbances. Again, the negative prediction for these children did not always occur. Some children did react unfavorably but many did not.

Anthony (1975) calls attention to the observation that people who are psychologically upset are not disturbed 24 hours a day, seven days a week, for twelve months a year. The idea exists that when somebody is evaluated who is emotionally disturbed, the evaluation findings represent their usual way of behaving and relating in all situations. Such an evaluation, mental status examination, is done under rather extraordinary and stressful circumstances. It is a situational context which normative persons would find disarming and stressful. Conclusions from such special examination procedures are made which may not be warranted. Indeed, when one naturalistically observes people who have various degrees of disorganized behavior, they are not disorganized all of the time. They have adequacies and can often function well as parents with their own children. Some may be able to spare their children from being recipients of their disturbed behaviors.

There was a child in one of Anthony's families whose mother had a delusion about food, namely, if you ate certain food it would kill you. This boy continued to eat the food that his mother considered to be dangerous. When he was asked how he did that, he said, "Well, I've eaten it many times and I'm not dead yet." This boy used his own reality testing to determine that his mother was not rational about what she believed and communicated (Anthony, 1975).

In summary, this is what various authors have to say about stress resistant children. Socially, they are described as personable, sensitive to others, empathic, well liked by peers, verbal, socially appropriate, well behaved in classrooms and ready to help others; often a non-family adult is important in their life, such as a teacher. In the cognitive realm, they think for themselves and have good attentional processes; they are problem solvers, reflective and playful; they make creative use of imagination and fantasy; they use information effectively, do well in novel situations and make reality/fantasy distinctions. Affectively, stress resistant children have capacities for frustration tolerance and gratification delay; they both express and control their emotions; they have optimism, a future orientation and a sense of humor. Their self characteristics include positive self regard, self-esteem maintenance, internal locus of control and acceptance of responsibility; they resist negative labels and do not assume a victim identification; they usually have well developed special interests and activities in addition to liking school (Anthony, 1975, 1978; Garmezy, 1972, 1979, 1981; Murphy and Moriarty, 1976; Rutter, 1979; Segal, 1978).

PERSONAL COLLABORATIVE STUDIES ON
ACUTE AND CHRONIC STRESS IN CHILDHOOD

In a previous study of acute predictable stress in the late 1940s (Jessner, Blom and Waldfogel, 1952), findings on children exposed to tonsillectomy and hospitalization have recently been reviewed. Of particular interest were 22 children, 16 percent of the random population of 143 children of various ages, who were identified as emotionally disturbed. Fifty percent of this group (12 children) displayed only mild reactions or improved behavior post operatively and post hospitalization. These findings on the twelve children were somewhat of an enigma to explain at the time of the original study. There was the element of surprise that emotionally disturbed children had done "remarkably well." Closer examination of the data obtained on these children showed the following set of factors as probably related to normative and coping adaptations: an improvement in child health status, a shift in parental attitude toward the child that was more positive, an experience where the children clearly perceived fantasy and reality boundaries, hospitalization as time limited punishment and atonement for wrongdoings and, most importantly, a positive response to stress as a challenge which led to coping and mastery.

A recent study of acute collective stress provides additional findings from an unpredictable event (Blom, 1981). In the fall of 1977, an intervention project was initiated following a pedestrian overpass accident at an elementary school in Lansing, Michigan. Assistance was requested to help a school population of 283 children, their families, teachers, school personnel and the surrounding community assimilate this catastrophic event and restore a previous equilibrium.

The accident occurred in the morning as children were going to school. A 40-ton crane truck struck a pedestrian overpass on which 16 to 25 children were walking. Six boys fell fifteen feet to the pavement below and five were seriously hurt. The accident was observed by about 100 children on the school playground.

This population was followed over a seven-month period of time. Matt, age 8, was convinced that he knew that the skywalk was going to fall and that if he had been more insistent with his parents and teacher, he could have prevented children from being hurt. For not doing so, he felt guilty and personally responsible. Treatment was provided to help Matt with his traumatic reaction. There were some children, parents and school personnel who had post-accident behavior symptoms and signs for a prolonged period of time. Yet, there were many who coped and a few who were heroes.

A major emphasis of the crisis intervention program was to foster an already developing self-help therapeutic community and to be readily available to those identified as being uncomfortable. The intervention team supported a normal group developmental phenomenon of altruism (Barton, 1969). Members were active helpers rather than professionals waiting to be called in their offices. The latter is the traditional professional posture of providing help for pathological behaviors.

Based on responses to a sent-home questionnaire, 81 percent of the child and parent population were showing diminishing or no behavioral reactions 4 to 6 weeks later. The other 19 percent were contacted as well as all the families with injured children. Again, the vast majority of the population was doing "remarkably well." This finding was shared through a fact sheet sent home regularly with the children. A seven-month follow-up survey showed that 7 percent of the children were emotionally upset, not much different than what would be expected in a typical elementary school population under average expectable conditions.

Pediatric hospital settings also provide an opportunity to observe children who respond to repeated episodes of biological stress "remarkably well." One such example was Tony, age 10, hospitalized for the fifth time with Cooley's anemia and cirrhosis of the liver (Blom, 1958). As part of understanding his coping capacities, Tony was asked to tell stories from a series of Thematic Apperception Test cards. One of his stories depicted his illness as a destructive process (which it was) and his treatment (which in reality was to be a surgical by-pass procedure to alleviate pressure on his liver). The story was of a sea monster (illness depicted as a destructive symbol) who grew higher than 6,000 feet (Tony had abdominal swelling from fluid in his abdominal cavity) and wrecked cities and crushed houses (Tony was aware of his jaundice, anemia and abnormal liver functioning). The army, navy and marines were not able to destroy the monster (Tony had repeated hospitalizations, previous surgical removal of his spleen, many consultations with specialists, special diets and medication without influencing the course of his illness). A scientist discovered a new kind of gas that had been tested on animals (a hopeful outcome). A woman knew about this discovery (perhaps his mother) and got the scientist to try it on the monster (a different operative procedure in a university hospital away from his community). The gas went all over the creature and killed him (a view of treatment that got rid of the illness and provided a successful result).

From personal experiences with handicapped children and their families in hospital and school settings over many years, it is possible to identify factors that are often associated with successful adaptation and coping. These facilitating factors will be found in parents, siblings, professional caretakers and the handicapped child within an interacting system.

Positive parental factors often result from their having past experiences of satisfactory parenting in their own lives as children. It is helpful if a mutual supporting marital relationship exists and if stable professional care and services are available to their disabled child. Also positive is the ability of parents to plan and anticipate the future. A positive philosophical or religious life view is supportive. Home assistance, respite care opportunities and a listening ear from friends are also important. Parent groups and early home training are reported as helpful. The situation is made easier if the handicapped child is not the first child and if accurate diagnosis was possible early in the child's life or illness history.

Positive sibling factors often develop from satisfactory experiences in caring for a disabled brother or sister. The display of sensitivity, concern and empathy supports this development. Siblings often show spurts in their maturation. Periodic appropriate expression of negative feelings toward the handicapped sibling which are accepted and tolerated is also constructive.

It is helpful if professional caretakers have a balance of objectivity and empathy and if they can tolerate being targets of anger and disappointment from the child with disability and from his/her family. Also important is the ability to relate to the current psychological state of the disabled child and family and to accept help without cure as a comfortable goal.

Positive factors in the handicapped child include the development of alternative skills and the recognition of courage and accomplishment by others. Satisfactions can be obtained from achievements at levels of adaptation different from others. Hope, assertiveness and appropriate risk taking are further positive characteristics. Relationships to other disabled children and a positive identity of being different also facilitate positive adaptation.

STUDIES OF STRESS RESISTANT CHILDREN

Over the last few years a group of us has been interested in "stress resistant" children. As part of a seminar on stress and coping of children, graduate students were asked to pilot interview children who were nominated by school professionals as doing "remarkably well" under adverse circumstances or stressful conditions. After obtaining school, parent and child consent, eight children were interviewed using a modification of a method developed by Garmezy. The children were seen at school and their parents at home. Additional information was obtained from their teachers and other school staff.

In order to reduce pathology bias, it was necessary to interview children by a method quite different from usual child psychiatric or psychological interviews. A method developed by Garmezy provides children a series of eight cards with different topics to talk about such as friends, home and family, school, myself, interests and activities, future imagination and wishes, and worries and feelings. The child is asked to sort the cards in an order of preference for discussion. On the back of each card, there are a series of questions for the interviewer to ask the child.

The children in this pilot study included the following:

    8-year-old girl with genetic blindness
    8-year-old boy from the inner city with many recent life
       stresses
    10-year-old native American boy in a foster home
    11-year-old French boy attending school in the United
       States
    12-year-old girl in a family with schizophrenic members
    12-year-old boy who was a hero during a school disaster
    14-year-old girl with congenital blindness
    16-year-old girl with muscular dystrophy

All the eight children were either completely or partially main-streamed in school. Two came from non-intact families. They also had clearly identifiable handicapping or stress conditions operating in their lives. They enjoyed being interviewed by graduate students who in turn experienced pleasure in talking with them. Given the limitations of a cursory study of a few selected children, a content analysis of the written interviews was done in an attempt to identify their behavioral characteristics.

The characteristics developed from these eight children correspond closely to those previously reported even though their adverse life circumstances were somewhat different in that they primarily had disabling conditions. Socially, they attracted and used the support of adults at home, school and community; they were friendly, personable and talkative; peers accepted them and their disabilities; they had friendships. Cognitively, they could identify what they liked least and most about their reality; their orientation was to the future; they were successful at and liked school. Affectively, these children seemed emotionally sensitive, empathic with others and insightful of their own feelings and those of others. From a self aspect, they were inner directed and thought for themselves; they could detach from the dysfunctional behaviors of others; they believed in their own control over life events; and did not view themselves with negative labels assigned by others.

Such a listing of characteristics does not capture the essence of what these individual children are like. Some specific illustrations do that more successfully. Connie, the 14-year-old girl with congenital blindness, said she did not want to be "thought of as blind;" she was first and foremost "a person." Indeed, her parents had fostered this identity and her many activities reflected that, such as horseback riding and skiing. When mobility training was discussed, Connie went along with the use of a cane but said that she wanted to have a dog. As she explained, "If I go out by myself and get lost, I can't tell my cane to take me home--but I can say that to my dog."

The 10-year-old Native American boy in a foster home had at least two strikes against him, being of minority status and residing in a foster home. Both of these situations have been identified as at-risk. Yet Johnny explained it this way--"I have two homes; when things get bad with my mother at home (on the reservation), I can come here; when it gets better at home, I can go back." Johnny seemed to be able to manage pretty well in two different schools as well.

The 12-year-old boy who was a hero during a school disaster is presented in more detail. Jack was in sixth grade and a member of the school safety patrol. He was the oldest of three children from a stable, religious family who did things together. The children had chores to perform and Jack received an allowance because of his age. Neither parent drank or smoked. Mother, age 31, was pregnant with Jack before marriage but had not kept this a secret, clarifying that she has always cared for him. Father worked in an auto factory on the night shift. Mother did not work and was concerned about her children's welfare and progress. She was an avid school supporter, openly talkative with her children, a bit pushy. She often called the school about situations concerning her children. There had been accidents that happened to the family in the past: the nine-year-old brother was hit by a car five years ago at the site of the school overpass accident, a cousin was accidently shot in a hunting accident and an aunt had died six months ago.

Jack was identified as a hero based on his behavior when the overpass at his school was struck by a truck crane. He was on the crosswalk and shepherded children away including carrying some off. He did not panic. Jack described his feelings and the events in the following way: "Everything was in slow motion; it hit me later what happened and then I froze; the crosswalk fell right at my feet as I moved to talk to a friend; I picked up some kindergartners and carried them off but I really can't remember it; the kids were in better shape than the adults; you see younger kids look up to older kids to set an example." Jack received recognition for his heroism in the newspaper, the safety council of the city and a state legislature resolution for heroism. He responded to this recognition in a comfortable, pleased manner.

Jack responded to the interview cards in the following order: 1) interests and activities, 2) friends, 3) home and family, 4) school, 5) myself, 6) future, 7) imagination and wishes, and 8) worries and feelings. He was interested in reading about and actively participating in many sports and was familiar with sports heroes. He liked to travel and play games of chance. He made hooked rugs and model cars. Jack also read a book series by John Fitzgerald, *The Great Brain* (1967), which is about a boy who is a schemer with good intentions and who gets himself out of difficult situations. He enjoyed listening to radio as well as watching television. His favorite television shows were "Mork and Mindy," "Laverne and Shirley," and "Three's Company."

Jack made friends easily. He had one boy friend of seven years duration. He also talked with a 20-year-old obese and shy neighbor girl who "needs a friend." Jack had a positive opinion of himself; he liked the appearance of his hair and being tall. He worried more than his brother and wished he could spend more time with his father. He was a good math student, in the 94th percentile, and enjoyed mathematics because it got him to think and work out problems.

Impressions of Jack were that he was bright and enjoyed problem solving. He thought for himself yet was sensitive and able to be empathic with others. He was interested in reading and in boy and adult heroes. Jack was friendly, personable and sociable. He seemed to deal effectively with other children and adults. He was successful academically and socially in school. Jack was responsible and accepted his parents' values.

He handled his social recognition of heroism with modesty and affirmation of his values.

As indicated previously, Jack was an avid reader of a book series, *The Great Brain.* In reading one of these books, one is impressed by the similarities between Tom in the stories and Jack in real life. Tom in the stories is 12-years-old and the middle of three children, all boys. Tom displays a number of consistent personality characteristics. He is intelligent, clever and ingenious. He has knowledge of facts and a good memory. He takes the initiative and capitalizes on situations for materialistic and abstract rewards. Tom has the respect of friends and lives up to his reputation. He deals with injustice and unfairness. He believes in his own power and the importance of setting a good example for younger children.

In the book, the "Skeleton Cave Incident" is a heroic tale where Tom's intelligent planning and means-ends thinking pay off. Two boys and a female dog (Lady) are lost in a cave. All efforts at finding and rescuing them by adults are unsuccessful. Concern is expressed about their welfare as time goes on. Tom goes to the barn to think about what to do. He comes out with a plan that was formulated as a result of hearing their male dog (Brownie) bark. He recalled that Lady was in heat, an important detail, and knows that Brownie would be able to track her scent in the cave. Tom takes Brownie to Lady's home to pick up her scent. In this way, he and others find the lost trio. However, Tom also thinks about how to get out of the cave as well. Therefore, he gets some beef liver from the butcher shop and rubs this on the soles of their shoes so that Brownie will have a scent to get out of the cave.

Tom in the story and Jack in real life are intelligent thinkers and problem solvers. They enjoy the respect and admiration of other children. They are concerned about injustice and unfairness and display courage and belief in their own powers.

THEORETICAL CONSIDERATIONS ON COPING AND DEFENDING

From the study of normative populations or studies of populations which have taken a normative view, Haan (1977) has made distinctions between behavioral styles which are defending and those which are coping. In the professional literature coping and defending are used with different meanings. They are frequently interchanged. Defenses may be further characterized as maladaptive or adaptive and as primitive or mature. Haan (1977) and others (Gilmore, 1974; Mechanic, 1974; Murphy and Moriarty, 1976) make distinctions between coping characteristics and defending ones. Haan (1977) has characterized the major difference between coping and defending as consisting of coping as actively dealing with inner and outer events in terms of overcoming and problem solving while defending involves protecting oneself against such events. Other differences have been identified as shown in Table 1.

TABLE 1

Characteristics of Coping and Defending

Coping	Defending
Search to Overcome	Repetition of Sameness
Continued Psychological Effort	Restriction in Effort
Solution Towards Mastery	Maintain Equilibrium
Progression	Regression
Alternative Choices	Limited Choices
Flexibility	Rigidity
Pull to the Future	Pull to the Past
Oriented to the Present	Oriented to the Past
Rationality--Good Perceptions	Irrationality--Distortions
Emotional Tolerance	Emotional Intolerance
Information Gathering	Information Reduction
Interpersonal Involvement	Intrapersonal Preoccupation
Hopefulness and Confidence	Fatefulness and Lack of Confidence
Shame When Not Meet Standard	Guilt When Not Meet Standard

Haan (1977) also places fragmentation on the opposite end of a continuum from coping indicating behavioral styles that neither actively deal with the environment and inner life nor successfully protect. It would be her contention that behavioral styles will not be solely defensive or entirely coping. There are mixtures of styles and changes in their use over and through time.

Using Haan's reasoning, it is possible to provide a coping alternative for the list of defense mechanisms and processes contained in Moore and Fine's Glossary of Psychoanalytic Terms (1967). This has been done in Table 2.

Murphy refers to the many different ways children cope with difficulties during development (Murphy and Moriarty, 1976). Normal children show great resilience and use both defending and mastering capacities. The same psychological mechanism may sometimes be used defensively to protect and at other times offensively to master. Murphy views development as proceeding from an interaction of individual vulnerabilities and strengths with stress and support of many environments over time.

A PERSPECTIVE ON NORMALITY AND COPING

The interpretation of these data and findings should not be a lack of concern for the negative effects of poverty, racism and handicapism in our society even though data indicate that within these environments there are children who are coping and positively adapting. One does need

TABLE 2

Contrasts Between Defending and Coping Mechanisms

Defending	Coping
Repression	Expression
Regression	Progression
Reaction Formation	Caring
Reversal	Directedness
Isolation	Integration
Undoing	Doing
Compulsion	Free Choice
Obsession	Problem Solving
Projection	Inner Locus of Control
Denial	Acceptance
Inhibition	Control
Asceticism	Morality
Acting Out	Constructive Actions
Intellectualization	Insight

to consider the kinds of opportunities which should be provided children in those environments to facilitate skills or behavioral characteristics that are associated with adaptation and satisfaction.

There are dangers of distorting the emphasis on normality and competence. There can be an inappropriate return to or continued reinforcement of rugged individualism and social Darwinism. There can also be an unrealistic view of coping children as being those who do not break or are invulnerable or are like steel dolls. Competence may be mistakenly equated to intelligence. Long-range follow-up studies by Sears of Terman's high IQ children from the 1920s have pointed to a range of successful-unsuccessful life outcomes along with variation in life satisfaction (Coleman, 1980).

There is a need to continue to study normal and competent children and their families over time, or cross sectional time. This should include the range of individuality from handicap, to at-risk, to normal potential, to special potential. Individuality also interacts with a range of environments from handicap, to vulnerable, to at-risk, to normal expectable, to quality of life. There also needs to be a further examination of what might be called the myth of early identification of and intervention with children at-risk. The evidence from life span developmental psychology supports the concept of multiple entry points of intervention as well as vulnerability at various ages. The studies of Inbar (1976), for example, point to middle childhood, commonly held as a stable period in child development, as a stage of vulnerability.

IMPLICATIONS OF COPING FOR INTERVENTION AND PREVENTION

In the example of Jack, the school accident hero, one was impressed by the potential influence of children's literature on the behavior of children. Children's literature often depicts stress events, tragedies and handicaps experienced by children. Fassler (1978) discusses and identifies books for children about death, separation, illness, life style changes and other stress events. She applies the insights from these books to the needs of children, parents and child professionals. Cianciolo (1975) has brought the many potentialities of children's literature to the attention of teachers. Unfortunately, these potentials have not been sufficiently utilized in the teaching of reading and in helping children to deal with stress in their lives.

Experiences have been developed and accumulated on how regular classroom elementary teachers can identify and process stress events in the lives of children in their classrooms (Blom, Cheney, and Snoddy, 1982). Ways of identifying stress events and their behavioral indicators or reactions and types of reactive teacher strategies can be taught to and practiced by teachers with considerable success.

However, the generation of prosocial, adaptive and coping behaviors in children by classroom teachers presents a number of complexities. These proactive teacher strategies belong to a larger group of teaching activities called psychoeducational programs in the classroom (Morse and Ravlin, 1979). These programs have existed for some time under various designations such as affective education, values clarification and decision-making skills. At one time they achieved a great deal of popularity and application. Currently, they are not so extensively used for many reasons such as undemonstrated effects, parent criticism, their artificiality, the return to basic academic skills, overselling programs, unrealistic expectations and lack of evaluation. In addition, many of these programs are based upon global positive mental health concepts that are not anchored in empirical studies of children. Some have come from transpositions of psychopathological studies and others from conceptualizations of ideal normality or well being that do not exist in reality.

The development of proactive interventions and strategies to generate and maintain coping behavioral styles in children should have an empirical base. It is here that existing and ongoing studies of "normal" and "stress resistant" children in real environments provide a particular opportunity. Such studies have the potential of developing proactive teacher interventions. In fact, the cognitive-behavioral training strategies reported in the literature represent the beginning of such efforts (Meichenbaum and Goodman, 1971; Spivak and Shure, 1974; Camp, Blom, Hebert and vanDoorninck, 1977).

There are also treatment implications from the studies on stress and coping (Kliman, 1978). A more sensible perspective on positive factors and strengths in people's lives needs to be emphasized. One can too easily become mired in the past instead of also focusing on present existential events in the lives of children and families. Attempts should be made to capture examples of competence in current and past lives and to provide psychodynamic understanding of coping processes (Blom, 1981). Regression should be limited and active problem solving encouraged. Stressing self-responsibility will foster problem solving and an inner locus of control over events and feelings. A more positive alternative explanation for events may offer a more optimistic perspective. Therapists and counselors should monitor their own preoccupation with pathology and be aware of the constant focus on the problems of patients. All of these aspects require a therapist to also be active and not just a good listener.

SUMMARY

This presentation has discussed the preoccupation of behavioral scientists with behavioral pathology and its consequences. Attempts have been made to redress that imbalance by calling attention to the overlooked data that the majority of children and adults cope with adversity, handicap and at-risk situations. Theoretical considerations on coping and defending based on such data have been offered as well as their implications to educational, treatment and prevention programs.

A modified quotation from Robert Louis Stevenson offers a serious concluding statement--"life is sometimes not a matter of holding good cards but of learning to play a poor hand well." It is also not just coping with adversity but learning from it and being able to obtain satisfactions and positive qualities in living. Existential fate deals different hands of cards at different times to all persons. Effective living needs to address that fate and to be aware that the fate of others might be our own.

REFERENCES

Anthony, E. J. Naturalistic studies of disturbed families. In E. J. Anthony (Ed.), *Explorations in child psychology.* New York: Plenum Publishing, 1975.

Anthony, E. J. The syndrome of the psychologically invulnerable child. In E. J. Anthony and C. Koupernik (Eds.), *The child in his family: Children at psychiatric risk.* New York: John Wiley, 1975.

Anthony, E. J. A new scientific region to explore. In E. J. Anthony and C. Koupernik (Eds.), *The child in his family: The vulnerable child.* New York: Wiley, 1978.

Barton, A. J. *Communities in disaster: A sociological analysis of collective situations.* New York: Doubleday, 1969.

Barzerman, M., Sheehan, C., Ellison, D. L., and Schlesinger, E. P. *Pregnant adolescents, a review of literature with abstracts, 1960-1976.* Washington, D.C.: Consortium on Early Childbearing and Childrearing, 1971.

Bleuler, M.   The offspring of schizophrenics.   *Schizophrenia Bulletin,* 1974, *8,* 93-107.

Block, J. in collaboration with Haan, N.   *Lives through time.*   Berkeley: Bancroft Books, 1971.

Blom, G. E.   Heather's story: Psychotherapy and the practice of the least restrictive alternative.   *Issue Paper UCIR.*   Michigan State University, January 1981.

Blom, G. E.   Psychological reactions of a school population to a skywalk accident.   In C. D. Spielberger, Sarason and Milgram (Eds.), *Stress and Anxiety,* Vol. 8.   Washington, D.C.:   Hemisphere Publishing Corporation, 1981.

Blom, G. E., Cheney, B. D., and Snoddy, J. E.   *MSU program cork: Drinking/non-drinking curriculum for teachers,* Cluster Two--Identification and processing of stress in children.   College of Education. Michigan State University: East Lansing, MI 1982.

Brazelton, T. B., and Als, H.   Four early stages in the development of mother-infant interaction.   *The Psychoanalytic Study of the Child,* 1979, *34,* 349-369.

Camp, B. W., Blom, G. E., Hebert, F., and vanDoorninck, W. J.   "Think aloud": A program for developing self-control in young aggressive boys.   *Journal of Abnormal Child Psychology,* 1977, *5,* 157-169.

Children's Defense Fund.   *America's children and their families: Basic facts.*   Washington, D.C.: Children's Defense Fund, 1979.

Cianciolo, P.   "Feeling books" develop social and personal sensitivities. *Elementary English,* 1975, *52,* 37-42.

Coleman, D.   1,528 little geniuses and how they grew.   *Psychology Today.* February 1980, 28-43.

Coles, R.   *Children of crisis.*   Boston: Little Brown, 1964.

Eddinger, L., and Forbush, J.   *School age pregnancy and parenthood in the United States.*   Washington, D.C.: National Alliance Concerned with School Age Parents, 1977.

Fassler, J.   *Helping children cope: Mastering life through books and stories.*   New York: The Free Press, 1978.

Fitzgerald, J. D.   *The great brain.*   New York: Dell, 1967.

Garmezy, N., and Neuchterlein, K.   Invulnerable children: The fact and fiction of competence and disadvantage.   *American Journal of Orthopsychiatry,* 1972, *42,* 328-329 (Abstract).

Garmezy, N.   Competence and adaptation in adult schizophrenic patients and children at risk.   In S. R. Dean (Ed.), *Schizophrenia: The first ten Dean Award lectures.*   New York: MSS Corporation, 1973.

Garmezy, N.   The study of competence in children at risk for severe psychopathology.   In J. Anthony and C. Koupernik (Eds.), *The child in his family: Children at psychiatric risk.*   New York: John Wiley, 1974.

Garmezy, N.   Children under stress: Perspectives on antecedents and correlates of vulnerability and resistance to psychopathology.   In A. I. Rabin, J. Aronoff, A. M. Barclay, and R. A. Zucker (Eds.), *Further explorations in personality.*   New York: Wiley and Sons, 1981.

Gilmore, J. V.   *The productive personality.*   San Francisco: Albion Publishing Co., 1974.

Haan, N. *Coping and defending.* New York: Academic Press, 1977.

Harris, J. D. *Normal children and mothers.* Glencoe: Glencoe Free Press, 1959.

Inbar, M. *The vulnerable age phenomenon.* New York: Russell Sage Foundation, 1976.

Jessner, L., Blom, G. E., and Wagonfeld, S. Emotional implications of tonsillectomy and adenoidectomy on children. *Psychoanalytic Study of the Child,* 1952, VII, 69-81.

Keniston, K. *All our children: The American family under pressure.* New York: Harcourt, Brace and Jovanovitch, 1977.

Kliman, A. S. *Crisis: Psychological first aid for recovery and growth.* New York: Holt, Rinehart and Winston, 1978.

Lazar, I., Hubbell, V. R., Murray, H., Rosche, M., and Royce, J. *Summary report: Persistence of preschool effects.* DHEW Publication #(OHDS) 78-30129, Ithaca, New York, October 1977.

Lazar, I., and Darlington, R. B. *Lasting effects after preschool.* DHEW Publications #(OHDS) 79-30178, Ithaca, New York, October 1978.

Mechanic, D. Social structure and personal adaptation: Some neglected dimensions. In G. V. Coelho, D. S. Hamburg, and J. E. Adams (Eds.), *Coping and adaptation.* New York: Basic Books, 1974.

Mednick, S. A., and Witkin-Lanoil, G. H. Intervention in children at high risk for schizophrenia. In G. W. Albee and J. M. Joffe (Eds.), *Primary prevention of psychopathology,* Vol. I, Issues. Hanover, NH: University Press of New England, 1977.

Meichenbaum, D. H., and Goodman, J. Training impulsive children to talk to themselves: A means of developing self control. *Journal of Abnormal Psychology,* 1971, 77, 115-126.

Moore, B., and Fine, B. *Glossary of psychoanalytic terms.* New York: American Psychoanalytic Association, 1967.

Morse, W. C., and Ravlin, M. M. Psychoeducation in the school setting. In S. L. Harrison (Ed.), *Basic handbook of child psychiatry, Vol. III, Therapeutic interventions.* New York: Basic Books, 1979.

Murphy, L. B. *The widening world of childhood.* New York: Basic Books, 1962.

Murphy, L. B., and Moriarty, A. E. *Vulnerability, coping and growth from infancy to adolescence.* New Haven: Yale University Press, 1976.

Nuechterlein, K. H. *Competent disadvantaged children: A review of research.* Unpublished summa cum laude thesis, University of Minnesota, 1970.

Psychiatric News. Advisory panel project need for 50,000 psychiatrists in 1990. Vol. XV, #17, 1980.

Psychiatric News. Children of alcoholics said impaired. Vol. XV, #16, 1980.

Roosa, M. W., Fitzgerald, H. E., and Carlson, N. A. Teenage and older mothers and their infants: A descriptive comparison. *Mother Infant Project,* Report 3. Institute for Family and Child Study, Michigan State University, January 1981.

Rutter, M. *Early sources of security and competence.* Wolfson Lecture at Oxford University, February 10, 1976.

Rutter, M. *Fifteen thousand hours.* Cambridge: Harvard University Press, 1979.

Rutter, M. Proactive factors in children's responses to stress and disadvantage. In M. Kent and J. Rolf (Eds.), *Primary prevention of psychopathology,* Vol. 3. Hanover, NH: University Press of New England, 1979.

Sameroff, A. J., and Chandler, M. J. Reproductive risk and the continuum of caretaking casualty. In F. D. Horowitz (Ed.), *Review of child development research,* Vol. 4. Chicago: University of Chicago Press, 1975.

Segal, J. *A child's journey: Forces that shape the lives of our young.* New York: McGraw-Hill, 1978.

Snapper, K. J., and Ohms, J. S. *The status of children, 1977.* DHEW Publication #(OHDS) 78-30133. Washington, D.C.: U.S. Government Printing Office, 1977.

Spivack, G., and Shure, M. B. *Social adjustment of young children.* San Francisco: Jossey Bass, 1974.

Stewart, K. R. *Adolescent sexuality and teenage pregnancy: A selected annotated bibliography with summary forewards.* Chapel Hill, North Carolina Population Center, 1976.

White, R. W. Motivation reconsidered: The concept of competence. *Psychological Review,* 1959, *66,* 297-333.

White, R. W. Competence as an aspect of personal growth. M. W. Kent and J. E. Rolf (Eds.), *Social competence in children.* Hanover, NH: University Press of New England, 1979.

BECOMING AN ADULT IN THE 1980s

John Paul McKinney

Department of Psychology
Michigan State University
East Lansing, MI 48824

INTRODUCTION

Leaving Childhood

In most cultures, childhood is a stage of the life cycle that is loved and revered, at least in words, if not always in actions. Children and childhood may be admired because it is in them that adult hopes for the future and the world are high. It is almost as if when everything else in life suggests despair, we look at our children and find our hope for the future once again resurrected. Therefore, it is in many ways difficult to give up children or their childhood for adulthood and maturity. It is for example, one of the most agonizingly painful and difficult tasks for a parent to lose a child to death, whether suddenly or slowly, in infancy or at any childhood age. It is also difficult for parents who are unable economically, psychologically or physically to care for their child to relinquish and commit that child to the care of somebody else. It is difficult for parents who are abusive or otherwise found incapable to give up their children. Finally, it is difficult for all of us at different times and in different ways to say good-bye to our own childhood or to our children and their childhood. In loving our children we tend to hold up their stage of life as an ideal to us all. "Unless you become as little children you shall not enter the kingdom of heaven."

Perhaps there are some--the true poets--who have in some measure been able to retain their childhood; but most people have had to grow up. One can't be a child forever. Moreover, there is the possibility of over-romanticizing that first stage of life. As one of my colleagues has written, "It ain't easy being a kid," (Helfer, 1977). In many communities and in many families being a child is tragically difficult. Unfortunately

89

the prospects for adulthood and future life in many of those situations are no better. The little adult outcome research that is available on the topics of emotional disturbance, juvenile delinquency, child abuse, mental deficiency, etc., points to dismal self-fulfilling prophecies. While childhood, then, may be no bed of roses for some, the future for those same youngsters often looks no brighter to them.

Regardless of whether childhood has been marked by pain and difficulty or by love and abundance, the transition to adulthood carries with it certain inevitable events. Aside from the physical changes at puberty and the concomitant sexual development, the transition to adulthood is marked by an increase of self responsibility and dominance, and by the possibility of engaging in sexual activity. In addition, there is a withdrawing from the family of origin and a greater investment in the peer group.

Cultural anthropologists have observed that this transition from childhood to adulthood is gradual in some cultures and abrupt in others. The differential status of the child and the adult are clearly and publicly marked in some cultures and vague in others. In some cultures the rights and responsibilities of adults are assured by legal fiat, i.e., the age of majority. In other cultures the rites and rituals associated with the transition from childhood clearly identify the individual as a new adult. In twentieth century America, however, none of the above conditions prevail. Laws specifying the age of majority vary from state to state, from time to time, and from event to event. The age at which a person can drive a car, vote, obtain a marriage license, and drink alcoholic beverages legally may all be different, although each of these events may be seen as one mark of adult status. Similarly, the age at which one can be tried in adult courts or can enter into legal contracts may vary from time to time and from state to state. If laws do not help define adulthood with clarity, what about religious or other rituals which characterize the end of chldhood. Unfortunately, there is nothing universal about such religious events as Confirmation and Bar Mitzvah, which signify to the whole community a new status for the adolescent involved. While such events may have great importance to the individual involved and to the community of believers, they do not automatically guarantee any change in status beyond that group.

A Period of Transition--Adolescence

What does, then, characterize the transition from childhood to adulthood in our culture? One answer is a period of transition known as adolescence. Some have argued that the period is one of conflict, i.e., a time when one hews out his/her own identity via a series of conflicts that results in the establishment of one's own set of values which may be at variance with those of parents and other adults. Some writers (e.g., G. Stanley Hall, 1905; Gustin, 1968) have proposed that adolescence is a period of turmoil and conflict while others have found more evidence of conformity (Constanzo and Shaw, 1966; Douvan and Adelson, 1966). While some have argued that this is a time of parent-child conflict, others have countered that such conflict is not only not inevitable, but may well be the exception rather than the rule (Hess and Goldblatt, 1957; Meissner, 1965; Bandura, 1964).

The period of adolescence is clearly not well defined either in terms of its duration nor in terms of its major characteristics. It has been argued elsewhere (McKinney, Fitzgerald and Strommen, 1982) that one of the defining characteristics of adolescence may be its lack of definition to the individual adolescent, to those around him, and to those who have studied this developmental period. The most characteristic marker may be a certain ambiguity with respect to rights and responsibilities, status and values.

This chapter will focus on four major developmental tasks of late adolescence and the maintenance of self-esteem which is involved in each of them.

DEVELOPMENTAL TASKS OF ADOLESCENCE

Separation: The Defining Issue of Adolescence

While a good deal is known about the dispersal of animals from their family groups, less is known about the separation of adolescent boys and girls from their families. I regularly ask the students in an undergraduate course in adolescence how many have not yet left home. Typically over half the class raise their hands. I then ask the students how many are not living at home. About half of them say they don't live at home, despite the fact that they also insist that they haven't "left home." Leaving home, they tell me, means financial independence, or emotional separation, or having a permanent address, or being married. The task is obviously multi-faceted.

Some writers have dealt with this issue from a clinical perspective, and emphasized the aberrant ways in which some adolescents leave home (Stierlin, 1974). Recently, however, some research has been devoted to the more normal adolescent separation process. Sullivan and Sullivan (1980) compared a group of young men who went away to board at college with a group who lived at home while they commuted to college. They tested the groups while they were still in high school and again after they had begun college. They found that the boarders away from home demonstrated an increase in affection toward their parents, as well as a perceived increase in communication, independence, and satisfaction, when compared with those who remained at home and commuted to college.

Hotch (1979) demonstrated there are different perceived styles of home-leaving. While some adolescents see the process as self-initiated (agents), others perceive it as something happening to them by virtue of external pressures (patients). Hotch found that these perceived styles could be predicted by a combination of the variables of relatedness with the family and self-sufficiency.

Some may argue that the separation process does not begin at adolescence. In fact, one of the major hallmarks of development is increasing separation and individuation. At each developmental stage, individuals encounter separation from an earlier stage of development as well as individuation or differentiation from other periods. The individual becomes an increasingly unique and different person with his/her own identity. For the developmental psychologist, two sorts of separation stand out: first there is the physical individuation which occurs at birth, weaning, walking or any other stage when increased independence is apparent; a second, and equally important kind of separation, is cognitive.

Piaget has called this latter type of separation "decentering." For example, in early infancy, the baby behaves as though an external object were one and the same with his/her own movements. For example, he/she may equate the mother's breast and his own sucking. The baby may identify the rattle with his own hand movements. An infant may look for a rattle in the place where he last threw it, despite the fact he may have seen the rattle lifted and put elsewhere after having thrown it. As the child develops cognitively, he begins to recognize objects as separate and constant. Still later he can further decenter by symbolizing the object. He may retain the object in its otherness by abstracting its essential qualities, and thus retain a concept of the object, even in its physical absence. And finally, he/she can identify the object with a word. In this way the child overcomes his sense of separateness from the rest of the world.

With advancing development children encounter increasing cognitive differentiation until the stage of formal operations which occurs in early adolescence. Again, a decentering occurs. The individual goes from a reliance on concrete information in the solution of problems to the use of formal operations. Formal operations consist of a higher level of abstraction with profound consequences for the development of scientific, moral, and political thought. In science, for example, the child can appreciate the relationship between relations. He or she can therefore hypothesize and can cognitively hold several variables constant while observing the effect of treatment on yet another variable. In other words, the adolescent can deal with the form of an argument or problem, not just with its content.

In the area of morality the adolescent can now consider the ideal as well as the real. Adolescents are not as bound by the immediate consequences of their actions but have internalized principles which guide their behavior. In the political arena, adolescents can consider what is possible as well as what is actual. They have developed an understanding of community and understand the prescriptive nature of authority. That is why they see authority as a positive rather than merely coercive force.

This change from concrete to formal operations involves a separation also. This separation occurs in at least two ways. First of all, there is a separation between subject and object. The individual at adolescence can recognize himself or herself, by virtue of his or her ability to decenter, as an object among objects. It is for this reason there is an increase in self-consciousness at this age. The adolescent often behaves as though for "an imaginary audience." Elkind (1967) has described this "imaginary audience" characteristic of adolescence as part of the ego-centrism of that stage.

A second type of separation involves the sense of separation of self from others, that is, as an object. This individual adolescent becomes distinguishable from other similar objects, i.e., unique. Elkind calls this the "personal fable." The individual considers himself unique and separate from others, in a sense that nobody else can either have nor understand his or her feelings which are considered unique. The adolescent assumes "It can only happen to me." One may also hear the other assumption which may turn out to be a tragic miscalculation..."it could never happen to me."

The sense of an "imaginary audience" results from under-differentiating one's own thoughts from those of other people. The adolescent, whose main concern is himself or herself, assumes mistakenly that everyone else has the same preoccupation. Thus, his or her life appears to be played out before this imaginary audience. The "personal fable," on the other hand, results from an *over*-differentiation. In separating himself/herself from others the adolescent overdifferentiates his/her own feelings from those which others may have and assumes he/she is completely unique. It may be difficult for that reason to counsel the adolescent and to establish understanding.

This dual separation in the transition from concrete to formal logic involves, as do many separations, going into new unknown psychological territory. The new territory is adulthood. Sullivan has observed that many early adolescents experience for the first time a sense of loneliness. The need for communication with one's peers is at an all-time high. This is attested to by the number of hours spent on the telephone, the desire to have friends stay overnight, and the letters and notes sent back and forth to one another even among those who see each other every day in school. The formation of gangs occurs during this period. Among many adolescents, there is a heightened interest in talk shows and in citizen band and short wave radios. Many of these are ways in which adolescent can communicate at a distance. One adolescent who was having difficulty in social relations at school, and who was reportedly disliked by his peers, and was a bully to younger children, took great delight night after night in contacting people all around the world with his short wave radio. A late maturing 15-year-old girl wrote long and daily letters to her dearest friend who lived one block away.

Some might ask, "Why do adolescents not turn to their family in an attempt to stave off loneliness?" When one is individuating from the family, looking there for emotional support may not help the growing up process. In a sense, one is always a "child" at home. The word, itself, refers not only to a stage of life but also to a relationship to one's parents. How does the individual overcome separateness? As mentioned earlier, the development of language distinguishes the infant from the young child and aids in overcoming the sense of separateness which is experienced when the individual distinguishes himself from other objects. In adolescence, it can be argued that the development of love for others serves the same function. First of all, affection for the same sex and later heterosexual love are ways in which separateness is overcome. In *The Art of Loving*, Erik Fromm (1956) defines love in precisely that way, i.e., "the overcoming of separateness." The confidant or "best friend" of the early adolescent serves the important function of validating the individual's self worth and acceptance.

The history of our interest in growing and separating reaches back into antiquity. Even though developmental psychology is a relatively new science, these issues and the concern about them are ancient. In the fourth century B.C., Plato wrote a description of development, and gave educational and pediatric advice in his *Republic* and *Laws*. He was clear, for example, about the meaning of education and its relationship to morality:

> Let not then, that which we assert instruction is, be undefined. For now, when we blame or praise the bringing up of each person, we say that one has been educated, but another uneducated; although the men have sometimes been very well educated for retail trades, and those of ship-owners, and for the profits from some other things of this kind. For of those, who, it seems, consider such things to be education, there would be now no account; but that (we say) is the education from childhood towards virtue, which causes a person to feel a desire of, and a love for, becoming a perfect citizen, and to know how to govern and to be governed with justice. Such a bringing up this discourse would, as it seems to me, define, and be willing to call it the only education; but that, which tends to the acquisition of wealth, or to any bodily strength, or any other cleverness, apart from intellect and justice, is a handicraft trade and illiberal, and not worthy to be called education at all (Plato, 1959, pp. 30-31).

Aristotle divided the "developmental" portion of the lifespan into three stages: the first stage went from zero to seven years; the second lasted from seven until puberty; and young manhood, from puberty until twenty-one.

The Greeks also included youth importantly in their mythology. Among the most important figures perhaps is Artemis, the goddess of youth. She was also known as the goddess of the hunt and the goddess of childbirth. We can make three important observations about Artemis: first of all, she goes by many different names; she is a multi-faceted patroness, with many aspects to her personality. Being worshiped in many places she seems almost like a different person in each. One search led to no less than 27 different titles for Artemis (Diana, Luna, Hecate, etc.). Secondly, the stories of Diana or Artemis are full of paradoxes. She is virginal and yet a mother. She is both a huntress and a guardian of animals. She is reportedly gentle, loving children and small animals, and yet can be vicious towards foes. Recall the story of Acteon, who was turned into a stag and hounded by the dogs for the sin of seeing Diana bathing naked in the stream. Artemis or Diana is, on the one hand, chaste and on the other, wild and impulsive. Finally, like the moon which she also represents, she is both constant and changing.

These three observations about Artemis parallel three analogous issues in modern adolescent psychology. First of all is the issue of *identity*. Despite psychological differentiation, individual adolescents struggle to maintain a sense of sameness with their previous experience and with their future aspirations. Secondly, the *paradoxes* within the adolescent personality have been a feature of that period which has attracted much research and theoretical attention. One such paradox is the desire to be unique and simultaneously to conform. Third, there is the issue of *simultaneous stability and change*, i.e., the struggle for sameness during a period of rapid change or, conversely, the desire for change when crystallization seems inevitable.

Identity Formation versus Diffusion

Among the psychosocial crises of development, identity versus identity diffusion looms largest during adolescence (Erikson, 1959, 1968). Although psychological differentiation has been occurring since birth, it begins to accelerate during adolescence. Personality becomes far more complex. For example, intellectual factors become more differentiated, and social choices are based on a greater variety and wider differentiation of personality variables. The adolescent also has more varied identification. Before adolescence, youngsters identify with concrete objects and persons; the adolescent, however, also identifies with ideals, goals and values. Studies in political socialization (Adelson and O'Neil, 1966) suggest that during adolescence, individuals develop a sense of community which is very different from the proscriptive and narrowly defined egocentric political thinking of earlier childhood. These new identifications for adolescents interact with the particular identification of the historical era during which they are growing. Adolescence, in other words, reflects--perhaps magnifies--the prevailing cultural norm.

Gillespie and Allport (1955) documented what they called the "privatism" of the values of American youth. Two things can be said about this observation. First, conservative political values were the order of the day in the 1950s when Gillespie and Allport were writing. The adolescents reflected adult values. Second, the high school and college students of the 1950s were often the sons and daughters of economic depression era parents. Many of their parents had begun their careers under highly unstable situational conditions of insecurity. If we compare those students of the 1950s with the adolescent generation of the 1960s, we are comparing them with the sons and daughters of those who began their careers after World War II, a victorious time period. Their sons and daughters, not surprisingly, were rebellious, revolutionary, idealistic, and marked by social concern. One need not over-romanticize or idealize these youth nor see them as unique in the history of civilization.

To some, the youth of the 1960s appear to be modern versions of Francis of Assisi, the 13th-century friar who chose a life of poverty and a life in community rather than what he considered the hypocritical lifestyle of his parents. Identifying with children and helpless people, St. Francis begged for food and lived in poverty, but always with a joy that has become apocryphal. The stories of his love for animals are many. He began the practice of creating the nativity scene at Christmas so that children could more fully participate in the event. If ever a saint could be considered a flower child, it was Francis. Put another way, if the flower children of the 1960s or any other era ever had a patron saint, it was Francis. In both instances, one occurring in the thirteenth and the other in the twentieth century, the rebellion of the adolescents was more a socio-cultural phenomenon than one of psychological development. In arriving at their own identity, adolescents very often reflect the values of the community or reflect a rejection of those values which they identify as hypocritical or somehow at variance with their earlier training.

In a study of adolescent value changes between the 1960s and the mid-70s, McKinney, Hotch, and Truhon (1977) compared the values of achievement and interpersonal morality in those two eras. By using a sentence completion technique which included the stems "I am proud of myself when..." and "I would be ashamed of myself if...", the behavioral values of a group of university students were studied. A factor analysis revealed that two primary values for the subjects were the value of achievement, which was a private or personal value not involving other people and morality, which always occurred as an interpersonal value. For example, to the stem "I would be proud of myself if...", the following responses would indicate a value of achievement "if I did well in school;" "if I graduated on time;" "if I could get a good job." To the same stem, another sort of response would indicate a value of interpersonal morality or social concern: "...if I helped somebody else;" "...if I didn't lie;" "...if I could be friendly to other people more of the time." The results of such responses taken from a group of students in 1969 and in 1975 are given in Table 1. It would appear that the high value placed on interpersonal morality in the 1960s was not overwhelming relative to the personal concern about achievement, at least among university students. Contrasting these data with those of 1975, however, the importance of the private value of achivement is more striking. It is important to remember the ideals of adolescents are as much a matter of historical and social context as they are of social and adolescent development.

TABLE 1

Behavior Values of College Students:
Responses to Sentence Stem,
"I would be proud of myself if..."

	1969	1975
Achievement Responses	76%	93%
Interpersonal Morality Responses	24%	7%

The term "identity" is used by Erikson to mean self sameness, i.e., personal continuity with previous life experience. The sameness occurs in the style of one's individuality as well as in the way one organizes his appropriate set of identifications into a meaningful, cohesive unit. Identity develops through interaction with the social environment, namely the significant others, and it also develops through efforts at reconciling the past with the present and the future.

The Paradox of Conformity and/or Uniqueness

One response to changes within the individual at adolescence occurs in answer to the inevitable question, "Am I acceptable?". The answer for many adolescents is a conformity to external standards. Costanzo and Shaw (1966), have demonstrated that conformity increases during early adolescence and then declines again in early adulthood. Costanzo and Shaw used the well known experimental paradigm first described by Asch in which subjects are asked to judge the length of two lines relative to a standard. While one line is very close to the standard, the other is clearly very much shorter or very much longer. The subject's task is to pick the line which is similar in length to the standard. However, the subject has in front of him or her the responses of several of the experimenter's confederates. While these responses would ordinarily be considered obvious errors in an experimental situation of this sort, the subject often conforms to the erroneous response of the "other subjects," that is, he or she will make the obviously wrong choice. Costanzo and Shaw studied conformity behavior in four different age groups: 7 to 9; 11 to 13; 15 to 17; and 19 to 21. Conformity behavior increased significantly from the 7 to 9 age period to the 11 to 13 age period and declined steadily thereafter with 19- to 21-year-olds nearly at the same level of conformity behavior as the 7- to 9-year-olds. Anyone who has walked through the corridors of a middle school or who has had a child of this age will not be surprised. The need to conform appears to result from a threat to self-esteem, induced at least in part by adolescent physical changes. Late maturers appear to be at a disadvantage in this respect, especially if they are males. For females, the most advantageous maturation rate, at least so far as self-esteem is concerned, is to be maturing right on time.

The Struggle for Simultaneous Stability and Change

During adolescence the delicate balance between change and stability in the development of the ego is disrupted. Questions about self-worth and the resulting conformity as well as rebellion are part of the adolescent phenomenon. A potentially more disturbing result of the conflict between the drives for stability and change is the sometimes crippling need for premature closure. The conflict can be resolved, in other words, by a premature denial of further change--a refusal to grow up--or by a sudden need for complete change--a renunciation of earlier values and behavior. On the one hand could lie an element in all sorts of regressive disorders from a petulant unwillingness to assume adult responsibility in otherwise healthy and normal children to such major adolescent disturbances as schizophrenia (Weiner, 1970) and anorexia nervosa (Bruch, 1978). On the other hand, the need for immediate and radical change can be the precipitant of delinquency, especially of an aggressive or sexual nature.

The need to maintain stability, i.e., not to grow up, has been treated in a literary way by James Barrie in the play, *Peter Pan.* Early critics (e.g., Hammerton, 1903) of that play suggested that its appeal could hardly be traced to a need to remain forever young, since everyone knows that children want desperately to be adults. But the play does have an appeal, especially among children, precisely, in my opinion, because it does touch on the other half of that stability--change dilemma. While the press not to assume adulthood has been too little researched, some clinical examples come to mind forcefully.

Mark was an 18-year-old diabetic who also suffered from a seizure disorder which was under adequate medical control. He had needed pediatric care since infancy. At that time, his mother, a physician, interrupted her medical practice to care primarily for her son and also an older sister. During early adolescence, Mark experienced some psychotic episodes with hallucinations and obsessions whose content dealt with authoritarian control. During therapy he denied any sexual impulses, calling any reference to sexuality "stupid." Although a bright boy who had done very well in school, he consistently failed "driver's education." Having graduated from high school, he enrolled at a local junior college. Suddenly a compulsion developed which sometimes prevented Mark from getting to school on time. He would walk toward the bus stop and then have to walk several steps back before beginning again. This pattern would be repeated several times, making the short trip to the bus stop from home a time-consuming and delaying affair. No such compulsion prevented Mark's coming home at night. One way of understanding these different behaviors is to view them as expressions of Mark's fear of and conflict over adulthood. His hallucinations and obsessions seem to represent struggles against hostile dependent control. His denial and devaluation of sexuality as well as failing to achieve driver's status were expressions of not accepting adult status. The bus stop compulsion was a direct portrayal of the wish to assume independence in conflict with the safety of dependence. Mark's struggle with independence was exacerbated by the realization that, after 18 years of parental dependence, pediatric supervision and medication monitoring, he would become more responsible for his own physical and mental well-being. He responded positively to psychotherapy although obsessional symptoms recurred at the time he went away to college a year later, another independent step.

Sally attempted to commit suicide shortly after her twelfth birthday while in the sixth grade. Angry at her mother for not letting her play with a much younger friend, she tried to overdose on Tylenol. Later in treatment, Sally commented, "I wish I was still in the fifth grade. Everything was good then." Her therapist asked for clarification. "After that I started to grow up. I didn't want to grow up."

A 15-year-old adolescent boy was referred to the endocrine clinic of a large city hospital. He was very short in stature and showed no pubertal maturation. When it was found that Joseph had an endocrine deficiency, hormone treatments were recommended. Joseph was told he would not grow taller or develop into puberty without treatment, but the choice was his. Relieved that a solution had been found, Joseph was scheduled for pre-treatment laboratory tests. But he became extremely afraid of hypodermic needles and could not proceed with the tests. He quickly developed a phobic aversion to the clinic and to the nurses and physicians with whom he had formerly been friendly. In fact, when taken to the clinic he would run away, sometimes not returning home for several hours.

Joseph also began to have problems at school, in part from his short stature and immature appearance for a tenth grader. At age fifteen, people were responding to him as if he were age 11 or 12. Teachers complained that he had stopped taking responsibility for his school work. Joseph began to run away from school. At home, his younger brother, who was taller and physically more mature, began to torment him. Again Joseph's response was to run away from home, always to return before nightfall. The thought of still being "a child" frightened and humiliated Joseph, but so did the thought of initiating change, for which his cooperation and decision were sought.

The Ubiquitous Issue of Self-Esteem

One dilemma which crops up in each of the developmental tasks of adolescence is the maintenance of self-esteem. Whether one focuses on separation, identity formation, conformity, or the simultaneous need for change and stability, one recognizes the adolescent's attempt to preserve both a reasonable public image of himself or herself, as well as a decent self-regard.

Conformity protects the adolescent from the fear of appearing weird as surely as the attempt to be unique staves off any threat of being lost in the crowd. The need to care for oneself, in both senses of that ambiguous phrase, looms large for adolescents. While they are learning to take care of themselves physically and financially, they also need to learn to care about themselves, to like themselves, their bodies, their feelings, their thoughts, and to develop their ability to contribute meaningfully.

The whole process of separation and individuation at adolescence (Blos, 1967) brings with it threats to self-esteem as the result of new drives without the old supports. Independence is won at a price. Not surprisingly, parents can provide a setting in which self-esteem can be either fostered or hindered. In a whole variety of ways, parents can support their adolescent's self-image by demonstrating an active interest in them. For example, parents who know their children's friends, even if they don't like them, are likely to have youngsters with higher self-esteem than those who are ignorant of this important aspect of their adolescents' lives (Rosenberg, 1965). Adolescents who participate in family discussions at the dinner table and who feel their opinions are respected by their parents have higher self-esteem than their peers who do not experience these advantages.

The Challenges Facing the 1980s Cohort

In some respects, becoming an adult in the 1980s involves unique challenges. Unemployment in the United States is higher than at any other time since the Second World War. Monetary inflation is occurring faster than at any time since the Great Depression. Young men and women graduating from high school cannot find work. Those hoping to go to college cannot find summer jobs to help support their own education. Government grants and guaranteed student loans are being cut back while interest rates are going ever higher. Therefore, many middle and lower class youngsters are unable to attend college, while others are having to reject acceptance at their chosen colleges because of a financial inability to attend.

The choice of a vocation, which youngsters at this age have always had to make, is complicated by the world's uncertain economic condition in a number of ways. College, if one has the financial resources to attend, is more likely to become a time of vocational preparation rather than a period of liberal education, a "psychosocial moratorium," to use Erikson's term. For those planning on marriage, two careers have become an economic necessity rather than a choice. The impact of this fact on families is already apparent. More couples choose not to have children, to delay having children, or to put young children in the care of someone else, a paid professional, while both parents earn money to support the family. Because this is a family style unfamiliar to many, since their parents enjoyed a different way of life, it is one they must work out for themselves without the benefit of models.

The rapidly changing economic scene has had another sort of impact on the process of growing up. It has become increasingly difficult to predict what life will be like from one decade to the next. Recently a colleague of mine was buying a new family car for the first time in several years. He commented to his wife on how much more expensive cars had become since they had purchased their last one. Their 12-year-old daughter, overhearing the conversation, remarked, "I'll never be able to buy a car. When I grow up they'll probably cost a million dollars." It is difficult to imagine the economics of a world even 10 years hence with such rapidly spiraling inflation rates as are occurring now.

Political instability is another challenge to the process of growing up in the 1980s. Corruption at the highest levels of government threatened to undermine our democratic way of life and continue to pose serious questions about the ideals we have imparted to our children. Recently, a young friend of mine was discussing his plans to go away to college after he graduated from high school. I acknowledged that was a big step and asked if he had any doubts or concerns. He was not afraid of a rigorous academic program, or of his ability to make friends and enjoy a decent social life. "What bothers me," he said, "is that in October I'll be eighteen and I'll be able to vote. I don't know how you can choose when you read conflicting stories and don't know who to believe." Political choices are never easy, but in an era of instability they are especially difficult, especially for the novice.

Knowing what to believe in the area of international politics is no easier. At times our foreign relations seem strained almost to the breaking point, while the United States and the Soviet Union continue to amass nuclear arms. The effect of such global insecurity on the process of growing up was brought home forcefully recently. A dinner table conversation turned to the issue of nuclear wars. The two boys, seventeen and eighteen years old, were soberly exchanging views about the serious consequences of a potential flare-up of what had so far been a limited war in South America. One of the boys mentioned the disasterous effect of any use of nuclear weapons when his twelve-year-old sister spoke up in an obviously worried tone, "But I don't want to die before I grow up." The boys turned to reassuring her that they were only considering very unlikely possibilities, not something either of them actually believed would happen. Their father was struck by the fact that their reassurances lacked a certain conviction.

Therapeutic Implications

For the parents, teachers, and therapists of the generation growing up in the 1980s, what implications do these challenges suggest? First, our sons and daughters need to know they are valuable and worthwhile people. Self-esteem is enhanced when parents are interested and concerned about their children and when they show confidence in their increasing responsibility for their own actions. Individuals with higher self-esteem are more able to face difficult decisions than those plagued with self-doubt.

Secondly, children need to be taught how to choose. Children with the strongest values are those who have learned to make free choices on their own and thus have developed a sense of internal control (McKinney, 1975). They know that their actions can affect the world they live in. From the time children can first walk and talk, they can be given choices and the consequences of their decisions, both good and bad, can be shown to them. In this way, the contingent linkage between their behavior and its social consequences can be made clear. The choices demanded of an adult, whether about politics, career, family, mate selection, or education, will then be less frightening. Indeed, such choices will be seen as part of a continuous, albeit enlarging, process that was begun in infancy.

Finally, perhaps it goes without saying that, whenever possible, consistency in our own behavior would be enormously helpful to our growing children. Teaching them honesty, while tolerating corruption in business, education, or government is confusing. Teaching them not to fight and suggesting that rational people solve disputes by discussion rather than force is a lie if, as a nation, we impose our will on others or support wars as a way of gaining our rights. Even little children have learned that their country spends more money on defense than on education. Teaching our children respect for their own and the opposite sex while at the same time exploiting sex for commercial purposes is a sure way to lose credibility. Suggesting early sexual experimentation in the media to children who are too young to deal effectively with the consequences of sexual behavior is cruel.

If childhood is a stage of life that we love and revere, we can help our children grow responsibly into adulthood. In some respects becoming an adult in the 1980s is no different from becoming an adult in any other era. It involves a separation from childhood and the security of that stage and it also involves all the challenges of passing through the transitional phase of adolescence. If the cohort growing up in the 1980s are unique by virture of their peculiar political, social and cultural history, they are also akin to adolescents of other eras in their need for a stable base from which to push off. If there are two gifts the parent generation can give to those preparing to leave home, the first is a climate in which self-esteem is fostered, not threatened. The second gift is a stable launching pad.

REFERENCES

Adelson, J., and O'Neil, R. P. Growth of political ideas in adolescence: The sense of community. *Journal of Personality and Social Psychology*, 1966, *4*, 295-306.

Aristotle. *Politica.* In R. McKeon (Ed.), *The basic works of Aristotle*, (trans., W. D. Ross). New York: Random House, 1941.

Bandura, A. The story decade: Fact or fiction? *Psychology in the Schools*, 1964, *1*, 224-231.

Blos, P. The second individuation process of adolescence. In R. S. Eisler (Ed.), *The psychoanalytic study of the child*, Vol. 22. New York: International Universities Press, 1967.

Bruch, H. *The golden cage: The enigma of anorexia nervosa.* Cambridge, Mass.: Harvard University Press, 1978.

Costanzo, P. R., and Shaw, M. E. Conformity as a function of age level. *Child Development*, 1966, *37*, 967-975.

Douvan, E., and Adelson, J. *The adolescent experience.* New York: Wiley, 1966.

Elkind, D. Egocentrism in adolescence. *Child Development*, 1967, *38*, 1025-1034.

Erikson, E. H. *Identity: Youth and crisis.* New York: Norton, 1968.

Erikson, E. H. Identity and the life cycle. *Psychological issues*, Vol. 1. New York: International Universities Press, 1959.

Fromm, E. *The art of loving.* New York: Harper, 1956.

Gillespie, J., and Allport, G. *Youths' outlook on the future.* New York: Random House, 1955.

Gustin, J. C. The revolt of youth. *Psychoanalysis and the Psychoanalytic Review*, 1968, *98*, 78-90.

Hall, G. S. *Adolescence: Its psychology and its relations to physiology, anthropology, sociology, sex, crime, religion, and education* (6 vols.). New York: Appleton and Company, 1904-1905.

Hammerton, J. A. *J. M. Barrie and his books, biographical and critical studies.* London: Marshall, 1902.

Helfer, R. E. Being a kid isn't all that easy. Lecture presented to medical students at Michigan State University, East Lansing, Michigan, 1977.

Hess, R. D., and Goldblatt, I. The status of adolescents in American society: A problem in social identity. *Child Development*, 1957, *28*, 459-468.

Hotch, D. F. *Separating from the family: A study of perceptions of home leaving in late adolescence.* Unpublished doctoral dissertation, Michigan State University, 1979.

McKinney, J. P. The development of values: A perceptual interpretation. *Journal of Personality and Social Psychology*, 1975, *31*, 801-807.

McKinney, J. P., Fitzgerald, H. E., and Strommen, E. A. *Developmental psychology: The adolescent and young adult* (2nd ed.). Homewood, Ill.: Dorsey Press, 1982.

McKinney, J. P., Hotch, D. F., and Truhon, S. A. The organization of behavioral values during late adolescence: Change and stability across two eras. *Developmental Psychology*, 1977, *13*, 83-84.

Meissner, W. W. Parental interaction of the adolescent boy. *Journal of Genetic Psychology*, 1965, *107*, 225-233.

Plato. *The Laws*. In G. Burns, *The works of Plato*. London: H. G. Bohn, 1859.

Stierlin, H. *Separating parents and adolescents*. New York: New York Times Book Company, 1974.

Sullivan, K., and Sullivan, A. Adolescent-parent separation. *Developmental Psychology*, 1980, *16*, 93-99.

Weiner, I. *Psychological disturbance in adolescence*. New York: Wiley, 1970.

CRITICAL ISSUES IN MORAL DEVELOPMENT

Diane I. Levande

School of Social Work
Michigan State University
East Lansing, MI 48824

INTRODUCTION

The early 1980s have begun with a vigorous concern about American families; a concern which is in large measure linked to serious questioning of contemporary values and a renewed interest in the moral upbringing of children. Noting the magnitude of public anxiety about the family, Charlotte Saikowski (1980) indicates that 45 percent of Americans think family life has grown worse since the mid-1960s, and over one-third of the population believes the situation will continue to deteriorate. Changing moral standards, decline in moral behavior, and uncertainty in the moral realm are frequently cited as causes of the numerous problems confronting families, problems ranging from the increasing divorce rate to the high incidence of domestic violence.

The call for renewed attention to morality was initiated even before the present movement to strengthen family life. Discussions of the factors prompting this heightened interest in the study of moral development include several alarming national events and trends in recent history, i.e., assassinations of public figures, Watergate, environmental pollution, the rising crime rate, and child abuse and neglect.

The goals of defining and encouraging moral behavior and revitalizing the family combine in the process of socialization, a task defined as primary for the family system. Socialization, broadly conceived, encompasses the numerous experiences in life that translate and transmit the values and expectations of one's family, social group, and culture. It has long been believed that the period of childhood, particularly the intensive parent-child interaction of the first years of life, is the most crucial time for learning the "shoulds" and "oughts" of living within the greater social system. That the family should be the primary molder of a child's moral character remains a dominant value position in American society.

The factors which prompt concern in the realm of morals and family life are frequently depicted as negative. There is, however, another important and motivating aspect which prompts continued quests for explanations and solutions to these dilemmas. Recent developments in knowledge related to understanding family systems and moral development have triggered new awareness of the complexity of interactions and relationships which define the human condition. New scientific paradigms in the form of theories and conceptual frameworks bring renewed hope for problem resolution and increased efforts to bring about a "goodness of fit" between the situation in need of adjustment and the means by which this transformation may be achieved.

The onset of the 1980s confronts us with a growing array of theories and intervention modalities designed to explain, predict, and nurture the development of moral thought and action. Related to the process of becoming moral, an intricate testing period of moving from theory into practice is underway. While one may applaud the focusing of attention on this vital aspect of human life, a number of major issues remain unresolved. These issues form the framework for progress in understanding and encouraging moral functioning for those involved in child nurturance. A review of selected critical issues in the process of becoming moral also form the major purpose and direction of this chapter.

PHILOSOPHICAL ISSUES

All theories which purport to explain human functioning carry with them certain assumptions about the essence of human beings and human societies. In our recent history, the philosophical assumptions of such theories have been largely unexplored; implicitly assumed rather than explicitly detailed. This may reflect the oft-noted dichotomy between values and facts and the assignment of each to their proper place; science deals in facts, philosophy in values. A challenging situation occurs when science applies its empirical method to the study of human values. This overlapping of disciplinary boundaries may account in part for the vigorous debates now taking place between social scientists and moral philosophers concerning the definition and process of becoming moral. The nagging suspicion that there is no such thing as a "value-free" science also plays a role in these deliberations. Thus it may be, as some have argued, that research into questions concerning values is itself saturated with elements of the concept it proposes to investigate.

In the following discussion the complicated relationship between scientific models which describe the process of becoming moral and philosophical systems which detail the nature and meaning of morality is clearly evident.

Morals and Values

It is interesting and at times confusing to note that scholarly articles, books and entire curriculum plans may repeatedly use the terms morals and values without clarification of similarities or differences in meanings. It is not unusual to find moral education and values education used interchangeably or to note the process of value acquisition being described in discussions of moral development. Do these two concepts and their derivatives describe the same phenomena? Recent tradition answers this question in the negative, though the separation of the study of values (axiology) from the study of moral values (ethics) was not accomplished until the latter part of the nineteenth century.

Axiology is usually explained as being broader in scope than ethics, including the study of moral values, as well as having a wide range of practical and aesthetic evaluations. Ethics might be thought of as one particular aspect of value theory which concerns itself with conduct or behavior in relation to such concepts as good and bad, duty and obligation (Werkmeister, 1967).

Frankena (1963) deplores the ambiguity and vagueness which surrounds the use of these terms. He insists that moral values or things that are morally good must be distinguished from nonmoral values or things that are good in a nonmoral sense. According to Frankena, the sorts of things that may be morally good or bad include persons, groups of persons, and elements of personality, i.e., character traits, emotions, motives, and intentions. Many things may be nonmorally good or bad, for example, physical objects such as cars and paintings; experiences like pleasure, pain, knowledge, and freedom; and forms of government such as democracy.

That Frankena's distinction between values and moral values may be open to challenge is not difficult to understand since until the fairly recent separation of axiology and ethics, "the good" was most often interpreted as "the morally good." There is, however, a certain sense in the numerous works concerned with morals, moral rules, and moral judgments that being moral has to do with one's conduct or behavior in relation to other human beings. Derek Wright (1971) suggests that we can all recognize the difference between the conventional rules of dress and eating at one end of the continuum, and the rules concerned with keeping promises, honesty, respect for the rights of the individual, and sympathy for those in need at the other end of the continuum. Wright indicates that, "Whether or not the former ever deserve to be called moral, the latter always do" (p. 13).

A large amount of research attention has been devoted to the study of values in America, beginning in the 1950s and gaining momentum in the following two decades. Works such as those by Allport, Vernon, and Lindzey (1951), Kluckhohn and Strodtbeck (1961), Williams (1971),

Rokeach (1973), and Feather (1975), primarily represented in the literature of sociology and social psychology, attest to the strength of interest in the value concept. During the same time frame, intense efforts have also been directed to investigations of moral development, behavior, and education, as represented in the works of Kohlberg (1963), Mischel and Mischel (1976), Hoffman (1970), Lickona (1976), Peters (1967), and Wright (1971). Attempts to bring these two areas of research together to understand how each might inform the other are just beginning. Feather (1980) indicates that a number of questions, such as whether the transition to a new stage of moral reasoning depends upon the emergence of particular values or whether certain values emerge only after a specific stage of moral development has been attained, await answers. He contends that the clarification of the relationship between morals and values is likely to be a significant area of study in the 1980s.

The Nature of Good

As noted above, controversy over what constitutes the good, the right, and the moral has raged on in a seemingly endless debate among philosophers. The connection between this debate on the one hand and scientific theories which attempt to explain moral development and behavior on the other has been left, for the most part, unexamined. That this silence concerning the philosophical assumptions of scientific theories seems to have ended, at least in the area of moral development, may be attributed in large part to Kohlberg's recognition and subsequent explication of the philosophical foundations of his stage theory of moral development. In his well known article, "From Is to Ought," Kohlberg (1971) states,

> These ideas outline our psychological theory of moral judgment, a theory which assumes certain philosophical postulates for the sake of psychological explanation. We must now consider what philosophic support we can give to these postulates themselves (p. 214).

The philosophical system for determining the moral which Kohlberg (1976) derives from his studies of moral development has as its foundation a structure of justice. He defines the core of justice as the distribution of rights and duties regulated by concepts of equality and reciprocity, and he believes that one's sense of justice is what is most distinctively and fundamentally moral. Kohlberg (1976) argues that,

> One can act morally and question all rules, one may act morally and question the greater good, but one cannot act morally and question the need for justice (p. 40).

A critique by William Alston (1971) reveals the magnitude of the disagreement among scholars concerning the selection of justice as the core component of things moral. Alston contends that a large number of distinct accounts of what makes a judgment, a reason, an attitude, a rule, or a principle moral have been put forward.   According to Alston, Kohlberg has simply selected one such principle but fails to show that this choice represents anything more than what seems most congenial or interesting to him.

Another critic, R. S. Peters (1976), conceptualizes the issue more bluntly,

> He (Kohlberg) suffers from the rather touching belief that a Kantian type of morality, represented in modern times most notably by Hare and Rawls, is the only one (pp. 288-289).

After presenting other conceptions of morality in which justice is problematic, Peters summarizes,

> It is either sheer legislation to say that Kohlberg's morality is the true one or it is the worst form of the naturalistic fallacy which argues from how morality is ordinarily used to what morality is (pp. 288-289).

The crux of this debate and the issue which will undoubtably continue to surface in the 1980s is rooted in Kohlberg's insistence that the most essential structure of morality is a justice structure. He recognizes other possibilities for defining the distinctively moral such as respect for rules or consideration of welfare consequences to others, and indicates that individuals must and do use these orientations. However, his highest stage of moral development, stage 6, cannot be reached without justice as its primary principle. As Kohlberg (1971) indicates,

> Only justice takes on the character of a principle at the highest stage of development, that is, as something that is obligatory, categorical, and takes precedence over law and other considerations, including welfare (p. 220).

It is not fair to characterize Kohlberg as inventing a new or unique ethical system on the basis of his empirical studies of moral development. The system he proposes, with justice as its core component, has substantial roots in classical ethical theory.   There are, however, other plausible theories of justification as Frankena (1963), Peters (1966), and most introductory textbooks on ethics point out.   The essential point is that Kohlberg indicates that his scientific investigations have at long last identified the one true ethical theory, something which philosophers have been unable to do in centuries of effort. A further problem arises from Kohlberg's contention (1971) that the form and basic content principles of morality are universal.   Thus, differences noted in moral principles between cultures, subcultures, social groups, and individuals represent, in this   view,   varying   levels   of   progress   through   Kohlberg's six moral stages. As Kohlberg states,

> Moral judgments, unlike judgments of prudence or aesthe-
> tics, tend to be universal, inclusive, consistent, and
> grounded on objective, impersonal, or ideal grounds (p.
> 215).

Once again, the contention that moral judgments are objectively valid, that they are not dependent on personal opinion, taste, or group allegiance, has a long history of support in traditional ethics. Another tradition, however, that of ethical relativism, holds that there is no objectively valid, rational way of justifying one value judgment against another, thus two conflicting judgments may be equally valid.

In the selection of a universal ethical system based on justice, Kohlberg, according to critics, errs by not recognizing the value judgments he makes in the interpretation of his empirical data. The validity of this criticism can only be determined by further research combined with theoretical clarification and philosophical analysis. This is not meant to imply that "more of the same" will eventually resolve these difficult issues, but rather to support the need for continued efforts to explicate and critique the value assumptions of scientific theories.

Virtues versus Principles

Another crucial issue in Kohlberg's conceptualization of becoming moral relates to his dichotomy between moral traits and moral principles. His dismissal of the "bag of virtues" approach to moral development in favor of a principled morality raises serious criticisms of other psychological theories of moral development and behavior which focus on the acquisition of desirable character traits. It also presents serious issues in child nurturance and education: how, for example, does one instill a moral sense without encouraging such traits as honesty or compassion?

The criticism on this issue has focused primarily on building a case for the necessity of encouraging moral virtues and habits as the basis for action on moral principles. As Frankena (1963) suggests,

> To be or to do, that is the question. Should we construe
> morality as primarily a following of certain principles or
> as primarily a cultivation of certain dispositions or traits?
> (p. 52).

Frankena proposes a resolution to this dilemma by suggesting that we regard both principles and traits as two complementary aspects of the same morality. He concludes that it is hard to understand how a morality of principles can exist without the development of dispositions to act in accordance with such principles. Equally, according to Frankena, a morality concerned only with conformity to rules is far too narrow a definition.

The renewed interest in the moral upbringing of children, which encompasses both family responsibility and educational endeavors, will continue to serve as a motivating factor for the specification of conditions which encourage moral development.   Within this atmosphere, research efforts which focus on the clarification and reconciliation of the principles versus traits issue are likely to intensify.

THEORETICAL ISSUES

Most discussions of theories of moral development and behavior from the psychological perspective focus upon three major schools of thought: psychoanalytic, behavioristic, and cognitive-developmental. Psychoanalytic theory, as elaborated by Freud, is often viewed as the first fully psychological theory of moral development.   Aronfreed (1976) indicates that Freud tried to distinguish between the functions of knowledge and feeling in the operation of an internalized conscience; a complex aspect of personality formation rooted in the intensive conflicts of the oedipal stage and subsequent development of the superego.

According to Aronfreed (1976), behavioristic theories began with little more than extrapolation from the patterns of learning displayed by animals, gradually escalating to explanations of human social behavior and its antecedents in child rearing. Recent developments in social learning theory, usually categorized as a contemporary branch of moderate behaviorism, have gone well beyond accounts of the immediate effects of rewards and punishments to argue that the internalization of conscience can be understood as the shaping of the child's behavior by such processes as imitative modeling and the self-generation of reinforcing events.

Though psychoanalytic and behavioristic conceptions related to the moral side of life have been part of the psychological tradition for a longer period of time, the current revival of interest in moral development must be attributed to the cognitive-developmental framework proposed by Jean Piaget (1932) and its more recent elaborations and significant changes stemming from the prolific work of Lawrence Kohlberg and his collaborators.   Much of the current criticism of the cognitive-developmental view comes, as we have seen, from the philosophical realm.   In addition, scholars representing other psychological perspectives have presented vigorous challenges to this theory based upon research and theory development from their respective schools of thought. All of this activity has led Aronfreed (1976) to conclude,

Among the social and philosophical issues that exercise a fatal attraction on psychological theory, it is doubtful whether any has been more seductive than the question of man's status as a moral creature (p. 54).

Cognition and Affect

One difference in theoretical perspective which has frequently been noted, especially between the psychoanalytic and cognitive-developmental views, involves the relative influence of cognitive and affective factors in the moral realm. In our everyday experience we commonly view the affective domain as a dominant force in establishing a moral view or judgment. Quite frequently emotion is viewed as a negative factor which somehow precludes us from making rational, well conceived moral decisions. Kohlberg (1971) indicates that his theory, unlike the "irrational emotive theory of Freud," views cognition and affect as different aspects of the same mental events. He notes that it is evident that moral judgments often involve strong emotional components. This condition does not, however, according to Kohlberg, negate or reduce the cognitive component in moral judgment. In fact, Kohlberg (1971) indicates that the quality of affect involved in moral judgments is determined by cognitive structural development and is part and parcel of the general development of the child's conceptions of a moral order.

In response to this position, Alston (1971) is quick to point out that Kohlberg's blunt dismissal of "irrational emotive" theories and his comprehensive attention to the place of cognition in moral development do little to clarify the role of affect. Alston argues that one can hold the view that any distinctive emotional state also has a cognitive side and still insist that the affective side plays a crucial role in moral development and moral motivation. Alston (1971) and others propose that a necessary condition for a person's taking a principle or rule to be moral must be related in some degree to rules internalized early in childhood with a special kind of emotional intensity not unlike that which Freud described in superego formation. Alston further hypothesizes that the necessary component for one to act in accordance with a moral principle is the anticipation that guilt will occur if one fails to do so. Thus the recognition and desire to avoid feelings of guilt become conditions for being moral.

Hoffman (1976), though disagreeing with the psychoanalytic explanation about the origin of guilt feelings, suggests that guilt may trigger a process of self-examination and restructuring of values which may help strengthen one's altruistic motives which, in turn, motivate moral functioning.

Though much of the debate in psychological circles on the place of the affective domain in the process of becoming moral seems to focus on the concept of guilt, affect certainly involves other emotions or feeling states. William Kay (1968) proposes a comprehensive theory for the incorporation of affect which he refers to as an attitudinal model of moral development. From his perspective, cognitive theory is not enough; it may explain moral thinking but an understanding of moral behavior involves more. As Kay notes, "It is one thing to know the good. It is another to do it" (p. 228). Kay hypothesizes that the stages of moral development include certain attitudinal patterns as well as cognitive abilities, and that any attempt to enhance moral development must include attention to at least four attitudinal stages. These stages are altruism, rationality, responsibility, and moral independence. Though Kay believes that these stages develop in sequence, beginning with altruism, he also indicates that moral maturity consists of the co-existence and interaction in a highly developed form of all four attitudinal patterns.

It is likely that the role which affect plays in the process of becoming moral will be a major area for research and theory building during this decade. Criticism of this neglected area in much of the literature on moral development has been particularly vigorous during the 1970s. Perhaps most people agree with Peters' (1970) when he speaks about the rational passions and argues that,

> Strength of character is often represented in such terms as saying no to temptation, standing firm, or being impervious to social pressure. Rational people are able to do this only if they are passionately devoted to fairness, freedom, and the pursuit of truth, and if they have genuine respect for others and are intensely concerned if others suffer (p. 6).

Structure and Content

A closely related theoretical issue concerns the idea that what one believes in the moral area (content) can be separated from how one thinks about these beliefs (structure). This particular dichotomy is a tenet of cognitive-developmental theory upon which Kohlberg's delineation of six moral development stages rests. This view is clearly borrowed from Piaget's stage theory of cognitive development which traces the structure of knowledge. Thus, it is not the content of one's beliefs but rather how one thinks about the content which accounts for age related developmental stages of moral growth. Here we see that the emphasis is once again on the cognitive components of things moral.

The issues at stake in the structure/content controversy are extremely volatile ones. The first question is whether content and structure can be separated. Regarding Kohlberg's content free principle of justice, Simpson (1974) argues that neither concepts nor processes can be divorced from their cultural content. She states,

> There is no such thing as process alone, or a concept emptied of the specific items which generalize to its whole, and a morality which defines the right in all situations defines the right in none (p. 93).

Some critics of the structure and content issue, however, seem to agree that the two components can be separated; the critical difference for them is one of emphasis. In other words, there are those who insist that the content of one's beliefs is far more important than the structure, because what one believes has much more impact on moral behavior than how one thinks about such beliefs.

The larger issue involved in this dispute relates to the concept of cultural universals. When Kohlberg describes the moral development stages as universal and invariant, we are confronted with a situation in which any person, group, or culture failing to demonstrate the predicted progress in the expected sequential order becomes somehow morally inferior. That various groups, including lower class children, females, members of preliterate cultures, to name a few, have been found to progress more slowly through the six stage sequence with fewer, if any, representatives achieving the post-conventional level of moral development than white, Western, urban males has fueled the fires of rebuttal and criticism. Kohlberg's comments on these findings seem to have done more to increase the heat than to calm the flames. For example, Kohlberg (1971), in noting that preliterates go through the lower stages of moral development more slowly than Western, urban children, and do not reach the level of post-conventional morality, suggests this may represent a mild doctrine of social evolutionism, such as was elaborated in the classic work of Hobhouse. The idea that primitive culture implies primitive thought, or in this case, a lower rung on the ladder of moral reasoning, has been seriously criticized. As Simpson (1974) argues,

> Rather than accept large numbers of human groups as somehow deficient morally, it seems more appropriate to ask whether the same paradigm is suitable for use as a moral index with members of widely differing cultures if the methods involved (e.g., formal operational thinking) require modes of classification and problem-solving not utilized within each specific group (p. 92).

Gilligan (1977) speaks of the continuing "problem of women" in theories of moral development. Freud supported the idea that women show less sense of justice than men and are more influenced by their emotions. Piaget found girls less explicit about agreement on rules and less concerned with the legal elaboration of rules than boys. Add Kohlberg's finding that women are most typically found at stage 3 (a morality based upon social relationships and approval by others), and the notion of female inferiority is once again confirmed. Based upon her research data, Gilligan (1977) identifies the feminine experience and construction of social reality as a distinct perspective which, rather than being seen as a developmental deficiency, reflects a different social and moral understanding which deserves investigation and elaboration as an important component of female psychological development.

The idea that the form or structure of moral development represents what is universal and invariant gives the impression the structure is dominant and dictates content, rather than either the reverse (that content dictates structure) or a balanced interaction between these two components. Again, we see the same imbalance or at least the lack of clarity that was discussed in the cognitive-affective issue. Particularly in the case of women, the traditional stereotype of females as less rational, more emotional beings than males would seem to interfere with their progress in the area of morals.

The frequently cited criticism of Freud that he failed rather miserably to take into account the concept of culture has for many strained the credibility of psychoanalytic theory. In writing about Freud's impact on modern morality, Holt (1980) argues that Freud's seriously restricted sample of subjects, drawn primarily from basically decent and trustworthy citizens who shared many of his own values, blinded him to any real consideration of the impact of culture or the influence of varying social environments. Since Freud found morality so ingrained in his restricted sample of human beings he came to view it as innate.

Simpson (1974) similarly accuses Kohlberg of placing more importance on biological development than on what is learned culturally about the nature of the world. Thus, it is indeed tempting to ask whether, in this instance, the cognitive-developmental view of becoming moral is not simply new wine in old bottles, or vice versa.

In elaborating the social learning approach to moral development, Mischel and Mischel (1976) clearly specify the degree of theoretical divergence concerning the importance of cultural content. These researchers indicate that the increasing cognitive and verbal competencies of the child follow an age-related sequence which in turn is reflected in age-related changes in moral reasoning. However, the content of moral judgments will depend on the culture in which the individual develops. Mischel and Mischel (1976) also contend that a stage system of moral development which judges selfishly or situationally motivated behaviors based upon consequences as less moral, or perhaps premoral, misses the point, since, "even the noblest altruism supported by the highest levels of moral reasoning depends on expected consequences" (pp. 97-98).

There are additional theoretical issues, such as the significance of studying moral behavior versus moral development, which will continue to be salient areas for debate and exploration. Some promising integrative work has also been initiated such as Garbarino and Bronfenbrenner's model (1976) of moral development and socialization which attempts to accommodate both the cognitive theories of moral stages and the typology theories of cultural variation. The intensity of these theoretical differences promises vigorous research efforts in the 1980s.

ISSUES IN APPLICATION

It is perhaps an artifact of the academic tradition which has dictated the order of presentation in this chapter from the philosophical to the theoretical to the application issues. In the realm of actual experience it must be recognized that these three areas are overlapping and interactive. In the best of all worlds each domain questions, challenges, and informs the other areas of investigation in a continuing pattern of interrelationship. That this particular pattern seems recognizable in the study of being and becoming moral is an exciting possibility. Those whose concern focuses on the nurturance and education of children are raising questions for theorists and philosophers about the meaning and applicability of their findings. In a similar manner, the philosophical and theoretical issues discussed in the preceding pages have profound implications for the encouragement and enhancement of moral functioning.

As indicated earlier, the initial nurturance of moral character has long been viewed as a primary function of the family unit. Parents, as agents of socialization, have the power, and, some believe, the right to impose their values on their children. However, the limits of parenthood and the rights of children have become significant issues in contemporary American society. Writing about this issue, Rothman and Rothman (1980) state,

> Of all the rights movements that have transformed the
> character of American society over the past two decades,
> none is more controversial than children's rights (p. 7).

Perhaps part of the sensitiveness of this issue relates to the belief that parents, as the principal molders of the child's character, are the persons to be held most responsible when a child is judged to have acted in a less than moral manner.

The Morality of Punishment

Until quite recently the primary focus of childrearing practices as related to moral development was on parental discipline, especially the question of punishment. Though the theoretical literature on this topic is vast, it is also ambivalent. Aronfreed (1976) believes this situation derives from failure to define punishment broadly enough, and suggests that when punishment is conceptualized to include rejection, disapproval, and other kinds of psychological discipline, not just the more obvious verbal and physical attacks, it clearly can be seen to be an inevitable part of childrearing. He states,

> It is in fact doubtful that socialization ever takes place
> without those inherently adversive events which a child
> must perceive as contingent on his own actions and
> intended by others to suppress his behavior (p. 57).

Aronfreed's data supports the position that punishment works best when it is used early in the onset of transgression. The later suppression of the punished act, even when there is no longer any objective danger of punishment, is attributed to the anxiety attached to internal precursors of a transgression which range from the simplest representational images to the most complex evaluative structures such as moral principles.

On the definition of punishment, Saltzstein (1976) argues almost the reverse position: that numerous studies of parental discipline and the effects of punishment have erred in defining these variables too broadly. On the basis of his work with Hoffman, he hypothesizes three categories of disciplinary measures: induction, which involves pointing out to the transgressor the consequences of his behavior for other persons; power assertion, which refers to physical punishment or any exercise of physical or material power over the child such as threatening loss of privileges; and love withdrawal, defined as the nonphysical expression of anger or withdrawal of love. In testing this hypothesis, Saltzstein and Hoffman found that higher scores on various indices of morality generally were negatively associated with the use of power assertion, positively associated with the use of induction, and unassociated with the use of love withdrawal. The positive results of the induction approach are attributed to its nonaggressive nature and the opportunity it provides for learning and role taking.

Even though some disagreement exists about appropriate disciplinary techniques for optimizing moral development, some general socialization guidelines seem to be emerging as indicated in the following section.

Encouraging the Moral

There is agreement that adults who care for children need to be reasonably consistent in what they approve and disapprove. The old maxim that actions speak louder than words becomes particularly significant in modeling appropriate moral conduct, and the giving of reasons suited to the child's level of development seems vital. If, as a number of theorists believe, some form of mild punishment is necessary in order to develop internal self-regulated controls, the other side of the coin cannot be overlooked either; that is, the reinforcement of "good" or prosocial behavior. Thus, children need to be rewarded for being honest, being cooperative, being compassionate (Levande and Levande, 1979).

The implications of these guidelines raise another issue of contemporary concern--the role of television as a teacher of moral behavior. Statistics which detail the amount of time spent watching television, particularly for young children, combined with the quality (or lack thereof) of media programming have prompted various kinds of monitoring actions by individual parents and concerned citizen groups. The frequency of violent and aggressive behavior, the absence of rewards for demonstrating character traits associated with moral behavior, such as altruism, honesty, and sympathy, and the lack of positive models for conflict resolution represent some of the areas which have special relevance for moral learning.

Some of the implications of theories of moral development as applied in the educational setting are also significant for the parent-child relationship. For example, Kohlberg and others involved in designing programs in moral education propose that in order to optimize student progress in moral development the level of the teacher's verbalizations must be one step above the level of the child. According to Kohlberg (1976), it is not only teachers who must achieve stage 6 (or at least stage 5) in his moral development framework, but mothers (parents) as well, since individuals at the post-conventional level of moral development tend to integrate moral messages with higher level reasoning and thus represent better moral educators.

A few problems exist with this position as Fraenkel (1976) points out when he asks,

> How can a teacher (parent) who reasons at stage 3 (conventional) be expected to present a stage 5 (post-conventional) argument to a stage 4 (conventional) student (child) if he or she cannot understand what such an argument is? (pp. 296-297).

Here lies a serious problem since Kohlberg estimates that only ten percent of the population reaches stages 5 or 6 in his moral development scheme. The probability that most parents (and teachers) reason at a lower stage is quite high.

It is also proposed that children learn principles of justice in the context of a just environment, that is, in an atmosphere of equality and reciprocity of interaction where moral conflicts are discussed and debated freely among equals. It is obvious that this stipulation has implications for the very nature of the parent-child relationship which, by definition, is not equalitarian. Neither are most marriages in U.S. society organized along equalitarian standards, though this may represent a contemporary ideal for some couples. Thus, according to this view, the actual parent-child interaction as well as the model presented by the mother-father relationship in most families is not conducive to motivating higher levels of moral development.

A particularly potent criticism involving these issues has been raised by Peters, Alston, and others who believe that too little attention is given to the conventional level of moral development (stages 3 and 4) in Kohlberg's theory. Peters (1976) argues that since so few of us are likely to emerge beyond the conventional level, it seems particularly appropriate that we be "well bedded down" in one or the other of these two stages. He also believes that a firm grounding in the earlier stages of moral development is essential in order for a child to learn from the inside what it is like to follow a rule. Peters notes that if this rule-following period is not learned well, the notion of following our own rules at the post-conventional stage of moral development is unintelligible.

These issues related to what is needed for optimizing stage progression have significant implications for child nurturance as has been indicated. It is also obvious that much work remains to be done on the clarification of these matters.

Moral Education

Almost all known cultures and societies have at least paid lip service to the notion that education should do more than teach social skills, increase knowledge, or improve intellectual ability. Many have tried to build methods of moral instruction into their educational systems under such headings as "bringing up children in the fear of the Lord," "educating the whole man," or "character training." In Western society, Socrates was perhaps the first to question the concept philosophically by asking whether virtue could be taught and, if so, how.

Over the years the focus and methods of moral education in American schools have varied with changes in the greater social system as well as new knowledge in the areas of theory and practice. The current educational attention to the moral realm stems in part from the recognition that education, like science, is not value-free. The activities of school life which carry moral messages have been enumerated several times. Thus, the first issue, and one which will continue to be a pressing matter in this decade, involves making the implicit explicit, or finding out what exists in the schools related to moral education. The second question involves defining what ought to be, a philosophical question to which there are no easy answers. Some school communities are now exploring these issues, involving teachers, administrators, students, parents, and concerned citizens in the process of defining what is and what ought to be.

A third issue involves the selection of a method for moral education. As noted in the last section, several implications of the cognitive-developmental framework for moral education are being researched. Programs based on the Kohlbergian approach, with some variation, stress the importance of group discussion of relevant moral conflicts in an environment of equality and reciprocity. It is proposed that the teacher represent moral reasoning at the post-conventional level, somehow conveying alternative rational arguments which are at least one level above those of the students. All this is expected, as well as being able to motivate and sustain serious discussion of abstract moral dilemmas, while not assuming the role of an authority figure.

The view of moral development elaborated by Kohlberg and others is an example of moving from theory into practice. The various programs now being tested in school classrooms are based on several years of empirical study into the way moral thought develops in children. Clearly this testing process is still in its initial stages, leaving a number of vital questions for further investigation. A second and perhaps more well known approach to moral education which is being used extensively in American schools is values clarification.

The history of the values clarification method differs from the cognitive-developmental approach in the sense that it gained recognition and viability first and foremost as a teaching methodology. It had its beginning in the work of Raths, Harmin, and Simon who observed behavioral problems in young people which they believed stemmed from a lack of deeply held values (Bereiter, 1978). This method is designed to promote the process of valuing through the use of guiding exercises, leading questions, and discussion topics. The term values has a broad meaning in this approach, more consistent with the study of axiology than ethics, with moral values given no special status.

Over the past decade and a half the values clarification approach has grown extensively, gaining many proponents and a number of variations. Reluctance by value clarification adherents to define either a philosophical or theoretical foundation until challenged repeatedly to do so, especially by advocates of the cognitive-developmental approach, has added fuel to the at times heated debates between these two schools of thought. Stewart (1975) enumerates several critical areas where values clarification, according to his analysis, falls dreadfully short. Two critical issues in particular illustrate the differences between these approaches and relate to a number of points discussed earlier in this chapter.

First, the value clarification method concentrates primarily on content with little or no attention to structure. Thus, this approach is viewed, especially by those who value a method which stresses intellectual development, as overwhelmingly concerned with the affective or emotional domain to the exclusion of cognitive functioning. According to Stewart,

> Values clarification strategies not only focus primarily on
> content and almost completely ignore structure, they
> largely concentrate on trivial content (p. 138).

Recalling Kohlberg's disdain for what he refers to as "irrational emotive" theories, this criticism is not an unexpected one. On the other hand, the values clarification strategies rapidly gained support from educators who believe that the affective domain must be paid attention to in the classroom. This raises again the question of how a balance might be achieved between content and structure, affect and cognition.

A second major criticism of values clarification relates to its philosophical base of ethical relativism. Though the strategies of the method are designed to help individuals clarify their own values, users of this approach are urged to employ a nonjudgmental attitude, allowing students to reach their own conclusions concerning the right or wrong of their thoughts and behaviors. Opponents of this philosophical view argue that it gives no direction or guidance in things moral since everyone is always right. According to critics, a morality without absolute or universal goods becomes a morality based on individual whim.

Value clarification advocates may legitimately argue from the philosophical position of ethical relativism, but in doing so, they must also acknowledge and respond to the crucial issues which this approach raises in regard to the assumptions it makes about the essence of human beings and the nature of social groups. This is equally true for those who advocate ethical positions involving absolute or universal principles such as the cognitive-developmentalists. To date, more effort has been put forth in the area of philosophical justification by the Kohlbergian advocates than by the value clarification adherents, though some foundations for the latter approach have been laid, most notably in the work of Kirschenbaum (1976).

In sum, the strengths of one approach become the weaknesses and criticisms of the other. This is not a choice between a superior method and a poor one, a right approach versus a wrong approach, or a good system over a bad system, though strong advocates of one or the other of these two approaches sometimes imply this kind of choice. For many educators it is not a choice at all, since Purpel and Ryan (1976) indicate that while moral education cannot be eradicated, it can be ignored. For others, as Colby (1976) argues, integration of these two approaches is both possible and desirable. And for some the choice involves still a different alternative, such as Scriven's (1976) cognitive moral education. Increasing concern with things moral at various levels, as this chapter has tried to document, does suggest that confrontation with these problems, ambiguities, and choices will become even more frequent in the near future for those who nurture children.

CONCLUSION

The transitions and uncertainties of contemporary life, especially those which directly impinge upon the form and function of the family, have prompted a growing concern about the nature of moral thought and action. In the study of human behavior, this concern has been translated into vigorous action in research and theory development on the process of becoming moral. The issues discussed in this chapter represent some of the unanswered questions in defining and nurturing moral development which, in turn, become the challenges for future work in understanding this important aspect of life.

There are other significant issues in the study of moral judgment and behavior which might have been included, thus this chapter reflects the constraints of space, time, and knowledge. Certain assumptions are also evident, including the belief that becoming moral represents a process worthy of study, and that confrontation with the unanswered questions will serve to illuminate the comprehensive efforts of the past and suggest directions for the future.

REFERENCES

Allport, G. W., Vernon, P. E., and Lindzey, G. *A study of values: A scale for measuring the dominant interests in personality.* Boston: Houghton Mifflin, 1951.

Alston, W. P. Comments on Kohlberg's "From is to ought." In T. Mischel (Ed.), *Cognitive development and epistomology.* New York: Academic Press, 1971.

Aronfreed, J. Moral development from the standpoint of a general psychological theory. In T. Lickona (Ed.), *Moral development and behavior.* New York: Holt, Rinehart and Winston, 1976.

Bereiter, C. The morality of moral education. *The Hastings Center Report*, 1978, *8*(2).

Colby, A. Two approaches to moral education. In D. Purpel and K. Ryan (Ed.), *Moral education...it comes with the territory.* Berkeley, CA: McCutchan Publishing Corporation, 1976.

Feather, N. T. *Values in education and society.* New York: Free Press, 1975.

Feather, N. T. Values in adolescence. In J. Adelson (Ed.), *Handbook of adolescent psychology.* New York: Wiley, 1980.

Fraendel, J. R. The Kohlberg bandwagon: Some reservations. In D. Purpel and K. Ryan (Eds.), *Moral education...it comes with the territory.* Berkeley, CA: McCutchan Publishing Corporation, 1976.

Frankena, W. K. *Ethics.* Englewood Cliffs, NJ: Prentice-Hall, Inc., 1963.

Garbarino, J., and Bronfenbrenner, U. The socialization of moral judgment and behavior in cross-cultural perspective. In T. Lickona (Ed.), *Moral development and behavior.* New York: Holt, Rinehart and Winston, 1976.

Gilligan C. In a different voice: Women's conceptions of self and of morality. *Harvard Education Review*, 1977, *47*(4), 481-517.

Hoffman, M. L. Moral development. In P. H. Mussen (Ed.), *Carmichael's manual of child psychology*, Vol. 2, (3rd ed.). New York: Wiley, 1970.

Hoffman, M. L. Empathy, role-taking, guilt, and development of altruistic motives. In T. Lickona (Ed.), *Moral development and behavior.* New York: Holt, Rinehart and Winston, 1976.

Holt, R. R. Freud's impact on modern morality. *The Hastings Center Report*, 1980, *10*(2), 38-45.

Kay, W. *Moral development.* London: George Allen and Unwin, Ltd., 1968.

Kirschenbaum, H. Clarifying values clarification: Some theoretical issues. In D. Purpel and K. Ryan (Eds.), *Moral education...it comes with the territory.* Berkeley, CA: McCutchan Publishing Corporation, 1976.

Kluckholn, F. R., and Strodtbeck, F. L. *Variations in value orientations.* Evanston, IL: Row, Peterson, 1961.

Kohlberg, L. The development of children's orientation toward a moral order. I: Sequence in the development of human thought. *Vita Humana,* 1963, *6,* 1-33.

Kohlberg, L. From is to ought. In T. Mischel (Ed.), *Cognitive development and epistemology.* New York: Academic Press, 1971.

Kohlberg, L. Moral stages and moralization. In T. Lickona (Ed.), *Moral development and behavior.* New York: Holt, Rinehart and Winston, 1976.

Kohlberg, L. The moral atmosphere of the school. In D. Purpel and K. Ryan (Eds.), *Moral education...it comes with the territory.* Berkeley, CA: McCutchan Publishing Corporation, 1976.

Levande, D. I., and Levande, J. S. The encouragement of pro-social behavior. *Middle School Journal,* 1979, *XX*(4), 12, 13, 31.

Lickona, T. (Ed.) *Moral development and behavior.* New York: Holt, Rinehart and Winston, 1976.

Peters, R. S. *Ethics and education.* Atlanta, GA: Scott, Foresman and Company, 1967.

Peters, R. S. Concrete principles and the rational passions. In N. F. Sizer and T. R. Sizer (Eds.), *Moral education.* Cambridge, MA: Harvard University Press, 1970.

Peters, R. S. Why doesn't Lawrence Kohlberg do his homework? In D. Purpel and K. Ryan (Eds.), *Moral education...it comes with the territory.* Berkeley, CA: McCutchan Publishing Corporation, 1976.

Piaget, J. *The moral judgment of the child.* London: Kegan Paul, 1932.

Purpel, D., and Ryan, K. What can be done? In D. Purpel and K. Ryan (Eds.), *Moral education...it comes with the territory.* Berkeley, CA: McCutchan Publishing Corporation, 1976.

Rokeach, M. *The nature of human values.* New York: Free Press, 1973.

Rothman, D. J., and Rothman, S. M. The conflict over children's rights. *The Hastings Center Report,* 1980, *10*(3), 7-10.

Saltzstein, H. D. Social influence and moral development: A perspective on the role of parents and peers. In T. Lickona (Ed.), *Moral development and behavior.* New York: Holt, Rinehart and Winston, 1976.

Scriven, M. Cognitive moral education. In D. Purpel and K. Ryan (Eds.), *Moral education...it comes with the territory.* Berkeley, CA: McCutchan Publishing Corporation, 1976.

Simpson, E. L. Moral development research: A case of scientific cultural bias. *Human Development,* 1974, *17*(2), 81-106.

Stewart, J. S. Problems and contradictions of values clarification. In D. Purpel and K. Ryan (Eds.), *Moral education...it comes with the territory.* Berkeley, CA: McCutchan Publishing Corporation, 1976.

Werkmeister, W. H. *Man and his values.* Lincoln, NE: University of Nebraska Press, 1967.

Williams, R. M. Change and stability in values and value systems. In B.
    Barber and A. Inkeles (Eds.), *Stability and social change*. Boston:
    Little, Brown, 1971.
Wright, D.   *The psychology of moral behavior*. Middlesex, England:
    Penguin Books, 1971.

PROGRAMS AND PRIMERS FOR CHILDREARING EDUCATION:

A CRITIQUE

Alison Clarke-Stewart

Department of Education
University of Chicago
Chicago, IL 60637

PAST AND CURRENT STATUS

If anyone were to inquire of any student of social progress, "What is the newest development in the educational world?" The answer would almost surely be schools for infants and a constructive program of education for parents.*(1)*

Organized parental education efforts have developed rapidly in this country;*(2)*[and]

books on the care and rearing of children find a ready market.*(3)*

Rapid change in social conditions, in housing, recreation, social mores ...makes a demand upon parents for a philosophy and methods based on today*(4)* [while]

The community, examining the child at the close of his preschool and most fundamental years, and finding him wanting, consistently lays the responsibility for this lack at the door of the home and further demands that the home remedy the situation.*(5)*

Scientists, of course, cannot take the place of mothers, but they can teach them many useful things and enable them to do intelligently not a little that they now do in accord with instinct or the advice of women no wiser than themselves.*(6)*

These statements taken from the annual *Yearbook* of the National Society for the Study of Education aptly reflect thinking in the United

125

States about the education of parents. Sponsored by federal agencies like the Office of Child Development and the Office of Education, promoted by book publishers and parent organizations, and supported by the Commissioner of Education's conviction that "parent education is the key to more effective education" (Bell, 1976), childrearing courses, books, pamphlets, shows, and home visits reached millions of parents in the 1970s. Among recent trends in education this focus on parents was significant, as efforts to inform parents and prospective parents increased dramatically in variety and scope over the decade.

But the attitude is not new. The foregoing quotations, while relevant today, were written not in the 1970s but over half a century ago. Parent education today may be supported by new data, take new forms, and be motivated by a new sense of concern, but the arguments and assumptions on which recent and current parent education efforts are based have not changed since the 1920s. These are that:

1. Parents are the most important influence on children's development and the early years are the most important period;
2. Schools are not doing an adequate job and are not as influential as the home;
3. Changing social conditions, such as poverty, stress, single parenthood, divorce, maternal employment and increasingly numerous associations outside the family, have led to increased parental uncertainty and anxiety;
4. Surveys show that some parents have not been successful in meeting their responsibilities to young children; and
5. New scientific knowledge about childrearing is available which, if disseminated, will effect behavioral change.

These arguments from the *Twenty-eighth Yearbook* (National Society for the Study of Education, 1929) are strikingly parallel to modern views. It is important, therefore, that we examine the recent parent education movement to see how far we have come and how far we have yet to go. This chapter provides a brief review of the "new scientific evidence" of the 1970s and critically examines its validity as an adequate and defensible basis for parent programs. It examines the effects of recent parent education programs and primers on children's development, asking "What can we conclude from our efforts thus far?" And it draws some conclusions as to how optimistic we can be about parent education as a social reform in the 1980s.

THE SCIENTIFIC EVIDENCE FOR PARENT EDUCATION

Animal Studies

The new scientific evidence that provided the impetus for recent forms of parent education may be divided into five types. The first type, research on the effects of early experience on animals, was used to justify all kinds of early interventions. When scientists manipulated the environments of young animals, providing systematically varied amounts of stimulation or deprivation, and gauging their impact on the animals' later performance, the results of their experiments were clearcut: Restricted rearing impairs development; more stimulating environments enhance it (see Bronfenbrenner, 1968; Hinde, 1970; Hunt, 1961; Palmer, 1969; Rutter, 1974; Thompson and Grusec, 1970). Animals in these studies, it was also found, were particularly vulnerable to environmental conditions present during infancy. These results were interpreted in terms of early "critical periods" and were used to justify early intervention for children in need.

The question is "Do these studies provide support for parent training programs?" Obviously they are limited by the fact that they dealt with nonhuman species. Although such comparative studies can be of value, one should be cautious about generalizing their findings to human subjects; human beings possess language, and verbal exchange is a central aspect of parent-child interaction and parent training programs. Even without this limitation, moreover, later studies with animals which varied the timing of the deprivation or stimulation experience showed animals to be more adaptable than had been first recognized (Cairns, 1977). The effects of rearing in isolation, for example, could be overcome in some instances by later experience with animals that interacted in reciprocal, playful, non-intense ways (Cairns, 1977; Gomber, 1975; Novak and Harlow, 1975). For these reasons, then, animal studies do not provide strong evidence to serve as a basis for parent education.

Extreme Environmental Effects

The second type of evidence to justify parent education came from studies of the effects of environmental extremes on human development. These were studies of children who were raised in severely depriving circumstances such as those occurring in orphanages and asylums or inherent in the isolation imposed by some psychopathic parents or caregivers (e.g., Bakwin, 1942; Dennis, 1973; Goldfarb, 1934; 1955; Pringle and Bossio, 1960; Provence and Lipton, 1962; Spitz, 1935; and see Ainsworth 1962; Bowlby, 1951; Clarke and Clarke, 1976a; Ferguson, 1966; Rutter, 1974; and Yarrow, 1961). Observations of such children demonstrated the results of extreme caregiving failure: These children, deprived or isolated from infancy or early childhood, were severely retarded in intellectual, language, and social skills in later years. When such children were adopted into good homes, however, their development was substantially improved (Dennis, 1973; A. D. B. Clarke and A. M. Clarke, 1977b; Kadushin, 1970; Lewis, 1954; Rathburn, McLaughlin, Bennet and Garland, 1965; Tizard and Rees, 1974). The conclusions reached from these studies were that early experience has a profound impact on children's development and that an environment which offers intellectual and social stimulation will enhance development. The extrapolation from this scientific evidence to parent education programs appears more reasonable than that from animal studies, but still it is limited by the severity and comprehensiveness of conditions compared in the studies of environmental extremes.

Studies of Social Class

The third kind of research to have an impact on parent education was research on social class--which was thought of as research on deprivation within "normal" limits. The discovery of "deficits" in the performance and abilities of poor children at the time they entered school was responsible in large part for the compensatory early education efforts in the 1960s and continued to motivate the parent training programs of the 1970s.

Linking socioeconomic status (SES) with presumed deficiencies in parental behavior is probably too simplistic to provide a sound basis for parent education, however. First, there were methodological problems in the studies of social class: socioeconomic status was often confounded with race, ethnicity, religion, and family structure, and studies were biased against low-income parents and children by the measures and methods used for assessment. Second, although the *mean* level of various kinds of parental behavior in different SES groups was statistically different, the *modal* behavior of parents and children in different groups was the same (Erlanger, 1974), and variability within classes was greater than that between classes (Deutsch, 1973). And third, the particular differences favoring the middle class (e.g., in mothers' affectionate, didactic, responsible, stimulating, and egalitarian attitudes and behavior) were not found in infancy, the period receiving the most attention by parent educators. So studies of social class do not provide the presumed mandate for training parents in poor families, either.

Parent-Child Correlation Studies·

The fourth kind of research used to support parent education was correlational research relating parental attitudes and behavior to children's behavior and competencies. The most direct evidence of this kind is provided by systematic observations of maternal and child behavior (see Clarke-Stewart, 1977a; Rutter, 1974; Schaefer, 1972). Early investigations had focused on the amount of time the mother was home, on gross behaviors and caretaking patterns such as feeding, weaning, and toilet training, or on global ratings of parental attitudes and the affective atmosphere in the home (see Caldwell, 1964). The results of these investigations were inconsistent or vague and of limited usefulness in developing specific guidelines for parents or program designers to follow.

Later observational studies of mother-child interaction in the 1960s and 1970s employed modern technological techniques for data collection and analysis. The results of these studies indicated that as early as six months of age infants' perceptual-cognitive competence is related to the amount of stimulation they have received through being attentively held, talked to, and played with by their mothers (Appleton, Clifton and Goldberg, 1975; Beckwith, 1971a; Beckwith et al., 1976; Rubenstein, 1967; Yarrow et al., 1975). Further, this relation continues and grows stronger as the child gets older (Bradley and Caldwell, 1976a; Carew et al., 1975; Clarke-Stewart et al., 1981; Elardo, Bradley and Caldwell, 1975; Engle, 1975; Hanson, 1975; Wenar, 1976). The more the mother provides appropriate play materials and intellectual experiences, and the more she shares, expands, and elaborates the child's activities, the better the child does in tests or behavioral assessments. Another maternal quality found to be consistently related to youngsters' behavior was contingent responsiveness (Beckwith, 1971b; Cazden, 1966; Jones and Moss, 1971; Endsley, Garner, Odom and Martin, 1975). Responding immediately and consistently when infants give specific signals (such as picking them up when they cry, or talking back to them when they vocalize) seems to foster their development of a generalized expectation that the environment is predictable and can be controlled (Lewis and Goldberg, 1969). This expectation encourages exploration of new situations and people and thus facilitates intellectual and social progress. Competence in these areas was also shown to be related to a pattern of parental discipline which is moderate, firm, rational, clear, and accompanied by frequent approval (McCall, Applebaum and Hogarty, 1973). Clearly, all these findings were relevant to programs or primers for parents.

One problem with the studies, however, is the representativeness of their findings. The studies have typically been done with small, white, middle-class samples; parent education is most often directed toward black, low-income families. The confounding influence of race in parent-child correlations is documented by those studies showing that the relationship between parental behavior and child competence is not the same in black and white families (Bradley et al., 1977; Clarke-Stewart, 1973; Elardo et al., 1977; Shipman, 1977); different processes appear to be important in homes of different racial groups.

Nor have most of the correlational studies separated out the factor of sex. Those few that have, however, show that in girls, independence and assertiveness are associated with firm, even abrasive, control, while for boys, the same kind of behavior is related to parental discipline best characterized as relatively lax and warm (Aldous, 1975; Baumrind, 1971, 1977; Rosenberg, 1977).

Since these investigations are correlational in nature, moreover, another problem is that they document *associations* between parental and child behavior, but not *causal direction*. The conclusion that it is the parents' behavior that is causing more or less optimal development in their children is not proved by statistically significant correlations. A finding from these same studies that was given less attention by parent-program planners was that children contribute significantly to their interactions with their parents and consequently to their own development.

Although lip service has always been given to reciprocity in parent-child relations, the popular assumption has usually been that the direction of influence is from parent to child. It had been known for some time that infants differ in their activity levels, persistence, reactions to new stimuli, and so on (Thomas, Chess, Birch, Hertzig and Korn, 1963), and there was some evidence that infant's behavior affects the mother's behavior as well as the reverse (e.g., Levy, 1958), but not until the 1970s was the task of documenting that reciprocity taken seriously. This was accomplished through graphic representations of second-to-second reciprocal cycles of mother-infant interaction e.g., mother jiggles/baby sucks or mother stimulates/baby is aroused (Brazelton, Koslowski and Main, 1974; Jaffe, Stein, and Perry, 1973; Stern, 1974) , and by additional evidence that individual differences in infants affect maternal behavior e.g., mothers vocalize more to heavier and more alert infants (Brown, Bakeman, Snyder, Frederickson, Morgan, and Hepfer, 1975) . The existence of bidirectional influences is undeniable, and casts doubt on a basic assumption underlying parent training programs that the way to the child's mind is through the parent.

Thus, although correlational studies of parent-child relations provide some supportive evidence for the potential value of parent education programs, they do not prove that changing parents' behavior in the direction statistically associated with advanced child development will assure increments in children's performance in a different population.

Experimental Studies

The final type of research that served as a justification for parent training followed the paradigm of the laboratory experiment; manipulating a single feature of the environment and measuring the effect of this manipulation on the child's immediate behavior. Most of these experiments used an adult experimenter as a parent substitute to stimulate, reinforce, or punish the child, or to provide a model for the child to imitate. Experimental techniques consistently demonstrated effects of the experimenter's systematic reinforcement of the ·child's behavior, effects which were related to the adult's nurturance, power, and enthusiasm (see Bryan, 1975; Harris, Wolf and Baer, 1967; Risley and Baer, 1973; and Stevenson, 1965). The question, though, is "What generalizability is there from these studies to real life?" Most studies utilized relatively trivial behaviors, like hitting a Bobo doll or donating a penny to a charity box, in highly constrained situations. Few studies looked at the transfer of these behaviors to different situations or a different stimulus or examined the long-term effects of the experimental manipulations. The generalizability of effects from lab and experiment to the complexity of home and family is still uncertain.

These five sources of empirical evidence--studies of animals, institutions, social classes, natural mother-child interactions, and experimental manipulations--provided a suggestive but shaky basis for the parent education movement.

THE RANGE OF PARENT EDUCATION PROGRAMS

But "movement" it was. Mid-decade, in 1975, a computer search by a federal inter-agency panel on early childhood revealed over 200 different programs for educating or training parents of young children were being federally funded. These 200 programs reflected enormous variety. Although they had common goals, parent educators did not always agree on how to change parents' or children's behavior.

Some programs emphasized the mother. One of these was the "Florida Parent Education Infant and Toddler Program" directed by Ira Gordon (Gordon, 1960; Gordon and Guinagh, 1977; Gordon, Guinagh and Jester, 1977). In this program, para-professionals visited poor mothers and their 3-month-old infants in their homes every week over a period of one, two, or three years. They taught the mothers games to play with their infants. In all of these games the principle of matching activities to the child's developmental level was stressed.

The "Parent/Child Toy Library Program" described by Glen Nimnicht (Nimnicht, Arango, and Adcock, 1977) also focused on the parent. Middle-income parents of 3- to 8-year-olds attended eight weekly sessions at a center, and through demonstration, discussion, and role playing, learned teaching techniques with toys that the researchers expected would enhance children's intellectual growth.

Another approach to parent training was to focus not on the parent but on the parent-child dyad. This approach is exemplified by Phyllis Levenstein's "Mother-Child Home Program," begun in New York in 1967 (Levenstein, 1970, 1977a, 1977b; Madden, Levenstein and Levenstein, 1976). In this model program, low-income mothers were visited at home by "toy demonstrators," who were social workers, middle-class volunteers, or mothers who had graduated from the program. The visits started when the child was two or three years old and occurred twice every week for seven months each year, over a one- or two-year period. The toy demonstrators modeled, encouraged and facilitated verbal interaction between mother and child as they played with toys and books provided by the program in a developmentally sequenced order.

The most intensive and comprehensive approach to parent training was seen in the Parent-Child Development Centers in Birmingham (Lasater, Malone, Weisberg, and Ferguson, 1975), Houston (Leler, Johnson, Kuhn, Hines and Torres, 1975), and New Orleans (Andrews, Blumenthal, Bache, and Weiner, 1975). These three programs differed in the ages and characteristics of participants, but all offered both intensive training in childrearing and comprehensive services for the entire family (including health care, social welfare, transportation, clothing, food, and general education). Parent training curricula were conveyed by diverse methods of instruction, including modeling, practice reinforced by other mothers, interviews with "model mothers," written materials, informal social discussions, group discussions, classes, workshops, home visits, and analyses of videotapes of the mother's interactions with her child. The broad goals of these projects focused on increasing mothers' abilities to cope with stressful environments and to facilitate and foster children's cognitive, socioemotional, and physical development.

This sampling of programs illustrates some of the variety in recent parent training and parent education programs. Programs focused on the parent, the child, or both. Their goals ranged from highly specific tasks for parents or children to broad cognitive, social, and physical goals for the children and affective, verbal and attitudinal goals for their parents. Children ranged in age from young infants to adolescents, and their parents came from a variety of groups including Indians, Mexican-Americans, teenagers, drug users, and child abusers. In federally funded programs most participating families were poor or had handicapped children. Program visits continued over periods of weeks or years, occurred daily or bi-monthly, and lasted from half an hour to a full day. They utilized individual teacher-parent sessions, group discussions, classes, television programs, or written materials, and they occurred at home or at a school, mobile health unit, or pediatric clinic. The staff were college students or graduates, para-professionals or professionals, mothers from the same neighborhood or from across town. The instructional approach was didactic (e.g., Kogan and Gordon, 1975), direct (e.g., Sonquist et al., 1975; Morris, London and Glick, 1976; Gordon, 1967; Levenstein, 1970), or indirect (Kessen, Fein, Clarke-Stewart, and Starr, 1975).

PARENT PRIMERS AND MANUALS

The "movement" also appeared in the public media with a marked increase in the publication of primers for parents, those "how-to" manuals that line the shelves of bookstores and supermarkets, and with more and more guest appearances by child development specialists on television. Pediatricians, psychologists, journalists, housewives, teachers, clergymen, working mothers, and single fathers all entered the how-to-parent market. Their offerings were abundant and diverse.

Book publication statistics showed a clear increase over the 1970s. The number of new books on practical child care published each year grew from about six a year at the beginning of the 1960s to more than 50 in 1979. Sales in the 1970s are estimated to have exceeded five million per year. In a 1976 study of a sample of 150 middle-class mothers of two- and four-year-olds (Clarke-Stewart, unpublished), all had read some child care books or articles and half had read more than five books. Since books are the most accessible and affordable source of expert guidance, it is not surprising that millions of parents turned to them, bought them, and read them.

TAKING STOCK OF BOOKS AND PROGRAMS

The important question about these books and programs, though, is not whether they were popular, but whether they worked, whether they were effective in modifying parents' behavior and changing the home environment to enhance children's development. It is time to take stock. We are at the beginning of a new decade. We should look at our track record and assess what we have found out and what we know about this kind of social reform.

First the Good News

Programs of education for parents that have been evaluated do have generally positive outcomes. The consistency of results showing positive outcomes from such a wide variety of programs is impressive. It is clear that parent training programs can have immediate effects on children's intellectual performance. Many programs, though not all, demonstrate significant if moderate IQ gains for program children relative to control or comparison children, gains which seem to peak at about three years of age (Andrews et al., 1975; Boger, 1969; Gordon et al., 1977; Gutelius, 1977; Lally and Honig, 1977a; Schaefer and Aaronson, 1977; and see Beller, 1979; Goodson and Hess, 1976; Horowitz and Paden, 1973; and White et al., 1973). In addition, gains in children's language, when measured separately from IQ, have been observed (Andrews, 1975; Boger, 1969; Lally and Honig, 1977b; Lasater et al., 1975). Fewer studies have assessed noncognitive factors, but those that have suggest that such variables as children's sociability, security, and cooperation may be increased by participation in a parent training program (Lally and Honig, 1977b; Lasater et al., 1975; Levenstein, 1977b).

There is also consistency of results for intellectual variables among longitudinal studies which have employed a post-program follow-up. Global measures of program effectiveness (placement in special education classes or grade failure) reveal consistent effects for most parent training programs through elementary school (Lazar et al., 1977a, 1977b). IQ gains are also maintained for a period of several years following the program but gradually decrease with time. There is a problem, however, in interpreting follow-up results, since the time elapsed between the program's end and the follow-up assessment is confounded with the child's age and educational experiences during this period.

Effects of parent training programs on the parents are less well known than child outcomes and not as consistent. Positive changes by the end of some programs have been noted in maternal behavior and attitudes. In these programs mothers were more talkative, didactic, responsive, and active with their children; they used more complex speech including questions with them; their attitudes toward childrearing were less authoritarian; and they felt more confident about being parents (Andrews et al., 1975; Benson, Berger, and Mease, 1975; Boger et al., 1967; Gutelius,

1977; Leler et al., 1975; Levenstein, 1977b; Love et al, 1976; Sonquist, 1975; Wandersman and Wandersman, 1976).

Now the Bad News

The bad news is that we do not know *why* these programs worked or how to design the most effective and efficient program. The problems of evaluation in this area are many and we have not yet done everything we can to overcome them. This is a situation which can and should be rectified in the 1980s.

One problem is that evaluation often has not been uppermost in parent programmers' minds. Research rigor is expensive and conflicts with the service purpose of most programs. Most programmers are convinced that they are doing good for parents--so why the need to prove it? In the inter-agency computer search mentioned earlier, fewer than one-quarter of the funded programs contained any kind of evaluation component, and when evaluation was included it was of the simplest kind possible (pre- and post-tests of children's performance with no control or comparison group). This lack of evaluation and control results not only from fiscal constraints but also from the opinion that assigning any family to a no-treatment condition when an assumed beneficial treatment is available is unethical, inhumane, or politically ill-advised. Some investigators have solved this problem with a "wait control" group, a group selected for the program at the same time and in the same way as the treated group but who must wait a period of time (their control group time) until a place in the program becomes available (Kogan and Gordon, 1975; Love, Nauta, Coelen, Hewett, and Ruopp, 1976; Martin, 1977). Other investigators have used older siblings as a comparison group (Karnes, Teska, Hodgins, and Badger, 1970; Madden et al., 1976). This nicely controls for parental motivation and family background, although, ideally, one would want to see the older siblings at the same age as the target children, which would be before the study began. Another partial solution is to use a "matched" comparison group (matched for sex, race, social class). The problem here is that these test-only subjects are often not offered the same invitation as families who are in the program, and they are frequently not pretested. When such comparison subjects are pretested, initial noncomparability on other than the matched variables (e.g., on IQ) often appears (Levenstein, 1977b; Slaughter, 1977).

But even creating a "real" control group often does not work in these studies in the real world. One group of investigators who used both a quasi-experimental design, including a matched comparison group, and a truly experimental format in which families were randomly assigned to treatment or control conditions, found that their parent training program (the Mother-Child Home Program) appeared significantly more successful when the quasi-experimental approach was employed (Madden et al., 1976). One possible explanation for this is that when control families live near the families in the program the curriculum may be diffused from program mothers to control mothers or from project children to control children (Bronfenbrenner, 1974; Gray and Klaus, 1970). Another is that the performance of the control subjects may increase over the duration of the study because of the repeated testing they undergo, a phenomenon known as the "climbing control group" (Andrews et al., 1975; Kogan and Gordon, 1975; Lambie, Bond, and Weikart, 1974). The problem of controls clearly is complex and deserves more attention and thought.

Another problem in evaluating parent training is subject attrition. In any study continuing over a lengthy time span it is inevitable that some families will drop out. It is even more likely if the benefits of staying in the study are not immediately obvious (as they are not likely to be for the control group). Attrition is not random. It may be related to the treatment (Slaughter, 1977; Stedman, 1977), to how well the child is doing (Lombard, 1973), to the parents' age (Morris et al., 1976), or to the child's initial ability (Lazar, Hubell, Murray, Roche and Royce, 1977a). This relation is complex and cannot accurately be predicted or controlled.

Assessment instruments used in evaluating parent training programs constitute another methodological hazard. Because most such programs were originally geared toward improving children's school performance, and because standardized IQ and achievement tests were readily available, it is not surprising that these became the major assessment tools used for program evaluation. It is now recognized that such tests have limitations. Reliance solely on IQ tests ignores possible socioemotional and motivational outcomes of programs and does not necessarily predict school achievement (Miller and Dyer, 1975). Nor is a single measure an adequate assessment, even of intelligence gains (Gray and Klaus, 1970; Klaus and Gray, 1968; Levenstein, 1977a, 1977b; Parkman-Ray, 1973; Slaughter, 1977). We need more complex and multivariate strategies for assessing the outcomes of parent programs. Included in such assessments should be measures of maternal attitudes and behavior. Change in the mothers' behavior has usually been assumed or ignored in parent program evaluations; investigators have generally not asked mothers about their goals or looked at their interactions with their children before or after imposing the program. It is also important to assess these outcomes of parent programs.

A further limitation of program evaluations is that even when adequate evaluations have been done, most researchers have been concerned only with demonstrating the *overall* effectiveness of their programs. They have not examined effects according to program dimensions such as length, intensity, curriculum, and mode of instruction, or according to subject dimensions such as child's or parent's age, ability, or background. In the evaluation of any single program, these components are all confounded because the program designer puts all his or her "best bets" into one complex program. It has been left to reviewers to try to compare outcomes associated with specific dimensions across programs. They have done this by taking a number of approaches: (1) ignoring confounding components and relating a common outcome to the position of each program on a given dimension, and then "taking a vote" to see whether the majority of programs showing a significant change are high, medium, or low on that dimension; (2) computing and testing the significance of the mean differences in outcome for each position on a given dimension; and (3) compiling raw data from different programs and correlating program dimensions with a common child outcome. The results of such attempts so far, however, have been disappointing. Of the 25 dimensions analyzed by the one study to utilize the last and best of these methods, only two were significantly related to program effectiveness (Vopava and Royce, 1978). In a review using the first approach (Goodson and Hess, 1976); the reviewers were cautious in interpreting their dimensional analyses and concluded that differential effects were the result of unidentified factors, while a third reviewer (Beller, 1979) claimed it was not possible to accomplish a dimensional analysis at the present time. As a basis for evaluating dimensional effects, manipulation and comparison of dimensions within programs while controlling other potentially confounding variables are needed.

This was attempted in a study by Kessen, Fein, Clarke-Stewart, and Starr (1975). This home-based program held constant the age and background of subjects, the length and intensity of the program, the training and qualifications of the staff, and the instructional approach. Evaluation, before the program began and at six-month intervals thereafter, was complex and comprehensive, assessing maternal attitudes and behavior and children's social, cognitive, and language development through tests, natural observations, and semistructured situations.

Beyond these constant variables, the study explored systematic variation in the curriculum content and the program focus. Subjects were randomly assigned to one of six groups. The first three groups were alike in their focus on the mother-child dyad but different in curricular goals and content. In the "Language Curriculum," the home visitor encouraged the mother to talk to the child, describing ongoing activities, playing language games, and labeling toys, objects, and pictures. When the child began to speak, the mother was encouraged to respond to and elaborate on his vocalization and to engage him in dialogues. The goal of this curriculum was to promote the growth of vocabulary and comprehension and to help the child appreciate the multifold uses of speech. For the second group, the "Play Curriculum," home visitors tried to help the mother arrange an environment wherein the child could discover and explore interesting and diverse objects suited to his or her developmental level. In this environment, interested and appreciative grownups would elaborate on the child's object interactions in nondirective ways and expand the activities he or she initiated. The third group received the "Social Curriculum," which was designed to provide the mother and child with frequent opportunities for playful, reciprocal interaction and to encourage continuation of such social episodes when the home visitor was not there. The home visitor first suggested activities for the mother and child to share and later joined in the activities, but always the focus was on the mother-child pair. The theme of this curriculum was the "enrichment of interpersonal connections" through mutual looking, playing, talking, responding, and expressing of affection.

While the Language, Play, and Social Curricula all focused on the mother-child dyad, two comparison groups focused on either the mother or the child. In the mother-focused group, the home visitor was friendly to the child but did not actively play with him or her; she directed her attention to conversation and activities with the mother. In the child-focused group, the home visitor was friendly to the mother but her activities consisted of conversation and play with the child; the mother was not encouraged to watch or participate. The curriculum for these two groups was a combination of the language, play, and social activities. The sixth and final group was a test-only control.

EFFECTIVE PROGRAM COMPONENTS

Summarizing research relating program outcomes to program dimensions reviewers have generally concluded that the content, goals, and philosophical orientation of the curriculum are not related to program effectiveness (Goodson and Hess, 1976; Lazar et al., 1977a; Vopava and Royce, 1978). A caveat to this finding is that almost all of the reviewed curricula have been "cognitive" in orientation and goals. In one review, for example, twenty programs were classified as cognitive, only five as language oriented and three as sensorimotor. Although no distinctions between curriculum content and program effectiveness can be drawn from these reviews, however, there is at least evidence that the absence of any curriculum--having only unstructured social visits or visits from a nurse --does not lead to gains in development (Badger, 1977; Gordon, 1967; Lambie et al., 1974; Levenstein, 1977b).

The Kessen et al. (1975) study also found no differences in children's IQ test performance related to which of the three curriculum groups they were in. Increases in children's functional competence (language production and symbolic or relational play) and mothers' articulate non-directiveness, however, were related to curriculum. The order of curriculum groups was Language, Play, and then Social. This finding further supports the observation that lack of a curriculum is ineffective, since the Social Curriculum offered relatively unstructured, social visits. The performance of children in the Social Curriculum group was significantly lower than that of children in the Language and Play Curriculum groups, and not different from the performance of test-only control subjects. Language and Play curricula subjects were not significantly different from each other. Perhaps this was due to the cognitive emphasis in both of these curricula. But if this is so, why is a cognitive curriculum superior? Possible explanations might include how closely the curriculum focused on the skills tested, how much it involved the mother, how compatible it was with her goals, how much it enhanced her (cognitive) understanding, or how easy it was for the home visitors to implement. (In the Kessen et al. study the Social Curriculum was most difficult for home visitors to implement, while the toys in Language and Play Curricula served as natural mediators of interactions.) Clearly the issue of the effectiveness of different curricula needs further investigation; investigation which includes a range of outcomes for both mothers and children, incorporates sensitive indicators of program content, and attempts to determine what makes one curriculum more effective than another.

Another program dimension about which more should be known is the focus of the program on parent or child. Some attempt has been made to examine this dimension in parent education programs. A small number of studies have compared the relative effects of mother-focused and child-focused programs. Of these, one (Lombard, 1973) found mother-focused superior to child-focused, another (Kessen et al., 1975) found child-focused superior to mother-focused, and a third (Stern et al., 1972) found no differences between child-focused and mother-focused programs, in terms of children's intellectual performance.

A few studies have compared mother-focused with mother-child-focused programs. When the mother watched the teacher instruct her child (mother-child focused), it led to greater child gains than when she merely attended parent meetings without the child (mother-focused) (Radin, 1972). When mothers were allowed to watch their children being tested there was less subject attrition (Stedman, 1977). And when parent education programs included home visits (mother-child focused) children gained more than when they consisted merely of group classes and discussions (mother-focused) (Brim 1965; Chilman, 1973; Goodson and Hess, 1976; McCarthy, 1972). For producing changes in *maternal* behavior, however, mother-focused programs may be more effective than mother-child focused (Beller, 1979; Kessen et al., 1975).

Most comparisons have been of mother-child-focused versus child-focused programs, assessed by comparing high and low parental involvement in the child's early childhood education program or by comparing home-based and center-based programs. These comparisons indicate that mother-child focused (high involvement or home-based) programs have a greater effect on the mother's attitudes and teaching (Adkins and Crowell, 1969; Adkins and O'Malley, 1971; Downey, 1969; Love et al., 1976; Radin, 1972). But these differences may simply reflect the fact that the mother has learned to give the "desirable" answer or exhibit the "desirable" behavior. No difference was found in the Kessen et al., study between maternal behavior to the child in child-focused and mother-child focused curriculum groups.

There is more evidence for the greater effectiveness of mother-child focused programs in enhancing *children's* development; more mother-child involvement produced higher or longer lasting gains in children's IQ in a number of studies (Adkins and Crowell, 1969; Adkins and O'Malley, 1971; Alford and Hines, 1972; Downey, 1969; Radin, 1972; and see Beller, 1979; Bronfenbrenner, 1974; Goodson and Hess, 1976; Lazar et al., 1977a). However, this evidence is not totally convincing, either. One reviewer (Bronfenbrenner, 1974) based his conclusion on a small sample of programs in which ages and frequency of visits were confounded; another comparison was between thirteen high-medium parent involvement programs and only one low involvement program (Lazar et al., 1977a); and a third report (Goodson and Hess, 1976) based its claim of superiority on gains of six versus eight to ten IQ points. Equally strong evidence exists for the claim that there is *no* difference between mother-child-focused and child-focused programs in fostering children's intellectual development (Gilmer, Miller, and Gray, 1970; Kessen et al., 1975; Miller and Dyer, 1975).

Some studies, moreover, have found that child-focused programs are *more* effective than mother-child programs for producing gains in children's test competence (Kessen et al., 1975), test orientation (Love et al., 1976), and school skills (Bronfenbrenner, 1974). In one combined home-visit and center program (Klaus and Gray, 1968), in fact, gains in children's tests performance occurred when the children were attending the center (child-focused) and disappeared when they had only home visits (mother-child focused). These results are somewhat inconsistent, but it seems most likely--and sensible--that to change the child's behavior, the child must be involved; whereas to change the mother's behavior, a mother-focused approach is effective.

Another dimension of program effectiveness is the kind of family that participates. Not surprisingly, it has been observed that parent programs are more effective when mothers are not working (Karnes et al., 1970) and not poverty-stricken (Bronfenbrenner, 1974; Chilman, 1973; Herzog, Newcomb, and Cisin, 1972; Klaus and Gray, 1958; White et al., 1973). Other family characteristics, too, such as the size of the household (Slaughter, 1977; Kessen et al., 1975) and the amount of contact with extended-family members (Kessen et al., 1975), seem to interact with treatment conditions in complicated ways. This is another complex issue that needs further exploration.

Characteristics of the child may also interact with program effectiveness. Differential effects have been noted for boys and girls (Gordon and Guinagh, 1977; Kessen et al., 1975; Lally and Honig, 1977b), but, unfortunately, data currently available are not sufficient to formulate any sex-related generalizations. The same is true for the interaction of children's initial intelligence or ability with program effectiveness (Goodson and Hess, 1976; Lazar et al., 1977a). Age may also be related to program effects. The problem in relating the child's age to program outcomes, however, is that age typically has been confounded with program length. Studies varying age of subjects at the beginning of the program show no significant age related differences in immediate effects (Andrews et al., 1975; Lambie et al., 1974; Levenstein, 1977a, 1977b; Morris et al., 1976), although there is some evidence that beginning at a younger age is better in the long run (Gordon and Guinagh, 1977; Karnes, Hodgins, and Teska, 1967; Karnes, Studley, Wright, and Hodgins, 1968; Vopava and Royce, 1978). Nevertheless, the consensus is that there is no "magic age" for starting parent training programs (Beller, 1979; Lazar et al., 1977a).

This raises the dimension of the length and intensity of the program. Positive results have been observed for early childhood programs varying in duration from a few months (Palmer and Siegel, 1977) to a few years (Gordon et al., 1977). Although some studies have found no differences between programs lasting one or two years (Andrews et al., 1975; Lombard, 1973; and Love et al., 1976), or two or three years (Klaus and Gray, 1968), when differences have been found (Gilmer et al., 1970; Gordon and Guinagh, 1977; Gordon et al., 1977; Levenstein, 1977) they favor the longer programs, and are usually reflected in longer lasting rather than larger gains, or in maternal or sibling changes rather than child changes. Caution must be applied, however, since, as previously mentioned, in several of these studies program length was confounded with child's age. Moreover, even if program duration ranging from one to three years is related to program effectiveness, programs lasting longer than this may not be additionally advantageous (Lally and Honig, 1977b). In programs lasting three years or less, consistency of involvement in the program also appears to be important. In Gordon's study (Gordon and Guinagh, 1977; Gordon et al., 1977), two contiguous years in the program were better than two nonconsecutive years.

A more intense program schedule and longer visits may also be more effective (Andrews et al., 1975; Gilmer et al., 1970; Kessen et al., 1975; Love et al., 1976), but the studies examining these variations generally have confounded program intensity with location, activities, focus, or age. Moreover, causal direction from visit length to program effect cannot be assumed. It may be that visits are shorter when the home visitor or mother is discouraged by the child's lack of progress or when the home visitor is unable to establish rapport with the mother, rather than that shorter visits produce smaller gains. According to the analysis by Lazar et al. (1977), there is no systematic effect of intensity of visits.

One final program dimension to be evaluated is the instructional technique and format. Program effectiveness may be related to instructional aspects of the program but, again, the evidence is not clear. There seems to be no difference in program outcome depending on staff qualifications (Gordon, 1967; Lazar et al., 1977a; Levenstein, 1977b; Love et al., 1976; Vopava and Royce, 1978; White et al., 1973) as long as there is a curriculum to follow (Lambie et al., 1974). The structure or specificity of the instruction may be related to immediate (Lazar et al., 1977a) or later (Goodson and Hess, 1976) outcomes for the child or the mother (Boger, 1967), but this evidence also is not strong. The format of the instruction may have a bearing on the program effectiveness.

Although parental group discussion and lectures are not very popular or effective in changing the parent's or child's behavior or attitudes (Brim, 1965; Chilman, 1973; Goodson and Hess, 1976; Gordon and Guinagh, 1977; McCarthy, 1972; Radin, 1972; and White et al., 1973), discussion that involves both group pressure and the mother's own child can be as effective as individual home visits (Andrews et al., 1975; Badger, 1977; and Slaughter, 1977).

In brief, there are no conclusive data to establish the superiority of any one method, focus, or curriculum in parent education. This is not to say that all programs are equally effective, only that we have not yet done an adequate job of systematically investigating program dimensions.

ASSUMPTIONS OF PARENT EDUCATION

Although some of the more simple assumptions on which early parent programs were founded have subsequently been disproved or discarded (e.g., that a brief program could serve as a permanent "inoculation" against later deficiencies), the parent program movement in the 1970s--as today--was based on a number of untested or unclarified assumptions. In addition to instituting more adequate and fine-grained evaluations to determine the effectiveness of programs and particular program components, researchers need to explore these assumptions.

1. *What the program designer intends is what really happens.* Home visitors, though given prior training in program techniques, have seldom been monitored in situations as they interpret and implement the program--and they should be.

2. *The message the parent trainer intends is what gets through to the mother.* The message that gets across may be distorted by the mother's uncertainty, anxiety, or ignorance, into a more simple-minded form--for example, the mother may hear "Play with your child!", but miss more subtle suggestions about how to play (Kessen et al., 1975). We need to know how the program is received.

3. *All mothers are equally ready for parent training.* Differences in mothers' attitudes prior to the program have been observed to be related to their involvement in the program (Schaefer and Aaronson, 1977), their behavior (Martin, 1977), and the child's progress (Schaefer and Aaronson, 1977). Consideration of individual differences in parents' needs is necessary.

4. *The mother's goals for herself and her child are the same as the program designer's--or would be if the mother knew better.* Compatibility between parents' and program's goals has been found to affect outcomes (Sonquist, 1975), but parents' goals have seldom been evaluated in parent training studies.

5.   *The mother changes or will change in the desired direction.* While
there is some evidence that desired changes in maternal behavior
occur (e.g., Lasater et al., 1975), there is also evidence that mothers
may change in the opposite direction from that intended--becoming
more directive (Kessen et al., 1975), more extreme (Chilman, 1973),
or less involved with their children (Badger, Hodges, and Burns,
1977). It may be, as Nimnicht et al. (1977) and Schlossman (1978)
have suggested, that the effect of parent training is to make the
mother more anxious or unsure, which could make her adapt the
program to strengthen rather than diminish her own natural pro-
clivities. Moreover, the most essential and desirable aspects of a
mother's natural behavior with her child--such as sociability, affection, responsiveness, and effectiveness--may not even be susceptible to change (Kessen et al., 1975). Naturalistic assessment of
the mother's behavior with her child before, during, and after the
program is important in order to find out what changes actually
occur.

6.   *Changing the mother's behavior causes the child's improved performance.* Studies have found that maternal attitudes or behavior
and children's IQ and behavior are correlated in intervention families (Andrews et al., 1975; Epstein and Evan, 1977; Gordon and
Guinagh, 1977; Lambie et al., 1974; Levenstein, 1977b; Schaefer and
Aaronson, 1977), as they are in "unimproved" families and that the
correlation between maternal education and the child's IQ is lower
in experimental families than in "unimproved" ones (Levenstein,
1977b). What is needed to test this critical assumption, however, is
analysis of the relation between changes in maternal and child
behavior over time.

Four studies offer evidence of this kind. In one study, researchers observed that mothers' behavior changed during training
sessions and children's behavior changed in the post-training period,
but no correlation was found between maternal change and child
change in individual mother-child pairs (Kogan and Gordon, 1975).
In a second study, researchers found that although mothers' behavior
changed prior to the time treatment effects were observed in
children's motor and cognitive performance, the time lags were
slight and could be at least partially attributed to asynchrony in
scheduling assessments (Andrews et al., 1975). These investigators
did not analyze for correlations between maternal change and child
change. The third study, by Kessen et al. (1975), examined both
changes in group means and correlational patterns and found no
evidence that changes in maternal behavior either preceded or
caused increments in children's performance. Indeed, it was found
that child changes preceded maternal changes on several factors.
Finally, in the fourth study, researchers found that the correlation
between children's IQ at the beginning of the program and maternal
stimulation at the end was stronger than that between maternal

stimulation at the beginning and children's IQ at the end (Forrester, Boismier, and Gray, 1977). Since the opposite direction of correlations was observed in a comparable study of families not participating in a parent training program (Clarke-Stewart, 1973), this correlational pattern may reflect a treatment effect. What is needed to settle this uncertainty is further breakdown by time periods within the duration of the program.

In sum, the results of these four investigations of mother-child changes, combined with the following findings: (a) that the behavior of children in exclusively child-focused programs influences the mother's behavior (Falender and Heber, 1975); (b) that mother-child interaction and children's behavior are more susceptible to program-induced change than are maternal behavior (Kogan and Gordon, 1975; Lally and Honig, 1977b) or attitudes (Lally and Honig, 1977b; Leler et al., 1975; Sonquist, 1975); and (c) that, as described earlier, child-focused programs are at least as effective as mother- or mother-child-focused ones in producing child gains, make it only too clear that we have no basis for the assumption that parent training programs "work" strictly or simply through the mother's influence on the child.

7. *The benefits of parent training will continue after the program ends because the mother has learned principles which she can adapt as the child gets older and as she interacts with later children.* Although younger siblings in parent-program families generally perform better than expected on tests of intelligence (Gilmer et al., 1970; Gray and Klaus, 1972; Klaus and Gray, 1968; Levenstein, 1977b; Miller, 1968), this apparent diffusion of the program is confounded by direct effects of the older sibling, the parent trainer, and her toys; it is not necessarily meditated by the mother's behavior. Although mothers report that they generalize the behavioral techniques they have learned to other family members (Hamm and Lyman, 1973; Shearer, undated), the degree to which they generalize apparently declines over time and place. It is greatest when siblings are close in age to the target child (Gray and Klaus, 1970) and in situations in which the behavior was taught (Gilmer et al., 1970; Levenstein, 1977b; Miller and Sloane, 1976). Evidence that mothers can adapt the principles learned in parent training programs as children get older has not been collected.

EVALUATION OF PARENT BOOKS AND MANUALS

If we know too little about the hows, whys, and effects of parent training, we know even less about the popular child care books. These books and articles have seldom been written with a scientific purpose, and their effects have not been measured. Links between the mother's knowledge gained from reading such books and her behavior toward her child have been assumed, however (Bronfenbrenner, 1958; Hunt, 1961;

Robinson, 1972). Bronfenbrenner, for example, argued the following from his reading of research on social class and childrearing over a 25-year period: popular childrearing literature was permissive; middle-class mothers read more; middle-class mothers were more permissive; therefore, reading leads to permissiveness.

Unfortunately, a variety of investigations have not found strong evidence for this presumed link between knowledge and behavior. There was not a sudden jump in permissiveness following publication of the first edition of Spock's *Baby and Child Care* in 1946 (Erlanger, 1974), nor was there any causal connection between childrearing advice in magazine articles and parental behavior over the four-decade period of the Fels longitudinal study (Crandall, 1977). Although one study (Clarke-Stewart, 1973) did show that mothers who were more knowledgeable about child development were more affectionate, talkative, playful, and responsive with their children, the mothers' knowledge about child development was also related to their general knowledge and to their IQ scores--factors that could account for both their specific knowledge about child development and their childrearing behavior. Since mothers in a survey in Chicago who were reading the popular child care literature (Clarke-Stewart, 1978b), did not expect to change their behavior before they read a childcare manual nor planned to do so after reading the book, inability to find a link between written materials and parental behavior is perhaps not surprising. Though fashions of childrearing in books and homes have waxed and waned together over the years, it is likely that both reflect changing times and values rather than that child development experts have a direct impact on parents' behavior. Books may be useful to parents, to raise their consciousness about their own behavior, to confirm that what they are doing is right, to describe the course of child development, or possibly to present an alternative or more elaborate view of childrearing. They do not, however, provide simple guidelines for parents to follow in daily, real-life interactions with their individual children, and most likely they do not effect behavioral change or social reform.

CONCLUSIONS

On the basis of this review of the research on parent education programs and primers we can draw several conclusions. First, the parent training endeavor is founded on a set of untested assumptons and unwarranted extrapolations from basic research. There is no clear mandate for parent training and no guarantee of success in this supposedly scientific base of the parent education movement. Second, changing parents' behavior is an enormously complex and uncertain task. It is unlikely to result from anything less than an intensive behaviorally oriented program involving both parent and child. And third, even if achieved, there is no assurance that the change in parents' behavior will advance children's development: The kinds of parental behavior that are most susceptible to change are not necessarily the ones most closely associated with development and the parental behaviors correlated with development do not necessarily cause it. Although positive outcomes for children have been obtained in a variety of parent education programs, it appears plausible that much of the observed advance in development comes from children's involvement with the parent trainers or their toys directly, rather than being mediated through the parents. What we need in the 1980s is not wholesale implementation of more parent education programs, but a further search for the most effective ways of facilitating children's development. As part of this search we need to systematically manipulate and monitor variations in parent programs. Only with this kind of rigorous experimentation and examination can we increase our understanding of how parental behavior affects children's development and promote better development in the next generation.

REFERENCES

Adkins, D. C., and Crowell, D. C. *Development of a preschool language-oriented curriculum with a structured parent education program* (Unpublished Final Report). Honolulu: University of Hawaii, Head Start Evaluation and Research Center, 1969.

Adkins, D. C., and O'Malley, J. *Continuation of programmatic research on curricular modules for early childhood education and parent participation* (Unpublished Final Report). Honolulu: University of Hawaii, Center for Research in Early Childhood Education, 1971.

Ainsworth, M. D. S. The effects of maternal deprivation: A review of findings and controversy in the context of research strategy. In *Deprivation of maternal care: A reassessment of its effects.* Public Health Papers, No. 14, 1962, pp. 97-165.

Aldous, J. The search for alternatives: Parental behaviors and children's original problem solutions. *Journal of Marriage and the Family,* 1975, 37, 711-722.

Alford, R. W., and Hines, B. *Demonstration of home-oriented early childhood education program* (Final Report). Kanawha County, W.V.: Appalachia Educational Laboratory, September 1972. (ERIC Document Reproduction Service No. ED 069 391)

Andrews, S. R., Blumenthal, J. B., Bache, W. L., and Wiener, G. *New Orleans Parent-Child Development Center* (Fourth Year Report OCD 90-C-381). New Orleans: University of New Orleans, March 1975.

Appleton, T., Clifton, R., and Goldberg, S. The development of behaivoral competence in infancy. In F. D. Horowitz (Ed.), *Review of child development research* (Vol. 4). Chicago: University of Chicago Press, 1975.

Badger, E. The infant stimulation/mother training project. In B. M. Caldwell and D. J. Stedman (Eds.), *Infant education.* New York: Walker, 1977.

Badger, E., Hodgins, A., and Burns, D. *Altering the behavior of adolescent mothers: A follow-up evaluation of the Infant Stimulation/Mother Training Program.* Paper presented at the Nassau County Coalition for Family Planning Conference, Westbury, N.Y., November 1977.

Bakwin, H.   Loneliness in infants.   *American Journal of Diseases in Children*, 1942, *63*, 30-40.

Baumrind, D.   Current patterns of parental authority.   *Developmental Psychology Monograph*, 1971, *4* (1, Part 2).

Baumrind, D.   *Socialization determinants of personal agency.*   Paper presented at the biennial meeting of the Society for Research in Child Development, New Orleans, March 1977.

Beckwith, L.   Relationships between attributes of mothers and their infants' IQ scores.   *Child Development*, 1971, *42*, 1083-1097. (a)

Beckwith, L.   Relationships between infants' vocalization and their mothers' behavior.   *Merrill-Palmer Quarterly*, 1971, *17*, 211-226. (b)

Beckwith, L., Cohen, S. E., Kopp, C. B., Parmelee, A. H., and Marcy, T. G.   Caregiver-infant interaction and early cognitive development in preterm infants.   *Child Development*, 1976, *47*, 579-587.

Bell, T. H.   *Formulating governmental policies on the basis of educational research.*   Address given at the University of Chicago, Chicago, April 5, 1976.

Beller, E. K.   Early intervention programs.   In J. Osofsky (Ed.), *Handbook of infant development.*   New York: John Wiley, 1979.

Benson, L., Berger, M., and Mease, W.   Family communication systems.   *Small Group Behavior*, 1975, *6*, 91-104.

Boger, R. P.   *Parents as primary change agents in an experimental Head Start program of language intervention* (Experimental Program Report), November 1969.   (ERIC Document Reproduction Service No. ED 013 371)

Bowlby, J.   *Maternal care and mental health* (World Health Organization Monograph No. 2).   Geneva: World Health Organization, 1951.

Bradley, R. H., and Caldwell, B. M.   Early home environment and changes in mental test performance in children from six to thirty-six months.   *Developmental Psychology*, 1976, *12*, 93-97. (a)

Bradley, R. H., and Caldwell, B. M.   The relations of infants' home environments to mental test performance at fifty-four months: A follow-up study.   *Child Development*, 1976, *47*, 1172-1174. (b)

Bradley, R. H., Caldwell, B. M., and Elardo, R.   *Home environment, social status, and mental test performance.*   Paper presented at the biennial meeting of the Society for Research in Child Development, New Orleans, March 1977.

Brazelton, T. B., Koslowski, B., and Main, M.   The origins of reciprocity: The early mother-infant interaction.   In M. Lewis and L. A. Rosenblum (Eds.), *The effect of the infant on its caregiver.*   New York: John Wiley, 1974.

Bronfenbrenner, U.   Socialization and social class through time and space.   In E. E. Maccoby, T. M. Newcomb, and E. L. Hartley (Eds.), *Readings in social psychology.*   New York: Henry Holt, 1958.

Bronfenbrenner, U.   Early deprivation in mammals: A cross species analysis.   In G. Newton and S. Levine (Eds.), *Early experience and behavior.*   Springfield, IL: Charles C. Thomas, 1968.

Bronfenbrenner, U.   *Is early intervention effective?   A report on longitudinal evaluations of preschool programs* (Vol. 2).   Washington, D.C.: Department of Health, Education, and Welfare, 1974.

Brown, J. V., Bakeman, R., Snyder, P. A., Fredrickson, W. T., Morgan, S. T., and Hepler, R. Interactions of black-inner city mothers with their newborn infants. *Child Development,* 1975, *46,* 677-686.

Bryan, J. H. Children's cooperation and helping behaviors. In E. M. Hetherington (Ed.), *Review of child development research* (Vol. 5). Chicago: University of Chicago Press, 1975.

Cairns, R. B. Beyond social attachment: The dynamics of interactional development. In T. Alloway, P. Pliner, and L. Krames (Eds.), *Attachment behavior: Advances in the study of communication and affect* (Vol. 3). New York: Plenum Press, 1977.

Caldwell, B. M. The effects of infant care. In M. L. Hoffman and L. W. Hoffman (Eds.), *Review of child development research* (Vol. 1). New York: Russell Sage, 1964.

Carew, J. V., Chan, I., and Halfar, C. *Observed intellectual competence and tested intelligence: Their roots in the young child's transactions with his environment.* Unpublished manuscript, Harvard University, 1975.

Cazden, C. Subcultural differences in child language: An interdisciplinary review. *Merrill-Palmer Quarterly,* 1966, *12,* 185-219.

Chilman, C. S. Programs for disadvantaged parents: Some major trends and related research. In B. M. Caldwell and H. N. Ricciuti (Eds.), *Review of child development research* (Vol. 3). Chicago: University of Chicago Press, 1973.

Clarke, A. D. B., and Clarke, A. M. Formerly isolated children. In A. M. Clarke and A. D. B. Clarke (Eds.), *Early experience: Myth and evidence.* New York: Free Press, 1976. (a)

Clarke, A. D. B., and Clarke, A. M. Studies in natural settings. In A. M. Clarke and A. D. B. Clarke (Eds.), *Early experience: Myth and evidence.* New York: Free Press, 1976. (b)

Clarke-Stewart, K. A. Interactions between mothers and their young children: Characteristics and consequences. *Monographs of the Society for Research in Child Development,* 1973, *38,* (6-7, Serial No. 153).

Clarke-Stewart, K. A. *Child care in the family: A review of research and some propositions for policy.* New York: Academic Press, 1977.

Clarke-Stewart, K. A. Popular primers for parents. *American Psychologist,* 1978, *33,* 359-369.

Clarke-Stewart, K. A., VanderStoep, L., and Killian, G. A. Analysis and replication of mother-child relations at two years of age. *Child Development,* 1979, *50,* 777-793.

Coleman, J. S., Campbell, E. Q., Hobson, C. J., McPartland, J., Mood, A. M., Weinfled, F. D., and York, R. L. *Equality of educational opportunity.* Washington, D.C.: U.S. Government Printing Office, 1966.

Crandall, V. C. *Changes in advice and their relations to changes in behavior.* Paper presented at the annual convention of the American Psychological Association, San Francisco, August 1977.

Davis, K. Extreme social isolation of a child. *American Journal of Sociology,* 1940, *45,* 554-565.

Davis, K. Final note on a case of extreme isolation. *American Journal of Sociology*, 1947, *52*, 432-437.

Dennis, W. Causes of retardation among institutional children: Iran. *Journal of Genetic Psychology*, 1960, *96*, 47-59.

Dennis, W. *Children of the creche.* New York: Appleton-Century-Crofts, 1973.

Deutsch, D. P. Social class and child development. In B. M. Caldwell and H. N. Ricciuti (Eds.), *Review of child development research* (Vol. 3). Chicago: University of Chicago Press, 1973.

Downey, J. *Project Early Push: Preschool program in compensatory education.* Buffalo, NY: American Institute for Research in Behavioral Sciences, 1969.

DuPan, R. M., and Roth, S. The psychologic development of a group of children brought up in a hospital-type residential nursery. *Journal of Pediatrics*, 1955, *47*, 124-129.

Elardo, R., Bradley, R., and Caldwell, B. M. The relation of infants' home environments to mental test performance from six to thirty-six months: A longitudinal analysis. *Child Development*, 1975, *46*, 71-76.

Elardo, R., Bradley, R., and Caldwell, B. M. A longitudinal study of the relation of infants' home environments to language development at age three. *Child Development*, 1977, *48*, 595-603.

Endsley, R. C., Garner, A. P., Odom, A. H., and Martin, M. J. *Interrelationships among selected maternal behavior and preschool children's verbal and nonverbal curiosity behavior.* Paper presented at the biennial meeting of the Society for Research in Child Development, Denver, Spring 1975.

Engle, M., Nechlin, H., and Arki, A. M. Aspects of mothering: Correlate of the cognitive development of black male infants in the second year of life. In A. Davids (Ed.), *Child personality and psychopathology: Current topics* (Vol. 2). New York: John Wiley, 1975.

Epstein, A. S., and Evans, J. L. *Parenting: Processes and programs.* Unpublished manuscript, High/Scope, Ypsilanti, Michigan, November 1977.

Erlanger, H. S. Social class and corporal punishment in childrearing: A reassessment. *American Sociological Review*, 1974, *39*, 68-85.

Falender, C. A., and Heber, R. Mother-child interaction and participation in a longitudinal intervention program. *Developmental Psychology*, 1975, *11*, 830-836.

Ferguson, T. *Children in care--and after.* London: Oxford University Press, 1966.

Forest, I. *Preschool education.* New York: Macmillan, 1927.

Forrester, B. J., Boismier, N. O., and Gray, S. W. *A home-based intervention program with mothers and infants.* Unpublished manuscript, George Peabody College for Teachers, Nashville, TN, 1977.

Gilmer, B., Miller, J. O., and Gray, S. W. *Intervention with mothers and young children: A study of intrafamily effects* (DARCEE Papers and Reports, 4, No. 1). Nashville, TN: George Peabody College for Teachers, 1970.

Goldfarb, W. Effects of psychological deprivation in infancy and subsequent stimulation. *American Journal of Psychiatry*, 1945, *102*, 18-33.

Goldfarb, W. Emotional and intellectual consequences of psychologic deprivation in infancy: A revaluation. In P. H. Hoch and J. Zubin (Eds.), *Psychopathology of childhood.* New York: Grune and Stratton, 1955.

Gomber, J. M. *Caging adult male isolation-reared rhesus monkeys (Macaca mulatta) with infant conspecifics.* Unpublished doctoral dissertation, University of California, Davis, 1975.

Goodson, D. B., and Hess, R. D. *The effects of parent training programs on child performance and parent behavior.* Unpublished manuscript, Stanford University, 1976.

Gordon, I. J. *Early child stimulation through parent education* (Final Report). Gainesville, FL: Institute for the Development of Human Resources, University of Florida, June 1969. (ERIC Document Reproduction Service No. ED 038 166)

Gordon, I. J., and Guinagh, B. A home learning center approach to early stimulation (Final Report, No. 5-RO1-MH-16037-04). Gainesville, FL: Institute for Development of Human Resources, University of Florida, December 1977.

Gordon, I. J., Guinagh, B., and Jester, R. E. The Florida Parent Education Infant and Toddler Programs. In M. C. Day and R. K. Parker (Eds.), *The preschool in action* (2nd ed.). Boston: Allyn and Bacon, 1977.

Gray, S. W., and Klaus, R. A. The early training project: A seventh-year report. *Child Development*, 1970, *41*, 908-924.

Gutelius, M. F. *Mobile unit for child health supervision* (Interim Report No. RO1-MH-9215). Ely, VT: March 1977.

Hamm, P. M., Jr., and Lyman, D. A. *Training parents in child management skills with the school as the agent of instruction.* Washington, D.C.: National Center for Educational Research and Development, February 1973.

Hanson, R. A. Consistency and stability of home environmental measures related to IQ. *Child Development*, 1975, *46*, 470-480.

Harris, F. R., Wolf, M. M., and Baer, D. M. Effects of adult social reinforcement on child behavior. In W. W. Hartup and N. L. Smothergill (Eds.), *The young child: Reviews of research.* Washington, D.C.: National Association for the Education of Young Children, 1967.

Heinicke, C. M. *Changes in the preschool child as a function of change in the parent-child relationship.* Paper presented at the biennial meeting of the Society for Research in Child Development, New Orleans, March 1977.

Herzog, E., Newcomb, C. H., and Cisin, I. H. Double deprivation: The less they have the less they learn. In S. Ryan (Ed.), *A report on longitudinal evaluations of preschool programs.* Washington, D.C.: Office of Child Development, 1972.

Hess, R. D., Block, M., Costello, J., Knowles, R. T., and Largay, D. Parent involvement in early education. In E. H. Grotberg (Ed.), *Day* care: Resources for decisions. Washington, D.C.: U.S. Government Printing Office, 1971.

Hinde, R. A. Animal behavior: A synthesis of ethology and comparative psychology (2nd ed.). New York: McGraw-Hill, 1970.

Horowitz, F. D., and Paden, L. Y. The effectiveness of environmental intervention programs. In B. M. Caldwell and H. N. Ricciuti (Eds.), Review of child development research (Vol. 3). Chicago: University of Chicago Press, 1973.

Hunt, J. M. Intelligence and experience. New York: Ronald Press, 1961.

Jaffe, J., Stern, D. N., and Peery, J. C. "Conversational" coupling of gaze behavior in prelinguistic human development. Journal of Psycholinguistic Research, 1973, 2, 321-329.

Jencks, C. Inequality. New York: Basic Books, 1972.

Jones, S. J., and Moss, H. A. Age, state, and maternal behavior associated with infant vocalizations. Child Development, 1971, 42, 1039-1051.

Kadushin, A. Adopting older children. New York: Columbia University Press, 1970.

Karnes, M. B., Hodgins, A. S., and Teska, J. The effects of short term instruction at home by mothers of children not enrolled in a preschool. In Research and development program on preschool disadvantaged children (Final Report). Washington, D.C.: U.S. Office of Education, 1969.

Karnes, M. B., Studley, W. M., Wright, W. R., and Hodgins, A. S. An approach for working with mothers of disadvantaged preschool children. Merrill-Palmer Quarterly, 1968, 14, 174-184.

Karnes, M. B., Teska, J. A., Hodgins, A. S., and Badger, E. D. Educational intervention at home by mothers of disadvantaged infants. Child Development, 1970, 41, 925-935.

Kessen, W., Fein, G., Clarke-Stewart, A., and Starr, S. Variations in home-based infant education: Language, play, and social development (Final Report, No. OCD-CB-98). New Haven, CT: Yale University, August 1975.

Klaus, R. A., and Gray, S. W. The early training project for disadvantaged children: A report after five years. Monographs of the Society for Research in Child Development, 1968, 33 (4, Serial No. 120).

Kogan, K. L., and Gordon, B. N. A mother-instruction program: Documenting change in mother-child interactions. Child Psychiatry and Human Development, 1975, 5(3), 190-200.

Koluchova, J. Severe deprivation in twins: A case study. Journal of Child Psychology and Psychiatry, 1972, 13, 107-114.

Koluchova, J. A report on the further development of twins after severe and prolonged deprivation. In A. M. Clarke and A. D. B. Clarke (Eds.), Early experience: Myth and evidence. New York: Free Press, 1976.

Lally, J. R., and Honig, A. S. The Family Development Research program. In M. C. Day and R. K. Parker (Eds.), The preschool in action (2nd ed.). Boston: Allyn and Bacon, 1977. (a)

Lally, J. R., and Honig, A. S. *The Family Development Research Program* (Final Report, No. OCD-CB-100). Syracuse, NY, University of Syracuse, April 1977. (b)

Lambie, D. Z., Bond, J. T., and Weikart, D. P. *Home teaching of mothers and infants.* Ypsilanti, MI: High/Scope, 1974.

Lasater, T. M., Malone, P., Weisberg, P., and Ferguson, C. *Birmingham Parent-Child Development Center.* (Progress Report, Office of Child Development.) Birmingham, AL: University of Alabama, March 1975.

Lazar, I., Hubbell, R., Murray, H., Rosche, M., and Royce, J. *The persistence of preschool effects: A long-term follow-up of fourteen infant and preschool experiments* (Final Report, Grant No. 18-76-07843). Office of Human Development Services. Ithaca, NY: Community Services Laboratory, Cornell University, September 1977. (a)

Lazar, I., Hubbell, R., Murray, H., Rosche, M., and Royce, J. *Preliminary findings of the Developmental Continuity Longitudinal Study.* Paper presented at the OCD conference, "Parents, children and continuity," El Paso, Texas, May 1977. (b)

Leler, H., Johnson, D. L., Kahn, A. J., Hines, R. P., and Torres, M. *Houston Parent-Child Development Center.* (Progress Report, Grant No. CG60925, Office of Child Development). Houston, Texas: University of Houston, May 1975.

Levenstein, P. Cognitive growth in preschoolers through verbal interaction with mothers. *American Journal of Orthopsychiatry*, 1970, *40*, 426-432.

Levenstein, P. The Mother-Child Home Program. In M. C. Day and R. K. Parker (Eds.), *The preschool in action* (2nd Ed.). Boston: Allyn and Bacon, 1977. (a)

Levenstein, P. *Verbal Interaction Project--Mother-Child Home Project.* (Progress Report, Grant No. RO1-MH-18471-08.) (National Institute of Mental Health) Freeport, NY: Family Service Association of Nassau County and State University of New York, June 1977. (b)

Levy, D. M. *Behavioral analysis: Analysis of clinical observations of behavior as applied to mother-newborn relationships.* Springfield, IL: Charles C. Thomas, 1958.

Lewis, H. N. *Deprived children: The Mersham experiment, a social and clinical study.* London: Oxford University Press, 1954.

Lewis, M., and Goldberg, S. Perceptual-cognitive development in infancy: A generalized expectancy model as a function of the mother-infant interaction. *Merrill-Palmer Quarterly*, 1969, *15*, 81-100.

Lombard, A. D. *Home instruction program for preschool youngsters (HIPPY).* Jerusalem: The National Council of Jewish Women and Center for Research in Education of the Disadvantaged, Hebrew University of Jerusalem, September 1973.

Love, J. M., Nauta, M. J., Coelen, C. G., Hewett, K., and Ruopp, R. R. *National Home Start evaluation* (Final Report, HEW-105-72-1100). Cambridge, MA: Abt Associates, March 1976.

Madden, J., Levenstein, P., and Levenstein, S. Longitudinal IQ outcomes of the mother-child home program. *Child Development*, 1976, *47*, 1015-1025.

Martin, B. *Modification of family interaction* (Final Report, Grant No. RO1-MH-22750). Chapel Hill, NC: University of North Carolina, Psychology Department, January 1977.

McCall, R. B., Appelbaum, M. I., and Hogarty, P. S. Developmental changes in mental performance. *Monographs of the Society for Research in Child Development*, 1973, *38* (3, Serial No. 150).

McCarthy, J. L. G. Changing parent attitudes and improving language and intellectual abilities of culturally disadvantaged four-year-old children through parent involvement. In J. B. Lazar and J. E. Chapman, *The present status and future research needs of programs to develop parenting skills.* Washington, D.C.: Social Research Group, George Washington University, 1972. (ERIC Document Reporduction Service No. ED 927-942).

Miller, J. O. *Diffusion of intervention effects in disadvantaged families.* Urbana: University of Illinois, 1968. (ERIC Document Reproduction Service No. ED 026-127).

Miller, L. B., and Dyer, J. L. Four preschool programs: Their dimensions and effects. *Monographs of the Society for Research in Child Development*, 1975, *40* (5-6, Serial No. 162).

Miller, S. J., and Sloane, H. N. The generalization effects of parent training across stimulus settings. *Journal of Applied Behavior Analysis*, 1976, *9*, 355-370.

Morris, A. G., London, R., and Glick, J. Educational intervention for preschool children in a pediatric clinic. *Pediatrics*, 1976, *57*, 765-768.

National Academy of Sciences. *Toward a national policy for children and families.* Washington, D.C.: Author, 1976.

National Society for the Study of Education. *Twenty-eighth yearbook: Preschool and parental education.* Bloomington, IL: Public School Publishing Co., 1929.

Nimnicht, G., Arango, M., and Adcock, D. The Parent/Child Toy Library Program. In M. C. Day and R. K. Parker (Eds.), *The preschool in action* (2nd Ed.). Boston: Allyn and Bacon, 1977.

Novak, M. A., and Harlow, H. F. Social recovery of monkeys isolated for the first year of life: I. Rehabilitation and therapy. *Developmental Psychology*, 1975, *11*, 453-465.

Parkman-Ray, M. *Analysis and modification of maternal teaching strategies in rural poor families.* Ithaca, NY: Cornell University, 1973. (ERIC Document Reproduction Service No. Ed 129-398).

Pringle, M. L. K., and Bossio, V. Early, prolonged separation and emotional maladjustment. *Journal of Child Psychology and Psychiatry*, 1960, *1*, 37-48.

Provence, S., and Lipton, R. C. *Infants in institutions: A comparison of their development with family-reared infants during the first year of life.* New York: International Universities Press, 1962.

Radin, N. Three degrees of maternal involvement in a preschool program: Impact on mothers and children. *Child Development*, 1972, *43*, 1355-1364.

Rathburn, C., McLaughlin, H., Bennett, O., and Garland, J. A. Later adjustment of children following radical separation from family and culture. *American Journal of Orthopsychiatry*, 1965, *35*, 604-609.

Rheingold, H. L. The modification of social responsiveness in institutional babies. *Monographs of the Society for Research in Child Development*, 1956, *21* (2, Whole No. 63).

Risley, T. R., and Baer, D. M. Operant behavior modification: The deliberate development of behavior. In B. M. Caldwell and H. N. Ricciuti (Eds.), *Review of child development research* (Vol. 3). Chicago: University of Chicago Press, 1973.

Robinson, M. *Parent/Child Development Centers: An experiment in infant-parent interventions and systematic testing of social innovations* (R and D Planning Memorandum). Washington, D.C.: Office of Research Plans and Evaluation, Office of Economic Opportunity, 1972.

Rosenberg, M. *The dancer from the dance: An investigation of the contributions of microanalysis to an understanding of parental socialization effects.* Paper presented at the Conference on Research Perspectives in the Ecology of Human Development, Cornell University, Ithaca, NY, August 1977.

Rubenstein, J. Maternal attentiveness and subsequent exploratory behavior in the infant. *Child Development*, 1967, *38*, 1089-1100.

Rutter, M. *The qualities of mothering: Maternal deprivation reassessed.* New York: Jason Aronson, 1974.

Schaefer, E. S. Parents as educators: Evidence from cross-sectional, longitudinal, and intervention research. In W. W. Hartup (Ed.), *The young child: Reviews of research* (Vol. 2). Washington, D.C.: National Association for the Education of Young Children, 1972.

Schaefer, E. S., and Aaronson, M. Infant education project: Implementation and implications of the home-tutoring program. In M. C. Day and R. K. Parker (Eds.), *The preschool in action* (2nd Ed.). Boston: Allyn and Bacon, 1977.

Schaefer, E. S., Furfey, P. H., and Harte, T. J. Infant education research project, Washington, D.C. *Preschool program in compensatory education: I.* Washington, D.C.: U.S. Government Printing Office, 1968.

Schlossman, S. L. Before Home Start: Notes toward a history of parent education in America, 1897-1929. *Harvard Educational Review*, 1976, *46*, 436-467.

Schlossman, S. L. The parent education game: The politics of child psychology in the 1970's. *Teachers College Record*, 1978, *79*, 788-809.

Shearer, M. S. A home-based parent training model. In J. Grim (Ed.), *Training parents to teach: Four models* (Vol. 3, *First chance for children*). Chapel Hill: University of North Carolina, undated. (ERIC Document Reproduction Service No. ED 102-778, EC 071-447).

Shipman, V. C. *Stability and change in family status, situational, and process variables and their relationships to children's cognitive performance.* Paper presented at the biennial meeting of the Society for Research in Child Development, New Orleans, March 1977.

Skeels, H. M., and Dye, H. B. A study of the effects of differential stimulation on mentally retarded children. *Proceedings and Addresses of the American Association of Mental Deficiencies*, 1939, 44, 114.

Slaughter, D. T. *Parent education for low income black families.* Paper presented at the General Mills American Family Forum, Washington, D.C., October 1977.

Sonquist, H. *A model for low-income and Chicano parent education.* Santa Barbara, CA: Santa Barbara Family Care Center, 1975. (ERIC Document Reproduction Service No. Ed 113-063).

Spitz, R. A. Hospitalism. *Psychoanalytic Study of the Child*, 1946, 2, 113-117.

Stedman, D. J. *Effects of evaluation on infant cognitive development.* (Final Report, No. RO1-MH-24005.) Chapel Hill, NC: Frank Porter Graham Child Development Center, August 1977.

Stern, C. *Increasing the effectiveness of parents-as-teachers.* December 1970. (ERIC Document Reproduction Service No. ED 048-939).

Stern, D. Mother and infant at play: The dyadic interaction involving facial, vocal, and gaze behaviors. In M. Lewis and L. A. Rosenblum (Eds.), *The effect of the infant on its caregiver.* New York: Wiley-Interscience, 1974.

Stevenson, H. W. Social reinforcement of children's behavior. In L. P. Lipsitt and C. C. Spiker (Eds.), *Advantages in child development and behavior* (Vol. 2). New York: Academic Press, 1965.

Thoman, E. B. Some consequences of early infant-mother-infant interaction. *Early Child Development and Care*, 1974, 3, 249-261.

Thomas, A., Chess, S., Birch, H. G., Hertzig, M. E., and Korn, S. *Behavioral individuality in early childhood.* New York: New York University Press, 1963.

Thompson, W. R., and Grusec, J. Studies of early experience. In P. H. Mussen (Ed.), *Carmichael's manual of child psychology.* New York: John Wiley, 1970.

Tizard, B., and Rees, J. A comparison of the effects of adoption, restoration to the natural mother, and continued institutionalization on the cognitive development of four-year-old children. *Child Development*, 1974, 45, 92-99.

Tizard, B., and Tizard, J. The cognitive development of young children in residential care. *Journal of Child Psychology and Psychiatry*, 1970, 11, 177-186.

Vopava, J., and Royce, J. *Comparison of the long-term effects of infant and preschool programs on academic performance.* Paper presented at the annual meeting of the American Educational Research Association, Toronto, March 1978.

Wandersman, L. P., and Wandersman, A. *Facilitating growth for all the family in adjustment to a newborn.* Paper presented at the National Conference on Family Relations, New York, October 1976.

Wenar, C.   Executive competence in toddlers: A prospective, observational study. *Genetic Psychology Monographs,* 1976, *93,* 189–285.

White, B. L.   *The first three years of life.*   Englewood Cliffs, NJ: Prentice-Hall, 1975.

White, S. H., Day, M. C., Freeman, P. K., Hantman, S. A., and Messenger, K. P.   *Federal program for young children: Review and recommendations.*   Washington, D.C.: U.S. Government Printing Office, 1973.

Wolins, M.   Young children in institutions: Some additional evidence. *Developmental Psychology,* 1969, *2,* 99–109.

Yankelovich, Skelly, and White, Inc.   *Raising children in a changing society* (General Mills American Family Report, 1976-77).   Minneapolis: General Mills, 1977.

Yarrow, L. J. Maternal deprivation: Toward an empirical and conceptual re-evaluation. *Psychological Bulletin,* 1961, *58,* 459–490.

Yarrow, L. J., Rubenstein, J. L., and Pedersen, F. A.   *Infant and environment: Early cognitive and motivational development.* Washington, D.C.: Hemisphere, 1975.

FOOTNOTES

(1) 28th NSSE Yearbook, 1929, page 7.

(2) 28th NSSE Yearbook, 1929, page 20.

(3) Editorial, *The New York Times,* November 1, 1925.

(4) 28th NSSE Yearbook, 1929, page 67.

(5) Forest, 1927, page 231.

(6) Editorial, *The New York Times,* October 29, 1925.

CHILD AND FAMILY ADVOCACY: ADDRESSING THE RIGHTS AND RESPONSIBILITIES OF CHILD, FAMILY AND SOCIETY

Gaston E. Blom, Joanne G. Keith, and Ilene Tomber

Child Advocacy Resource Network
Michigan State University
East Lansing, MI 48824

WHEN:

- a state legislature passes a bill to outlaw any reference to illegitimacy of a child on all legal documents

- a local group supports the development of a child abuse council for its community

- a school district helps its students become involved in the decision making process by establishing a student run court on discipline

- day care providers form a state coalition to support licensing and regulations for all centers

- a child psychiatrist criticizes the stereotypes and negative expectations of handicapper children held by many human service professionals

- a family adopts four foster children to hold another family together

SOMEONE HAS ADVOCATED FOR CHILDREN

157

INTRODUCTION

Sixty-three million children under 18 years of age are living and growing up in the United States today (Bureau of the Census, 1978). Each of these children is unique; no two have identical genetic endowment or life experiences. Each is in a process of change. For most children this change is within the range of normal human development but for many it is not. It is for *all these children* that we propose child advocacy to redress the wrongs and foster the quality of life.

Americans view themselves as a child and family centered society. However, a gap still exists between what Americans believe and what actually exists. There are unmet needs, unrecognized rights, and poor quality of life for too many of the nation's children and families. Citizens not only need to be aware of the gap between belief and reality but also need to examine the causes for that gap. Anti-child attitudes exist in terms of those who see children as the exclusive property of parents, abuse them, deny them both protection and decision rights, fail to ensure them adequate health care, and view children solely as a future resource for parents and society. There is also a more insidious ignoring and neglect of many children and families. In our society adults have multiple roles as spouses, parents, family members, citizens, neighborhood members, volunteers, and workers. Conflict arises among these many roles and all too frequently parenting may be sacrificed in the resolution of such conflict.

In this presentation, the authors will first examine the gap between belief and reality about America's children through summarizing what is happening now to the nation's children and their families and reviewing what has been done recently at the national level for them. Then beliefs about children and societal changes will be discussed as they affect the welfare of children in the past, present, and future. A statement on the rights and responsibilities of children, families, and society follows. The authors then present some aspects of effective child advocacy.

WHAT IS HAPPENING NOW TO
AMERICA'S CHILDREN AND FAMILIES

Ninety-nine percent of all children live in families and historically the family has been the primary caregiver responsible for the emotional, psychological, social, and economic well-being of the child (Bureau of Labor Statistics). Therefore, the most effective advocacy for children will first examine and develop support with and for the family. The one percent who do not live in families live in institutions with little if any consistent caregiving, and represent 640,000 children; support for these children is also a primary target for advocacy (Edelman, 1979).

For all children several basic resources are necessary to enhance development: caring, competent, and consistent caregivers; time with adults and other children for learning and growing; and financial resources to provide adequate food, shelter, and health care. These resources remain far from adequate for many children. For other children there has been a reduction in the availability of these basic resources because of rapid changes occuring in society and in families.

Most children (78%) live in two parent families. However, the percentage of children living in two parent households has decreased since 1970 when 85 percent of children in families lived with two parents. The number of children living with only one parent has increased from 12 percent in 1970 to 19 percent in 1979. The largest increase was among children living with their mother only. The remaining five percent of children live in families where someone other than a parent is the family head (Bureau of the Census, 1978). What may be overlooked is that by the time a child is 18, forty percent will have lived in a single parent household for some period of time. In nearly half these cases there will be a divorce (Keniston, 1977).

Living in a single parent home in and of itself may not be necessarily detrimental to children; however, if this means the child has gone through traumatic emotional separations through the divorce or death process, the child's welfare may be in jeopardy. Although 40 percent of single parents remarry (Masnick and Bane, 1980), are the children better off when the parent remarries? How do children cope with multiple households? Is there a significant amount of child care given by a non-custodial parent or by a step-parent?

Families are growing smaller with fewer children. In 1977, the average number of children per family was 2.00--down from 2.29 in 1970 (Bureau of the Census, 1978). With fewer children this could mean more time and resources available for care and support of children. However, during this same period of time there has been a drastic increase in households in which all adults are employed full time, which could indicate more money but less time available for children.

In 1978, almost half of all children had mothers in the labor force--an increase of 15 percent in numbers since 1970. As expected, older children were more likely to have a mother in the labor force; 52 percent of those families with children 6 to 17 years were employed outside the home compared to 39 percent of mothers with younger children. There has been at least a 10 percent increase for both groups of children--those in school and preschoolers. These increases have occurred in a relatively short period of time at a rate so rapid that figures are obsolete by the time they are published (Bureau of the Census, 1978).

Society has been caught unprepared for this increase in maternal employment and provides little support for the families involved. There is the issue of childcare and the social, emotional, and physical needs for young children throughout the day. There are the questions of after-school care for children in school: Are they alone? Can they safely take care of themselves? How do they use their time?

The economic resources available to a family give a rough estimate of access to opportunities, goods, and services for children. It is true that the average income increased 35 percent from 1973 to 1977. However, the inflation rate and taxes have accelerated, giving families little or no change in purchasing power since 1967. Food, housing, medical care, and transportation, basic necessities for children's growth, have increased in price between 1967 and 1980 more than 250 percent! The projections for the future do not suggest the lessening of these increases. Increased housing costs and interest rates impact especially on those families currently buying into the housing market, i.e., especially young families, many of those with young children. Energy and food costs represent larger percentages of income for lower income and young families (Masnick and Bane, 1980).

For all families in low socio-economic levels, providing basic necessities for children is difficult. This is illustrated through problems of access to quality health care. Some refer to America's health care system as consisting of one for the middle and upper classes and another for lower socioeconomic groups. The latter usually receive illness care at public hospitals and clinics by anonymous and constantly changing physicians. The former attend private outpatient doctor offices by appointment where they see the same physician. Lower socioeconomic groups have great health needs and yet receive the poorest delivery of services. It is estimated that 7 to 14 percent of children do not have a regular source of medical care and that 30 percent are not fully protected against prevalent childhood diseases. In addition, children have the least health insurance coverage of any age group. Dental care appears to be an even greater luxury with 30 percent of children never having seen a dentist. Sixty-three percent of lower class urban children have not received any dental care. Mental health services do not even approximate the need for evaluation, treatment, and consultation. It has been estimated that 90 percent of children who need such services do not receive them (Keniston, 1977).

While American public schools can point to many accomplishments, education needs to further address its unfinished business. There are five percent of school-aged children (1.5 million) not enrolled in school and another four percent who are suspended. Headstart serves less than one fourth of its intended population of poor children. Of those in school, 25 percent drop out before graduating from high school, and 20 percent do not acquire functional literacy skills (Children's Defense Fund, 1979; Snapper and Ohms, 1977).

If available time and adequate financial resources are highly important to the development of children, certain groups of children are in greater jeopardy and need of support: children of single parent households, minority families, and families of low socioeconomic status. Employment of mothers is far greater among single parents; this is coupled with significantly lower income. About 61 percent of all children in female-headed families had mothers in the labor force compared with 48 percent in husband-wife families, and the rate of increase between 1970 and 1978 was slightly faster for mothers of young children under six (Bureau of Labor Statistics, 1978).

One specific group of children in single parent homes which seems to be in even greater jeopardy are those born into homes of unmarried teenage women. In 1977, 300,000 children were born into these families and this has increased between 1970 and 1977 (Children's Defense Fund, 1979).

Long and short term unemployment in families varies over time and across regions. But the black unemployment rate has been double that of whites (Keniston, 1977). Other minority groups including Mexican Americans, Native Americans, and women have been drastically under-represented in better paying jobs and overrepresented in low paying jobs. Women's pay has been found to be 57.2 percent of men's (Keniston, 1977).

This overview of trends in American families raises many issues about the welfare of American children. More specifically, children can be identified where the need for advocacy and support is clearly apparent. These are children at risk of developing present and future emotional, mental, health, social, and educational difficulties.

There are children at risk because of environmental conditions such as experiencing a parental death (5.7 million) or parental divorce (7.0 million) or parental alcoholism (15 million) or parental physical or sexual abuse (1.0 million); at risk also are children living in poverty (10 million) or in foster homes (500,000) (Westman, 1979). Perhaps these conditions may be causally related in part to child runaways, officially reported as one million a year. There is another large group of children who are at risk because of congenital and acquired handicaps (10 million). These handicaps include mental retardation, speech and language disorders, learning disabilities, physical and sensory impairments, and emotional disorders (Westman, 1979).

WHAT HAS BEEN DONE RECENTLY AT THE NATIONAL LEVEL FOR AMERICA'S CHILDREN

Formal and informal efforts have existed for a number of years to periodically look at the issues and problems of America's children and families. Dating back to 1909, White House Conferences were held about every ten years to take stock of our gains and problems. Most of these efforts reflected on past decades rather than planning for the future. Recommendations seemed more directed at solving past dilemmas rather than dealing with issues and concerns of the decade to come (Beck, 1973).

Ninety percent of these recommendations remain unfulfilled (Senn, 1977). While these conferences were well intended, they fell short of what they were supposed to realize. Perhaps the most critical failure was in not developing ongoing mechanisms and processes to examine the problems and quality of life of children and families within a balanced framework of private and public initiatives and responsibilities. No articulated family--child--society policy was developed. Many programs and policies were developed that had good intentions, but they were not sufficiently monitored and evaluated. This resulted in continuing or discontinuing programs based on inadequate information. New problems and consequences arose that had not been anticipated. The balances between private and public responsibility and voluntary and mandatory services were often not sufficiently considered.

The International Year of the Child, 1979, and the White House Conference on Families, 1980, represented similar recent efforts to renew national commitments, to celebrate children and families, and to take stock of national gains and problems concerning them. As previously, many people were concerned about the role of society in individual lives. Some people emphasized the return to a stable, less flexible continuity in life style and life values. Others stressed the need to acknowledge and positively respond to the reality of many societal changes. Again, the focus was on the differences rather than on the commonalities of people's concerns for children and families, and on the search for an appropriate role for society in the partnership with child and family.

A particular focus of interest during the International Year of the Child was on the rights of children (U.S. National Commission IYC, 1979). The year 1979 was recognized as the 20th anniversary of the United Nations Declaration of the Rights of the Child, passed by the United Nations General Assembly in 1959. This document contained a series of important principles concerning the lives and status of children. While they are stated as rights, they really represent a commonly shared series of needs, interests, and moral and ethical values about children. These rights or principles include: special protection, opportunities, and facilities to develop in a healthy and normal manner with freedom and dignity; entitlement to a name and nationality from birth; adequate nutrition, housing, recreation, and medical resources; special treatment if handicapped; an atmosphere of affection and security in the care of parents wherever possible; education; priority protection and relief in disaster; and protection against neglect, cruelty, exploitation, and discrimination (Declaration of the Rights of the Child, 1977). A somewhat similar bill of rights for children in the United States was endorsed by the 1970 White House Conference on Children, some 10 years after the United Nations declaration.

Most individuals would not disagree with this series of principles or rights of children. And most people would agree that the family represents the best structure to ensure that these principles or rights are

practiced and protected. Beyond these statements one encounters disagreement and controversy.   At times during these last two years
polarized and conflicting views were expressed on the causes of and
proposed solutions to identified problems, on what constituted the nature
of quality of life ingredients, and on the appropriate roles of society in
problem solving and fostering quality of life. What became lost in the
conflict, polarization, and politicization was the common shared concern
of most Americans related to the rights and responsibilities of children,
families, and society.

HOW BELIEFS ABOUT CHILDREN AND SOCIETAL CHANGES HAVE AFFECTED THEIR WELFARE

Views of children and childhood have changed throughout history.
There was never a singular view of children at a given historical time.
However, in the past, children were often seen as miniature adults who
were able to do adult work when they were big or strong enough, and
therefore an economic resource. Many children died at birth and during
infancy from undeveloped health care, infections, and accidents.   Maternal mortality was also high and childbearing had a particular high risk
as well. Many cultures valued boys over girls, viewing them as a more
valuable economic resource.

With the industrial revolution the need arose for a smaller work
force with more than manual skills. This, coupled with advances in the
control of disease, has led to a different way of looking at children. At
this time, childhood came into its own as a life stage, and with it a
purpose and need for universal education rather than education only for
the wealthy and powerful. Adolescence, as Aries (1972) conceptualizes it,
followed as a life stage. It was created out of the need for more
advanced educational skills in society. So childhood and adolescence, as
distinct life stages, were creations of historical change and social
adaptation.

These historical views still hold in many cultures and within
particular individual families today. Children may be treated as a future
resource. Sometimes childhood illness and health do not receive sufficient attention because of problems in health care delivery. Parents
may fail to attach to children because of problems in caring and
nurturing. They may have strong preferences for boys. Children from
disadvantaged and minority groups may not take advantage of universal
education because of negative cultural expectations and family pressures
to work.

Current views of children and childhood held by parents and adults
also differ. These views influence childrearing practices and the role
expectations of children. Many adults think of children largely as a future
resource, and consider present family and social influences only as they
will affect children's futures. While this view often expresses a positive

concern for the child as a future adult, important roles for children in the present are not recognized or given opportunity for expression. Children can be an important source of revitalization, creativity, and idealism for parents, other adults, and society. They can stimulate and strengthen the force of caring for others in the presence of destructive and self-centered forces of the adult world.

Some adults view childhood as a state of innocence, vulnerability, and impressionability. Therefore, children are important and valued but are easily influenced by learning experiences in their environment. Discipline, control, and training are seen as very important in child-rearing. Childhood is also viewed as a paradise to be envied, and in contrast as a time of struggle and conflict.

In reality, no single view of childhood is accurate and comprehensive. There are many interacting aspects of children as unique individuals, changing over time and being influenced by environments. It is not possible to present a unified, integrated, scientifically based, agreed upon concept of the child, child development, and established methods of childrearing. While there are some broad areas of agreement, a great deal is left to tradition, intuition and belief in what worked for one's self.

There have been changes in family roles and norms over time and quite dramatic ones during the last ten years. One of them has been the movement of women into the marketplace. A number of motives are cited for this shift in women's roles such as inflation, technological take-over of household production, control of conception, and the consequent search for meaningful activity. The movement today toward self-awareness and self-fulfillment has made women more status conscious and has led to a sense of embarrassment and deprivation if they are not looked on as economically and personally productive. When they find themselves outside the job market, whether related to sex, age, skill, or ethnic back-ground, women often feel superfluous in an American society that is achievement and production-oriented. Terkel (1975) wrote, "A housewife is a housewife, that's all. Low on the totem pole. I can read the paper and find out...Somebody who goes out and works for a living is more important than somebody who doesn't. What they do is important in the business world. What I do is important to only five people" (p. 33).

Two other societal trends have undoubtedly impacted upon children and families and will continue to do so: increased electronic technology (Toffler, 1974) and natural resources shortages. Television is one example of the technological influences which has already had a profound impact.

Television was first introduced in the United States in 1939, but daily television programming did not begin until after World War II. However, by 1972, 95 percent of American homes had a television set, more than any other electrical appliance (Liebert, Neale and Davidson,

1973). Quite early in television's fantastic development and growth, the television set was recognized as a new and influential family member in the American home. It has been estimated that the current high school graduate has watched television longer than she/he has been in the classroom. An average elementary school child watches television 15 to 25 hours per week while an average high school student watches 12 to 14 hours (Murray, 1980). The American child has become a media literate.

By 1950 concerns were expressed by parents and educators about the impact on children of television violence, sexual and ethnic role stereotypes, and sexually stimulating scenes and themes. There were further anxieties about advertising directed at children and the general influence of television on intellectual and social development. These concerns have continued for 35 years with very little response by the broadcasting industry to parental advocacy pressures and to research data which have in a number of ways supported parental anxieties. An important proviso is that research has also demonstrated prosocial effects including the communication of knowledge and information (Murray, 1980).

In the long struggle with the television industry there has been conflict between private action (individual or collective group decisions to monitor programs) and public policy (regulations concerning types of programs, their scheduling, and the amount and type of advertising viewed by children). Currently, the Federal Communications Commission and the Federal Trade Commission are deliberating proposals and decisions resulting from the advocacy of the Action for Children's Television. Concerns have been expressed about freedom of the press as guaranteed by the first amendment to the constitution. But concerns have also been communicated about an industry which has been too responsive and acquiescent to its sources of profit, i.e., the advertising of products.

As part of social change, the complexity of culture and the size and unresponsiveness of both governmental and nongovernmental institutions make it difficult for people to be and to feel in control of the destiny of their lives. Studies of the Carnegie Council on Children (Pifer, 1978) have demonstrated that the average American family does not feel it has the power to sufficiently make or influence the decisions affecting their children. Events such as inflation, rising taxes, and unemployment contribute to a basic mistrust of government and the heightening of individual narcissism.

WHAT ARE THE RIGHTS AND RESPONSIBILITIES OF CHILDREN, FAMILIES AND SOCIETY

America is a heterogeneous culture, one with many commonly shared values and also a significant number of values which vary and even conflict within individuals and subgroups. This heterogeneity represents both a weakness and a strength.

Weakness occurs when an attempt is made to deny or reject the pluralism of others and to impose a single value system on all. Strength lies in the acceptance of the rich diversity of history, backgrounds, experience, and opinions of people. The conflict which inevitably arises from diversity and difference can foster constructive, positive change for individuals, families, groups, and society.

For example, in today's world, polarization and conflict exist between younger and older generations; conflict also exists between persons brought up during different historical eras such as the 1960s and the 1970s. Yet, it is possible to deal with these phenomena through a constructive process whereby the stability and continuities of the past, which need to be maintained, interact with the newness and discontinuities of the present which support change. This is a constant dialectic process in our democratic society which can foster growth, adaptation, and satisfaction. If American society fails to understand and appreciate that process, then a perspective on defining and redefining the rights and responsibilities of child, family, and society is lost. Instead, society remains focused on disagreement and becomes embattled. Then the common search for positive goals for children and families within society no longer exists.

Children in our country represent a group of minority age status whose rights and interests are for the most part represented by adults who hold a position of proxy consent in relation to them. Children rarely can be advocates for themselves or have decision rights until they reach a socially defined legal age. There is very little recognition that children have gradual increasing competence which goes through a process of development. The standard view of a child is a person whose competence has not yet developed and is therefore incapable of speaking for and being responsible for himself or herself. It would seem more reasonable that the child should participate in decisions affecting his/her life appropriate and reasonable to the level of development of competence. Such a child development view is neither anti-family or anti-society. It is a sound principle to obtain prior training and experience for later decision-making at legal age. However, at present insufficient training and experience are provided in schools, homes, and communities to develop effective decision-making skills for children. The child also has a right to know, to be informed, and to be listened to about situations and decisions that directly affect her/him.

Caldwell (1980) has discussed the interactive balance of rights and responsibilities of child(ren), parent(s) and society. These three elements --child, parent, society--are part of a reciprocating system in which each element influences and is influenced by the others.

Caldwell also distinguishes between protection rights and choice rights of children. Protection rights foster growth and developmental potential and delay the assumption of choice rights. The United Nations

Declaration of the Rights of the Child (1959) consists of protection rights--health, name, nationality, nutrition, housing, recreation, education, affection, and security. Most of them are provided through parents together with a supportive society and a few rights are ensured by society directly. Choice rights are related to a child's level of maturation and competence. They involve consent, action, responsibility, and decision-making and are usually conferred in adolescence or young adulthood.

Children's responsibilities to parents and society are an important aspect of the balance--to assimilate the values of society and to fulfill the duties of childhood (to mature, learn, respect and honor parents). Parent responsibilities or duties to children (to rear, provide, love, protect, and train children) are closely related to children's rights. Society also has responsibilities to provide resources for parents, establish protection for children, and provide alternatives when parents fail. What is lacking from society is a comprehensive and coherent social policy supporting parents and children and the human services needed for both.

Social policy is made and modified over time through a dynamic interaction and expression of rights and responsibilities of children, parents, and society. A process or mechanism to achieve that interaction and expression for policy development is child advocacy.

WHAT IS EFFECTIVE ADVOCACY

What is Advocacy

Advocacy is not a new idea, nor is it revolutionary or radical. It has been practiced as long as people have displayed care and protection for each other. Advocacy is viewed as a continuous ongoing process which addresses the balanced rights and responsibilities of child, family and society. It is this process which has not been sufficiently practiced or which has not been effective for a variety of reasons. Advocacy as a process can achieve a renewal today with greater sophistication and knowledge. Furthermore, it is critical to do so if the needs of America's children are going to be adequately addressed and the quality of life for children and families, now and in the future, significantly improved.

For many people today, the concept of advocacy has come to have negative connotations. Advocacy actually has positive caring definitions. It has been defined as acting in behalf of one's own interest, pleading the cause of others, assuming a degree of responsibility for acting in behalf of others, and defending or maintaining a cause or a proposal.

Aims

Advocacy has a number of aims. One is to change conditions that are harmful or undesirable to both children and families and to prevent such conditions from occurring or developing. But in addition to ameliorating or preventing problems, it has a goal of promoting quality of life environments and positive potentials and opportunities for individuals. Advocacy should also provide a mechanism for formulating public policy which should include planning human services. It should orient human services professionals in their professional and personal roles. Lastly, advocacy should have a less formal social aim to motivate voluntary action, opinion, and service. Volunteerism without charity and denigration of recipients is one of the strong positive features of American life. Yet, volunteerism clearly needs revitalization and recommitment today through the voice and activities of the private sector.

Forms

There are many forms of advocacy that may be either educational (non-adversarial) or legal (adversarial). They include: individual (case), group (class), issue, and systems change advocacy. Advocacy may focus on special groups of children and their families such as the handicapped, migrants, refugees, latch key children, foster children, and other forgotten/neglected groups. It may focus on special issues of concern for children and families such as child abuse/neglect, poverty, corporal punishment, minority status, health care, welfare, and day care. It may also be directed toward changes in the various systems that work with children such as the public schools, the courts, and social service agencies.

Advocacy need not be just problem focused but can be concerned about improving quality of life conditions such as providing adequate transportation, parks and playgrounds; reducing/eliminating pollution; and improving the design and cleanliness of our living environment. It can also be concerned with promoting positive and caring attitudes towards children and families by fostering positive intergenerational relationships and positive attitudes of respect.

Advocacy can be initiated by an individual in behalf of his or her own interests. In fact, this is the most common form of advocacy on the part of parents in relation to their children. In addition, many individuals involve themselves in similar advocacy efforts for those outside their own family. There is a growing ombudsman movement which makes available procedures for individuals to correct harmful and undesirable conditions and actions that affect them. There is, however, a limit to a single individual's power to influence and change the system which may be producing problems. Such individual action requires skill, knowledge, and access to the power structure. There are a few notable exceptions to this generalization as exemplified by the action of a single national leader such as John F. Kennedy in relation to the mentally retarded children and Martin Luther King in terms of striving for equal educational opportunity within mainstream education for black children. However, there is still a need to train and educate parents in effective individual advocacy efforts. Often this is how people become motivated to move toward advocacy in a broader context--i.e., trying to make the system work better for all concerned, not just their own child/family.

While not disregarding the importance of individually initiated efforts, advocacy can often be most effective when initiated by a group(s) at local, state, and national levels. Some groups are organized around a common set of concerns and problems, such as parents having children with learning disabilities or a similar handicap or chronic illness. When coalitions of such groups join together with other citizens not directly affected, professionals, and decision-makers, the results can be more effective. Unlike single issue groups, child advocates often diffuse and fragment their efforts by competing with each other.

Human service professionals in more recent years have become advocates for those they serve, recognizing they can no longer remain aloof from policy making and program development. However, in today's world they have also become targets of the advocacy actions of others, a role with which they are unfamiliar and uncomfortable. Being both the initiator and target of advocacy as well as forming coalitions with families and children are somewhat new roles for professionals.

Blom (1981) indicates in his account of psychotherapy of Heather, a 19-year-old young woman with Down's Syndrome, how his role encompassed being therapist, advocate, and friend. These roles are often traditionally viewed as contradictory by mental health professionals. In Blom's experience with Heather (helping her to make special education decisions, establish relationships with others, get married, and become a sexual partner), the outside world of agencies and professionals presented indifference, opposition, and barriers to her achieving as normal a life as possible. It was therefore necessary not only to be supportive as a friend to Heather, but also to be an advocate through taking positions and stands that were not neutral in relation to those who would question and oppose Heather's rights.

The great majority of advocacy activity is non-adversarial and involves conscience raising, educational efforts, and voluntary action. An informed and committed citizenry is a necessary ingredient leading to the next step in effective advocacy, legislative and legal action necessary for effective change.

Advocacy Process

Advocacy involves a process which needs to be and can be taught in order for it to be effective regardless of its forms, focus, and initiation. One aspect is issue or problem identification which not only has to be stated clearly, but which should also be selected according to criteria that provide the potential for support, interest, responsiveness, and success. These criteria would include need, social receptivity, the current historical time context, potential commitments from private and public leadership, and possibilities for coalition building from other individuals and groups.

The first step in the advocacy process is establishing a knowledge base for the selected issue. Already existing data need to be obtained and utilized and new data generated. Data need to be disseminated in such a way that they are not just dry statistics. It is possible to become numb to numbers unless they are humanized through actual life story examples. Numbers are also more effective the closer they touch people's lives and sensitivities. For example, in considering the question of programs for the high number of latch key children--children who are at home unattended by any caretaking or protecting adults--people may be persuaded by a study of home fires in a large metropolitan city that shows 17 percent involved an unattended child (Edelman, 1979).

The advocacy process also involves knowledge of the community-- its needs, resources, both private and public, and power structure. So there is a necessary knowledge base on the potentials for action as well as the issue. Thinking through the development of more than one strategy for action or decision is an important part of the process. There are always alternative options and it may be possible to clarify their advantages and disadvantages. Multiple strategies may be most advantageous under certain circumstances. Strategies may involve the private or public sector and voluntary efforts; identifying decision makers and obtaining access to them; demonstration projects, public education efforts, and disseminating information; modifying rules and regulations regarding existing laws, codes, and procedures; changing existing legislation or creating new legislation; and working at local, state or national levels. This phase of the advocacy process might be considered action planning.

Coalition building is an essential aspect of the advocacy process by itself. The more diverse support, formal and informal, that can be mobilized in agreement and focused on a selected advocacy issue, the greater opportunity exists for its success. As mentioned previously, well meaning and well intentioned advocacy initiatives often fail because they represent small fragmented efforts lacking broad support and existing in the presence of equally important issues with which they must compete. For example, efforts to rewrite a juvenile code in Michigan have been repeatedly pushed in the background while issues such as tax reform, inflation, and prison riots are given high priority.

Various organizations have developed materials which provide specific and detailed guidelines for the advocacy process (Children's Defense Fund, 1978, 1979; Education Commission of the States, 1977; League of Women Voters of the United States, 1976; League of Women Voters of Michigan, 1981).

Once action or actions are taken, it is still necessary to monitor them for both actual compliance and their intended or unintended effects. Very little effort is taken to establish ongoing monitoring and evaluating procedures regarding efficacy and unanticipated undesirable outcomes. Some of the problems which we face today regarding children and families have resulted from well intentioned original decisions which have had unfavorable results, some of which could have been corrected had we been more observant earlier. Juvenile courts, aid to dependent children, and child labor laws were created as solutions to problems of the past. As often happens with social change, new problems are created if social policy solutions go unmonitored, become rigidified and exploited, and are not reinterpreted in the light of new social realities.

INDIVIDUALS AND GROUPS RESPONSIBLE FOR ADVOCACY

Currently, child and family advocacy represents a significantly important area of knowledge and experience that needs to be identified and developed.

Child and family related policy and decision-making about problems and issues are political products, economic realities, and social responses. There are numerous decisions, formal and nonformal, that affect children and families--the state of the economy, length of the work day, tax policy, and housing determinations. In addition, there are decisions and policies that are of direct consequence to children and families such as day care options, education, and support services. Who or what group is seen or sees itself as being responsible for influencing decisions and policies that affect children and families?

Universities should develop interdisciplinary advocacy groups with teaching, training, research, and consultative functions. Colleges and universities also need to be more responsive to the information needs about child and family issues within their communities.

As indicated, policies and decisions have both indirect and direct effects. Therefore, mechanisms should be established by local, state, and national governments to anticipate the effect on children and families of proposed policies, decisions, and legislation. How it will affect children and families is a question decision-makers must ask. Human services for children and families should emphasize prevention of illness, disability, poverty, and other pathology indicators. Positive indicators of quality of life should be fostered.

All professionals who carry responsibility for children should learn advocacy skills. Without advocacy they tend to focus too exclusively on what is wrong with children. As a consequence, human service professionals can become overly attached to the clinical aspects of their work at the neglect of prevention of problems and enhancement of quality of life.

Communities should employ voluntary means to deal with the problems, issues, and quality of life of their children and families. Initiatives can be taken by schools, churches, clubs, 4-H, and other citizen groups. Coalitions should be developed to promote and monitor the range of necessary community child and family services and to foster quality of life environments and opportunities for all citizens. Citizens must be given greater opportunity to participate in community problem solving together with professionals and government representatives. Children and youth must have a clear opportunity to be listened to and participate in the institutions of which they are a part. Society can be strengthened if citizens experience and feel control over the forces which influence their lives in their community (MSU, IYC report, 1980).

SUMMARY

America needs to address what is wrong and reinforce what is right for children and families in America through developing advocacy processes and mechanisms. The concept of family should be broadened to include the myriad forms which exist today. We should think about all children, not just our own or those of our neighborhood. There should not be forgotten children for whatever reason. Every child needs some adult who cares for him/her in a personal way. The community should provide a supportive network for all children and all families. Children are not only family members or future adults, but persons in the present with reasonable and appropriate rights deserving of dignity, respect, and protection. Children are also an important and necessary source of revitalization to a society. We must not be just problem focused in our efforts for them. We must remind ourselves of Hubert Humphrey's statement about the uniqueness of America's Declaration of Independence which includes the pursuit of happiness as one of our nation's aims. The authors see child advocacy process and policy as the mechanism to problem solve and develop quality, satisfied lives for children in the present and as adults in the future.

REFERENCES

Aries, P. *Centuries of childhood: A social history of family life.* New York: Random House, 1965.

Beck, R. White House conference on children: An historical perspective. *Harvard Educational Review,* 1973, 53, 653-669.

Blom, G. E. *Heather's story: Psychotherapy and the practice of the least restrictive alternative.* Issue paper, University Center for International Rehabilitation, Michigan State University, January 1981.

Caldwell, B. M. Balancing children's rights and parents' rights. R. Haskins and J. J. Gallagher (Eds.), *Care and education of young children in America: Politics, policy and social science.* Norwood, NJ: Ablex, 1980.

Children's Defense Fund. *America's children and their families: Basic facts.* Washington, D.C., 1979.

Children's Defense Fund. *For the welfare of children.* Washington, D.C., 1978.

Children's Defense Fund. *Where do you look? Whom do you ask? How do you know? Information resources for child advocates.* Washington, D. C., 1979.

Declaration of the Rights of the Child. United Nations, New York, Office of Public Information, November 20, 1959, Reprinted May 1977.

Edelman, M. W. *Children without homes.* International Year of the Child. Presented at Michigan State University, November 15, 1979.

Education Commission of the States. *The children's political checklist.* Denver: Education Commission of the State, Report 103, September 1977.

Keniston, K. *All our children: The American family under pressure.* New York: Harcourt, Brace, Jovanovich, 1977.

League of Women Voters of Michigan. *Legislative action handbook.* Lansing, MI: January 1981.

League of Women Voters of the United States. *Making an issue of it: The campaign handbook.* Washington, D.C., 1976.

League of Women Voters of the United States. *Public action kit (PAK).* Washington, D.C.: 1976.

Liebert, R. M., Neale, J. M., and Davidson, F. S. *The early window: Effects of television on children and youth.* New York: Perganon, 1973.

Masnick, G., and Bane, M. J. *The nation's families: 1960-1990.* Cambridge, MA: Joint Center for Urban Studies of M.I.T. and Harvard University, 1980.

Michigan State University. *The university, the community, and Michigan's children.* Final report of the Michigan State University International Year of the Child Committee. East Lansing, MI: December 1980.

Murray, J. P. *Television and youth: 25 years of research and controversy.* Boys Town, NE: The Boys Town Center for the Study of Youth Development, 1980.

Pifer, A. *Perceptions of childhood and youth.* Reprinted from the Annual Report of the Carnegie Corporation of New York, 1978.

Senn, M. J. E. *Speaking out for America's children.* New Haven, CT: Yale University Press, 1977.

Snapper, K. J., and Ohms, J. S. *The status of children, 1977.* DHEW Publication No. (OHDS) 78-30133. Washington, D.C.: United States Government Printing Office, 1977.

Terkel, S. Just a housewife. In J. Farago and S. Farago (Eds.), *The family.* New York: Pocket Books, 1975.

Toffler, A. *Future shock.* New York: Bantam Books, 1974.

United States Department of Commerce, Bureau of the Census, 1978. Population profile of the United States, 1977. *Current Population Reports,* series P-20, No. 324.

United States Department of Commerce, Bureau of the Census, 1978. Estimates of the population of the United States by age, sex, and race: 1970-1977. *Current Population Reports,* series P-25, No. 721.

United States Department of Commerce, Bureau of the Census. Unpublished data--family relationship and presence of parents for persons under 18 years old, by age and race. March 1978.

United States Department of Labor, Bureau of Labor Statistics, 1971. Children of women in the labor force. *Special labor force report 134*, March 1970.

United States Department of Labor, Bureau of Labor Statistics, 1978. Unpublished data--Children of working mothers.

United States National Commission. International Year of the Child, 1970. *Preliminary report to the President*, November 30, 1978. Washington, D.C.: U.S. Government Printing Office, 1979.

Westman, J. C. *Child advocacy: New professional roles for helping families.* New York: The Free Press, 1979.

CHILD NURTURANCE: AN AGENDA FOR THE 1980s

Robert P. Boger, Gaston E. Blom, and Larry E. Lezotte

Michigan State University
East Lansing, MI 48824

INTRODUCTION

The initial chapter of this book sets a tone that runs through all of the following chapters. This chapter adapted from Edward Zigler's keynote address at the Michigan State University IYC Conference spoke of "gaps"--gaps between rhetoric and reality when it comes to child nurturance in America. On the one hand, America professes to be a child oriented and caring society; on the other hand, the evidence reflected by the various social indicators mentioned by Zigler and others clearly conveys a contradictory message. This concluding chapter focuses further on these "gaps" and suggests what can be done if we are going to live up to our professed societal goals for our nation's children.

The history of the United States is one of a nation struggling to overcome "gaps" that have existed in the social order. Although we have a long way to go, we do have improved public policies, legislation, and regulations designed to reduce and ultimately eliminate unequal treatment based upon race, age, sex or handicap. We cannot make the same statement about our nation's children. No national policies have emerged that takes what is known regarding effective child nurturing and uses that knowledge as a framework for a national agenda for action.

A PHILOSOPHICAL BASE FOR CHILD NURTURANCE

As a nation we desperately need an ethical and philosophical framework that raises our consciousness regarding our most precious resource--our children. Such a framework would set in place minimum standards for child nurturance that all would be expected to follow and outline national goals for child nurturing that would move us as a nation beyond minimum standards and toward child nurturing and pedagogical

175

excellence; the social and human costs of continuing without such a framework are too great to be tolerated further.

Compared to other democratic nations and compared to our own nation in other social arenas, the United States has taken an extreme position regarding its children and their families. Collective national action is absent and in its place is projected a *laissez faire* attitude and approach to child advocacy that are overly dependent on volunteerism and charity. These community self-help dimensions, though laudatory, are not enough by themselves. They must be part of a larger plan which perceivably does not exist.

While "anti-child' attitudes openly exist in some quarters, they are a distinct minority. Rather, the more insidious problem we face is "indifference". The nation appears to be content having haphazard childrearing policies and practices continue uninterrupted or unchanged even though we know that large numbers of children at best do not profit from them and at worst are severely harmed by them.

It is also important to point out that our troubled children are *not* the primary result of unloving parents. Subtle but definite attitudes exist that if families are having trouble rearing their children it is because they are fundamentally inadequate at what they do, don't care, or just do not try hard enough. These not so subtle attitudes, fostered at all levels of our society, are false. *The first item on our agenda for the 1980s, therefore, must necessarily be that of overcoming our traditional indifference and misunderstanding about the needs of our nation's children and the families that provide their primary support.*

A proactive concern for the children in our democratic society will be evident when decision-making at all levels of the society, from the individual parent to the federal government, consistently reflects explicit consideration of the following question, "How do our various decision options affect our children--now and long term?" Consideration of this crucial question should not be limited to the traditional arena of social policy, health and education. It should be explicitly considered in the economic, environmental, transportation, ecology, military policy and energy arenas as well.

The rationale for suggesting that our society explicitly weigh available decisions relative to their consequences for children is based on the philosophical belief that a significant criterion for judging excellence in society is indicated by the manner in which that society cares for its dependent members. Clearly, national policies regarding children are indicative of national "shortfall" in this regard. Something is ethically and morally wrong with a society of our capabilities that shows such little regard for its children. We are not suggesting that child oriented policies are the only basis on which to make such judgments, but the long-term moral and intellectual health of our nation demands that we not leave to chance such an important policy domain.

Proactive child nurturing is not only morally justified but it also makes good economic sense. Proactive nurturing is society's investment in *its* own future. We have a substantial knowledge base on which to draw in attempting to maximize the return on this investment in human capital. The question is whether or not we are prepared to make the commitments to do so. It is our position that society be confident in its own future only if it is confident that it has done for its children the best it knows how to do. On the other hand, it is also our position that no greater uncertainty and insecurity can be created in society than that generated by treating with indifference our future treasure in human capital--our children.

Many points have been raised in the preceding chapters. Some have stressed recent positive developments and the promise they hold for a brighter tomorrow, if only we build upon them. Others have emphasized the negative blights, such as child abuse and the insensitive, short-sighted policies of the American broadcast television industry. The press on families brought about by the continuing heavy economic recession of the early 1980s adds further to these negative impacts on children. The grim infant mortality and child health statistics outlined by Zigler and Heller in Chapter 1, have become even more grim under the press of the fiscal realities of the past two years. A 1982 report by the Michigan Department of Public Health entitled "Infant Deaths in Michigan: Analysis and Recommendations" indicates areas of Detroit to have an infant mortality similar to impacted areas of Latin America. We can put men on the moon, but we cannot keep our own children alive. With all of the economic stress on the nation's families, federal and state support for America's children remains a low priority with increasingly limited support. More and more, child nurturing support is reflected as totally the family's responsibility whether or not the family system has the resources (money, time or parental mental health) to enable quality child nurturance. One of our most precious freedoms in America is the freedom of parents to rear their children according to their own beliefs and philosophies. The family *is* the primary system in child nurturance but families must be supported--they cannot do it alone in today's technological, urban oriented society.

BRIDGING THE GAPS

What is needed to bridge these oversights regarding the well-being of our nation's children? First and foremost we need a change in national attitude--we must begin to care and we must begin to put this caring *before* other concerns. The well-being of the nation's children must become the bottom line!

Seemingly, we need to become more proactive--we need to build on our national strengths and assets. The "gap" can be narrowed when we are able to exploit the opportunities that can be found in problems created by social change itself. A few examples will serve to illustrate this phenomenon.

Children and the Elderly

As people live longer the number of senior citizens increases accordingly. The needs and concerns of the elderly may appear on the surface to be at odds with those of children. However, when one goes beyond the surface, the basis for mutual interests becomes readily apparent. The children need and would profit substantially from nurturing by our more elderly parents and grandparents. On the other hand, the sense of loss that often comes to the elderly when their own families move on and they find themselves alone can be largely overcome by the pleasures they could derive from a nurturing relationship that they might have with one or more children. The particular form that such exchanges could take might range from volunteers in the schools and neighborhoods to more structured roles as part-time employees in agencies and institutions that serve children.

What is important to the advancing of the agenda is that all parties recognize that each party has something to give and something to gain from the exchanges that could be promoted to overcome the ever increasing "generation gap."

Children and Technological Change

As suggested in previous chapters, we are on the edge of a communications, technological revolution that is unprecedented in history. The development of computers, communications satellites and television could serve to advance the agenda for children or they could become an ever increasing part of the problem, as much of broadcast television is at the present time.

The availability and dissemination of more information is clearly a "plus" for children if it is used wisely. The problem is that our nation's children could become "information" rich and "experience" poor. Who will help our children cope appropriately with their new information? Will it be available to all? Perhaps the advocates and leaders of the technological revolution could further advance their own interests as well as the interests of our children if they were to think more about the need to develop delivery systems that advance both our knowledge and appropriate uses to which that new knowledge should be put.

Suppose the following example were to be realized. A group such as the National Geographic Society prepares a documentary on some topic. Further, suppose that schools are encouraged to make a copy of that program and use it as a basis for a curricular lesson on the same topic. Furthermore, suppose that the schools (teachers and students) share with the program sponsor the questions raised by the program. Feedback system of this sort could serve as a basis for future programs. Here again, the realization that both children and program developers have something to give and something to get in the exchanges made possible by technological advancements will further reduce the "gap" that now exists in this area.

In addition to these proactive approaches to the massive techno-logical changes occurring in the 1980s a change in attitude on the part of the broadcast television industry is essential.   The massive evidence indicating the serious negative effects violence on television is having on American children must no longer be ignored by the television industry. Immediate action was called for by the Surgeon General of the United States as early as 1974.   The network leaders, when called before Congress, agreed--but little is done and the situation is now one of critical proportion. Only sleep and work consume more of our time than television.   It is reported that the average child graduating from high school will have spent almost twice as much time in front of the television set as he will have in the classroom. During this time he will have witnessed over a hundred-thousand violent episodes.   The result of this is one of lasting and serious harm, increased potential for violent ac-tion, and the *waste* of a fantastic potential for positive child nurturance.

Children and Family Structures

Changes in the family structure have produced the trend toward smaller families, usually two children or less, have created a new societal phenomenon. As a result of this change, ever increasing numbers of our young children spend ever increasing amounts of their time interacting with other children of the same, or nearly the same, age.

If we look to the knowledge base that clearly establishes the efficacy of cross-age tutorial models for instruction and if we listen to the problem that teachers have in providing individualized instruction we can imagine how exchanges between children of different ages could advance the interests of all parties. Should such exchanges be developed we would see that cooperation can serve to reduce one more mani-festation of the "gap" in child nurturing in America.

Smaller families should provide the benefit of increased quantity and quality of parent/child transaction. However, this often does not result because of divorce and/or the increasing employment demands on mothers as well as fathers. Programs of child care and support, which are family oriented and sensitive to the interface between the family system and other educational and community support systems, are needed to bridge this gap.

Parent Support

There is a growing recognition of the need to provide new parents and adolescents who are possibly soon to be new parents with information on infant capabilities and parent/child transaction that will enable them to begin child rearing with a positive foundation. National and state support for programs designed to assist parents in establishing realistic expectations of infant behavior and initiating positive parent/child transaction during the early perinatal period is growing and deserves our full support. Through such efforts, much can be gained in bridging the gap between what parents conceive to be ideal parenting and what, too often, is far less than ideal actual parent function. Primary prevention of child abuse and less parent/child dysfunctions can be well served by furthering this national trend.

COLLABORATIVE ADVOCACY

While it is true that children under 18 years of age constitute 30 percent of our population, they are nevertheless politically powerless. The question is, "Who can and should represent the needs of our nation's children?" In the first instance, the answer must be parents; beyond parents, we all must be concerned and committed and human service professionals must assume a special leadership position in child advocacy.

Since the call for leadership touches many human service institutions and organizations, new arrangements are needed. We need cooperation and collaboration among the traditional and sometimes competitive professional groups and agencies. Advancing the interests of our nation's children must be an integrated effort. Too often in the past, the major impediment appeared to be agency self-interest and boundary maintenance. This being the case, another item on our societal child nurturance agenda for the 1980s should be that of transcending self-interest. Professional disciplines, institutions, governmental agencies, religious groups, and other supporting institutions and groups must all work to put aside self-serving, self-protecting approaches for those that are more cooperative and integrative in nature.

Another major challenge in advancing this agenda is finding appropriate ways of involving children in the decision-making process. They deserve a voice in those decisions that will shape their destiny. Children have unique and special perspectives which should be listened to. They deserve to be respected for their developing competence. Adults who would be advocates for children must learn to listen to them and respond to them and not simply speak for them.

THE "WE" RATHER THAN THE "ME"

The pressure on American society in the early 1980s seems to be resulting in some positive notes for change. The "me" era of the 1960s and early 1970s, which focused so much on self-actualization and self-indulgence, is giving way to a more "other" oriented approach to societal issues--including child nurturance. Evidence of this is to be found in the increasingly "we" oriented approach of both parents to the early months (prenatal, perinatal and postnatal) of child nurturance within the family. The central role of the father in early child care is no longer the exception and the negative biases attending such functions are disappearing. Another example can be found in the increase in volunteerism and non-governmental support for families--even in times of increasing fiscal pressure. As we have noted, this "boot strap" approach is not enough by itself, but the self-help philosophy positively supports a sense of community and individual self-esteem.

With this "other" oriented climate, there is also another influential minority. They stress a conservative and parochial approach to community function and support of "others" in society. This is evidenced in moral education and attempts to legislate and regulate certain forms of behavior. There is a current trend away from ethical relativism and/or values clarification in some areas of society. The revival of conservatism and religious fundamentalism stresses moral absolutes and superiority. They denigrate, as immoral and amoral, the view that various behaviors and perspectives may be of equal ethical validity.

SUMMARY

The bridging of the gaps between what we believe and what we do in nurturing of our children are widening. Our hopes for changing the direction of this process and increasing overall positive care and nurturing of American children are based upon changes in attitudes and the full use of what we know. Evidence supports actions that all agree are appropriate and needed. What is lacking is a spirit of cooperation, coupled with commitments to make America's children--our human capital of the future--our first rather than our last priority.